A History of Education for the Many

Radical Politics and Education

Series editors: Derek R. Ford and Tyson E. Lewis

With movements against oppression and exploitation heightening across the globe, radical activists and researchers are increasingly turning to educational theory to understand the pedagogical aspects of struggle. The Radical Politics and Education series opens a space at this critical juncture, one that pushes past standard expositions of critical education and critical pedagogy. Recognizing the need to push political and educational formulations into new theoretical and practical terrains, the series is an opportunity for activists, political thinkers, and educational philosophers to cross-disciplinary divides and meet in common. This kind of dialogue is crucially needed as political struggles are increasingly concerned with questions of how to educate themselves and others, and as educational philosophy attempts to redefine itself beyond academic norms and disciplinary values. This series serves to facilitate new conversations at and beyond these borders.

Advisory Board:
Jodi Dean *(Hobart and William Smith Colleges, USA)*
Margret Grebowicz *(University of Silesia, Poland)*
Davide Panagia *(University of California, Los Angeles, USA)*
Patti Lather *(Ohio State University, USA)*
Nathan Snaza *(University of Richmond, USA)*
Stefano Harney *(Singapore Management University, Singapore)*

Also available in the series:
Experiments in Decolonizing the University: Towards an Ecology of Study, Hans Schildermans
Rethinking Philosophy for Children: Agamben and Education as Pure Means, Tyson E. Lewis and Igor Jasinski
Against Sex Education: Pedagogy, Sex Work, and State Violence, Caitlin Howlett

Forthcoming in the series:
Education, Society, and the Philosophy of Louis Althusser, David I. Backer
Queers Teach This!: Queer and Trans Pleasures, Politics, and Pedagogues, Adam J. Greteman
A Voice for Maria Favela: An Adventure in Creative Literacy, Antonio Leal

A History of Education for the Many

From Colonization and Slavery to the Decline of US Imperialism

Curry Malott

BLOOMSBURY ACADEMIC
LONDON • NEW YORK • OXFORD • NEW DELHI • SYDNEY

BLOOMSBURY ACADEMIC
Bloomsbury Publishing Plc
50 Bedford Square, London, WC1B 3DP, UK
1385 Broadway, New York, NY 10018, USA
29 Earlsfort Terrace, Dublin 2, Ireland

BLOOMSBURY, BLOOMSBURY ACADEMIC and the Diana logo
are trademarks of Bloomsbury Publishing Plc

First published in Great Britain 2021
This paperback edition published in 2023

Copyright © Curry Malott, 2021

Curry Malott has asserted his right under the Copyright, Designs
and Patents Act, 1988, to be identified as Author of this work.

Series design by Adriana Brioso
Cover image © bortonia/iStock

This work is published subject to a Creative Commons Attribution
Non-commercial No Derivatives Licence. You may share this work for non-commercial
purposes only, provided you give attribution to the copyright holder and the publisher.

Bloomsbury Publishing Plc does not have any control over, or responsibility for,
any third-party websites referred to or in this book. All internet addresses
given in this book were correct at the time of going to press. The author and
publisher regret any inconvenience caused if addresses have changed or sites
have ceased to exist, but can accept no responsibility for any such changes.

A catalogue record for this book is available from the British Library.

Library of Congress Cataloging-in-Publication Data

Names: Malott, Curry, 1972- author.
Title: A history of education for the many: from colonization and slavery
to the decline of US imperialism / Curry Malott.
Description: London; New York: Bloomsbury Academic, 2021. |
Series: Radical politics and education |
Includes bibliographical references and index. |
Identifiers: LCCN 2021007710 (print) | LCCN 2021007711 (ebook) |
ISBN 9781350085718 (hardback) | ISBN 9781350085725 (ebook) |
ISBN 9781350085732 (epub)
Subjects: LCSH: Education–United States–History. | Education and
state–United States–History. | Democracy and education–United
States–History. | Education–Social aspects–United States–History. |
Poor–Education–United States–History. | Education and globalization.
Classification: LCC LA205.M35 2021 (print) | LCC LA205 (ebook) | DDC 370.973–dc23
LC record available at https://lccn.loc.gov/2021007710
LC ebook record available at https://lccn.loc.gov/2021007711

ISBN: HB: 978-1-3500-8571-8
PB: 978-1-3502-1516-0
ePDF: 978-1-3500-8572-5
eBook: 978-1-3500-8573-2

Series: Radical Politics and Education

Typeset by Integra Software Services Pvt. Ltd.

To find out more about our authors and books visit
www.bloomsbury.com and sign up for our newsletters.

Contents

1	Orienting a History of Education for the Many	1

Part 1 Turning the World Upside Down

2	Colonialism in the So-Called New World	13
3	The Trans-Atlantic Slave Trade and the Balance of Forces in the Colonies	35

Part 2 From Counter-Revolution to People's Revolution

4	The Reactionary Character of 1776 and the Movements of the Many	55
5	Monopoly Capitalism and Three Systems of Education	85
6	African American Agency and the US Civil War	107
7	From Monopoly Capitalism to US Imperialism	121
8	The Russian Revolution and a New Era in Educational Theory	131

Part 3 Rise and Fall of a Global Proletarian Counter-Weight

9	The Great Depression and the Mood of the Many	147
10	From Mass Education to Mass Incarceration	165

Part 4 History's Future and the Role of the Many

11	A Unipolar Imperialist Power	177
12	An Emerging Counter-Force	191
	Conclusion: The Dialectics of History	205
	Notes	208
	References	209
	Index	220

1

Orienting a History of Education for the Many

A History of Education for the Many is similar to much of the literature in that it follows a chronological order. However, it is unique among history of US education survey textbooks in both scope and method. Rather than presenting the history of education's chronological ordering as either a disconnected or loosely connected series of policies more or less passively following a changing society over time, the present volume examines change over time dialectically.

What this means is that educational policies, for example, are understood to be the result or outcome of a larger society-wide, highly complex balance of forces. That balance of forces, broadly speaking, for *A History of Education for the Many,* has been between the exploited, the colonized, and the enslaved, on one hand, and the enslavers, the colonizers, and the exploiters, on the other. The ongoing, back-and-forth, pushing-and-pulling between the balance of such forces moves historical development in different directions.

The present volume is therefore differentiated from the field because dialectics understands social formations to be finite entities that, without predetermination, rise and fall. Whereas mainstream history of education texts present US education and the larger society in which it is situated as almost inevitable entities that will deterministically forever exist, *A History of Education for the Many* charts educational development through the rise and now fall of US capitalism. Consequently, dialectics allows us to perceive a potential future beyond the system the current balance of forces finds expression.

Unlike mainstream history of education texts, *A History of Education for the Many* pays attention to the ways education has been mobilized as an instrument all sides of social antagonisms have employed to either maintain or end systems of oppression. Consequently, this book pays particular attention to social movements and *collective* action as the mechanism that advances *collective* interests.

Finally, *A History of Education for the Many* offers a unique view of the dialectical development of social control by examining the role of the police (i.e.

state violence) along with education or ideology over time. Again, what emerges is an understanding that the future of the history of education, along with the larger society in which it is a part, is not predetermined or guaranteed.

What follows is a discussion of the theoretical framework used to construct this history of education for the many. Beginning with the notion of *orientation*, this first chapter concludes with a more detailed discussion of dialectics.

Introduction

Histories are not simply mirror images of the past. Rather, histories are narratives or stories written from particular points of view or orientations. For example, the story of a conflict or contradiction can be told differently depending upon what side of the conflict or contradiction is doing the telling. Each side of a conflict or contradiction, in other words, has its own orientation. To be oriented is to know what direction one is facing and how to proceed accordingly. To be oriented is to be situated in space and time. How a particular thing relates to or is situated relative to other objects gives it an orientation. In this book, the history of education is understood as part of a larger conflict at the heart of the Spanish and then English colonization of what would become the United States of America.

This colonization was the product of particular social formations or state apparatuses at particular stages of their historical development. Challenging the assumption that the state is a neutral entity that either reflects the views of the polity or manages the conflict between competing social classes is the position that the state is an inherently repressive apparatus serving the interests of the class that is the ruling-class. For Marxist philosopher Louis Althusser (1971/2014), "the state is a repressive 'machine' that enables the dominant classes ... to ensure their domination over the working-class in order to subject it to the process of extorting surplus-value" (70) (i.e. exploiting workers).

However, theorists have pointed out that because of the relative autonomy of the state, there is no guarantee that "the political outcomes of the state will serve the needs of capital" (Jessop 2001). This approach has resulted in "more detailed accounts of the complex interplay of social struggles and institutions" (Jessop 2001: 5). Building on this approach Jessop (2004) notes that "instead of treating the state as a simple instrument of class power or as a unified rational subject, one must examine its institutional forms, how they shape the political class struggle, and the latter's transformative impact on the state apparatus" (489). Similarly, Therborn (1978) theorizes the idea of mediation to articulate this complex dialectical relationship between the rulers and the ruled. However, for Therborn it is not necessarily the class character of the state that is indeterminate. Rather, it is the capitalist-class's ability to maintain and enforce state rule that is indeterminant. Outlining this position Therborn (1978) elaborates:

> Mediation, like representation, is traversed by the class struggle; how it functions in practice is determined by the constellation of forces arising out of the class struggle. But the state is never a neutral or passive mediator. Its fundamental class character is determined by the class character inscribed in the material rule-making, rule-applying, rule-adjudicating and rule-enforcing apparatuses, as well as by the reproductive mechanisms of the ruling-class which circumscribe the radius of state intervention. Mediation here signifies not arbitration, by exercise of class power through the state. The class state does not go between the classes in order to separate fighters, but to connect them, in an asymmetric relationship of exploitation and domination.
>
> (219–20)

Considering such detailed assessments of the state, it is clear that the state does not just consist of offices, departments, legislatures, and so on, but it also includes a population or citizenry and a physical geography or land-base, including bodies of water and air space. Nothing about states are static, permanent, timeless, or predetermined. Education, as an integral component of the state, has both developed as the state has developed, while simultaneously contributing to that development.

One of the primary functions of the state is to enact and enforce laws regarding everything from private property, who it regards and who it does not regard as its citizens, what constitutes its national boundaries, and how it monopolizes sanctioned violence. Central to this book is the issue of how the state compels people to submit to its laws and contribute to their functioning (Therborn 1978). For the purposes of this book, we can think of the means of control in two broad, interrelated categories: ideological and repressive. In two words, education and the police. Whereas the police serve no other major function outside of repression, public education not only manufactures social control and social reproduction (i.e. job training), it can also be mobilized to reveal and counter systems of oppression as a form of class struggle of the ruled. This book traces the balance of forces between the repressive state and people's resistance from colonial to contemporary times.

In 1976 Samuel Bowles and Herbert Gintis acknowledged these two broad forms of social control and reproduction emphasizing the central role of education noting that "to attribute reproduction to force alone borders on the absurd" (127). In addition, Bowles and Gintis argue that "under normal conditions" state force remains a latent potential mobilized only during times of heightened class struggle. Historically situating this normalizing trend in state theory Jessop (2001) notes that "the modern state actually resorts less often to violence to control the populace: surveillance and disciplinary normalization do much of the work of regularizing activities in time and space" (15).

While these tendencies are perhaps more accurate in regards to the treatment of the white working class, for Indigenous, Latino, and Black working-class communities, police repression, despite the effectiveness of *surveillance* and *disciplinary normalization* (i.e. force), is a daily occurrence. Bringing the role of state repression back into the historical discussion of social reproduction and working-class resistance, as is done in this book, adds a layer of analysis into this history of education of the *many*.

Even though the development of the class contradiction/conflict since Columbus's arrival in 1492 has been complex, at its most general level we can describe it as a highly unstable system consisting of two broad sides, *the few* and *the many*. The few, or the 1 percent, came to the Western hemisphere as enslaving, capitalist European colonizers in competition with each other. On the other side, the many are the masses of workers and the oppressed and colonized from Indigenous peoples, African Americans, Latin Americans, Asian Americans, Arab Americans, European Americans, etc., or the 99 percent. A history of education told from *the many's* side of the conflict reveals its orientation when situated next to a history of education told from the point of view of *the few*. Orientation, therefore, is first of all about locating a place of departure to begin from. The place of beginning impacts the appearance of what is *there*.

For example, from the point of view of the capitalist state apparatus the police are all who keep the chaos of criminality in check. The collective experience of the many, especially Black America, reveals the opposite. That is, the existence of the police plays a central role in preventing the emergence of safe and sustainable communities. Because the primary task of the police is to protect capitalist property relations and the so-called right of the 1 percent to appropriate the wealth produced by workers, entire communities are kept in deep poverty and patrolled daily by an occupying army of police. Guarding society as it exists the police are always ready to suppress periodic outbursts of rebellion (Correia & Wall 2018; Vitale 2018).

The zero point of orientation, the *here*, defines the relative distance to *there*. From the relationship between *here* and *there* emerge *this side* and *that side* of the conflict or contradiction. For the police state and the capitalist-class it serves rebellions are unjustified riotous chaos. For this history of education for the many rebellions are an expression of the system's inability to solve its contradictions. From the logic of the police state rebellions are always to be pacified through the combined use of force and cooption (i.e. the ideological manipulation of cops taking a knee). On the other side of the antagonism rebellions are positive, and when successful, develop into revolutions capable of resolving the contradictions the capitalist state is unable and unwilling to resolve. The fate of rebellions, and the development of history more generally, is therefore determined by the complex interaction of competing forces and the tactical choices each side makes.

It is important to note that from a dialectical perspective nothing is fixed or static as all existing entities are in a perpetual state of development and change. Sides of conflicts are therefore not fixed or predetermined, or have independent existences apart from each other, as their interconnected movement and change are driven by a complex, multifaceted contest between forces, the outcome of which is historical development.

Relevant here is Harry Harootunian's (2015) argument that historians tend to mistakenly replace *history as the object* with an incorrect *idea* of it. For example, he challenges conceptions of space that treat history as moving through predetermined stages. The idea that all social formations (i.e. societies) are basically the same, proceeding through identical and predetermined stages suggests that the way capitalism emerged in Britain from feudalism into capitalism would be replicated in other contexts. Harootunian also challenges the idea that so-called stages proceed linearly, each signaling a new beginning disconnected from previous stages, thereby distorting the continuity across time and space with no single social formation ever fixed, final, or complete. Lenin (1920/2016) contributes to our understanding of historical complexity noting that "history generally, and the history of revolutions in particular, is always richer in content, more varied, more many-sided, more lively and 'subtle'" than the most sophisticated commentators "imagine" (76).

Since orientation is so central to our understanding of the history of education, its meaning is explored further before proceeding to a focused engagement with dialectics.

On Orientation

To be *in* the world is to be objectively oriented in it, which is related to, but does not necessarily determine, one's subjective orientation. The perspectives that emerge from orientations therefore are partial and not immovable. To be oriented is to tend to perceive one side of something and not others. What is hidden is not just the result of spatial or ideological issues that cause an inability to comprehend everything all at once. What is hidden also tends to be the result of temporal factors or what has already happened that accounts for the object's arrival. If arrival is determined by the historical development of the larger totality,[1] then historical narratives are crucial for filling in the gaps of the past.

While the determinants that determined what *is* cannot be altered after the fact, how the past is understood and analyzed is an open debate. With this insight, we do not "take objects," such as systems of capitalist schooling and the police, "as given," failing to account for the "conditions of their arrival" (41). This is another way to articulate the gap between an object and the idea of it. Replacing the object with the idea of it can create the illusion that the object has fixed, final, and inherent qualities.

The orientation of the many, in part, is determined by their awareness of the *conditions of their arrival*. The capitalist has advanced a historical narrative that would have the many believe they possess innate qualities rendering their status eternal. Similarly, Harootunian's (2015) analysis of stagism is critical of the way it portrays the individual as self-made and without a history or conditions of arrival. Reorienting the historical narrative so the frame of perception is wide enough to capture the legacy of primitive accumulation,[2] indoctrinating education, state repression, and the long legacy of the many's resistance is fundamental.

Being conscious of one's conditions of arrival suggests an awareness of self as an embodiment of "sedimented histories" (Ahmed 2006: 56). In other words, the policies and practices (i.e. suspending Black students at four times the rate as white students for the same things) that give schooling an orientation are the result of a long and ongoing contested history of conflict (i.e. outlawing literacy for enslaved Africans) that accumulates over time like sedimentation on the bottom of a lake. What it means to be a student, teacher, or administrator at any given time is an always contestable embodiment of this sedimentation. What makes this sedimented history contestable is that the future is never predetermined or already known. While sedimentation mediates the shaping of time, its ongoing influence is vulnerable to subversion, resistance, and revolutionary transformation.

Harry Harootunian's (2015) metaphorical use of the palimpsest[3] points to a non-synchronous synchronicity, or a past that is contemporary. Rather than conceptualizing historical development as moving through separate, unrelated stages, Harootunian offers another way to think about how repetition creates continuity, thereby giving bodies orientation. The idea that the past is present can be mobilized to understand the ways in which the liberation movements of bygone eras become visible during times of crisis when the illusion of the permanence of capitalism is shattered.

The drive to contest, more generally, stems from the nature of the arrival of the many whose "corporeal schema" has been "interrupted." The laboring body of the many, or the body of labor, is a body not "at home" (Ahmed 2006: 157). The capitalist world is a world of capital. The laboring body provides the substance for all new capital while itself suffers from perpetual and fluctuating *want*. The capitalist who feeds off the labor of others, flush with capital, is a body at home in capitalism, while the worker is not at home here.

The mobilization of racialization has played a central role in dramatically increasing the severity of oppression. If colonialism makes the world white and therefore makes it home for those bodies made white, then the body not at home is framed as a body whose labor produces less value. Within this framework the so-called Black body is portrayed as not only less valuable, but deviant and criminally prone, and therefore subjected to the daily repression of the police as an occupying army.

The colonial basis of whiteness as justification for super exploitation and state violence represents the ideological orientation of physical space. The European ruling-class idea of "the East" as the object, as the horizon, or as the line marking the separation between so-called "civilization" or "Godly society" and "savagery" treats "the East" as if it "were a property of certain places and people" (113). The effect is the creation of an *other* whose history of arrival is grotesquely distorted to justify extreme abuse, violence, murder, dehumanization, and exploitation. Struggles around defining, re-defining, and policing orientation are therefore central to considerations involving the history of education for the many.

Dialectics

Dialectics is a theory of motion (i.e. change, movement, development, etc.). It is a theory that grasps how many of the competing social forces driving the movement of society are often hidden or mystified. Dialectics gives us a way of uncovering these hidden forces. The dialectic is powerful because it breaks through the illusion that isolated facts speak for themselves. Only by situating facts or ideas in the historical totality of society do they begin to make real sense. To comprehend the movement of time itself, we must conceive of the interaction of forces as much more than the interaction of static and independent entities. When the parts of the totality change, their relationship to the totality changes, and they themselves change. Dialectics presents reality as an ongoing social process; nothing is ever static or fixed. What follows is an introduction to the major components of dialectics, including the unity or interpenetration of opposites, sublation, and the negation of the negation.

The Interpenetration of Opposites

What compels entities to be in a constant state of non-deterministic motion are their internal contradictions, or the forces generated by the unity of opposites. The most central or essential contradiction within feudalism was between peasant and feudal lord; in slavery, it was between the enslaved and the enslaver; and in capitalism, it is between labor and capital.

Labor and capital are opposites because they have contradictory drives. For example, historically, labor has spontaneously sought to decrease the rate of exploitation by collectively bargaining for higher wages, better conditions, benefits, and so on. When successful, these decrease profit margins. Capital, on the other hand, seeks to always increase the rate of exploitation, and when successful increase the rate of profit.

Labor and capital are therefore compelled by opposite and antagonistic drives. This antagonism can be mediated by unions and state regulation on one hand, and police repression and anti-labor laws on the other, but it can only be overcome through the abolition of the relationship (i.e. the negation of the negation).

Labor and capital therefore do not have an independent existence apart from each other. To be a worker is *by definition* to be exploited by the capitalist-class, and to be a capitalist is *by definition* to exploit workers. The relationship between labor and capital is therefore *internal*. As a relation of exploitation, capital is a unity of contradictions. The dialectical development of this relationship over time is the movement of the balance of forces within capitalism.

Sublation

When something is sublated, it is both overcome yet preserved. In other words, something that has been sublated "retains even that which is negated" (Ford 2018: 1). Ford (2018: 9) explores a critique of the conception of sublation arguing it locks the subject into altering pre-existing options, alternatives, or outcomes. The notion of exodus, on the other hand, opens up possibilities unimaged within the narrow limits of what is. For the purposes of this book, we might note that the way in which capitalism might be sublated to better meet the needs of the many is not predetermined. What we can say, following Ford (2018: 8), is that "the possible," in whatever way, "always encompasses its own negation" (Ford 2018: 8).

We might think of Harootunian's use of the palimpsest metaphor as another way to describe sublation, thereby critiquing linear, stagist conceptions of history. That is, the faded, ancient text on the palimpsest with new writing transcribed on top of it has been overcome yet preserved in an altered form. The old text, in other words, has been sublated and is therefore characterized by both continuity and newness.

It is precisely because social formations, such as capitalism, do not develop automatically, mechanically, or in a predetermined fashion, even though their internal logics orient their development in particular directions, sublation will always retain an element of indeterminacy.

Ideas, such as histories of education, and education itself, as well as the police violence of the state organized to repress the people's movement toward sublation, are fundamentally important as they impact the balance of forces either stalling or advancing sublation.

The Negation of the Negation

The tendency toward *the negation of the negation* is arguably at the heart of dialectical development. It refers specifically to the way that phenomena and structures produce their opposites. However, the idea that the internal development of entities produces their opposites should not be misunderstood as a form of stagism or predetermination. In regards to oppressive systems from feudalism, slavery to capitalism, the oppressed have an interest in transforming them into their non-oppressive or less-oppressive opposites whereas the oppressors have an interest in preserving or extending them. When something undergoes the process of the negation of the negation, it has developed into something qualitatively distinct from what it was. Things can only develop out of things.

Conclusion

Approaching the history of education dialectically this book examines how education itself is always the product of a particular balance of forces between and within the primary and antagonistically related social classes in capitalist society. How have teachers and other workers leveraged power and control over their work when the existing state is an apparatus of capitalist-class power? Unions, mass movements, and successful, prolonged uprisings come to mind.

It is the intention of this text to demonstrate how each era and therefore each chapter develops from each other as a result of a fluid and shifting balance of forces. The story told here begins at the dawn of the sixteenth century.

Part One

Turning the World Upside Down

2

Colonialism in the So-Called New World

Introduction: Connection to the Previous Chapter

A History of Education for the Many charts the development of education through the rise and fall of US capitalism. This is the story of the quantitative development of a society inching ever closer toward the negation of the negation. What these United States of America will be sublated into is unknown. However, we do know that it will be the dialectical product of a struggle between competing class forces.

Our place of departure is the struggle for dominance between sixteenth- and seventeenth-century Spanish and English colonialism mediated by the resistance of manacled Africans and Native Americans.

Critical Role of Capitalism

"Although we come across the first beginnings of capitalist production as early as the fourteenth or fifteenth century, sporadically, in certain towns of the Mediterranean, the capitalistic era dates from the sixteenth century" (Marx 1867/1967: 715).

The story here begins at the dawn of the capitalist era at the end of the fifteenth century in the European Mediterranean from which Christopher Columbus would engage in four voyages west to the so-called new world. Revolutionizing the Columbus narrative, historian Gerald Horne (2020) departs from both the discovery myth and the lost-at-sea myth and in the process obliterates all fantasies of European supremacy. Recontextualizing the desperation thesis Horne (2020) demonstrates how the superior Ottoman forces drove Madrid and Western Europeans to the Western hemisphere. Horne (2020) brings attention to the role of the Ottoman Empire as the premiere, dominant global force of the sixteenth century, even after being expelled from the Iberian Peninsula at the end of the fifteenth century.

Painting a picture of an era engulfed in a whirlwind of human movement, migration, and enslavement, Horne (2020) unveils a sixteenth century where European powers, far from dominant, are struggling to survive. For example, as the Ottoman Empire rose to dominance "Christians, sensing the directions of the prevailing winds, began defecting to the Ottoman side" (Horne 2020: 22). The Ottoman fleet, Horne (2020) reports, reflected the larger composition of the Ottoman Empire with Turks serving as commanders, Greeks and Bulgarians as oarsmen, and what Horne (2020) calls "specialists" drawn from "the heart of Christian Europe: Genoese, Catalans, Sicilians, Provençals [and] Venetians" (22).

As Madrid was moving to repress and enslave Africans for the so-called new world by the mid-sixteenth century the Ottomans had essentially conquered Eastern Europe, North Africa, and today's Middle East. Even though fleeing west opened the door for further Ottoman expansion, ultimately, the wealth accumulated in the colonies was so vast that it "allowed Madrid and their immediate neighbors to reverse what appeared to be insuperable advantages enjoyed by the Ottomans" (Horne 2020: 23).

Feudalistic State Power

The form of state power that served as the model in the colonies was that which was dominating Europe at the time—a form of feudalism based on inherited power with the Roman Catholic Church as its international center. In fact, the Catholic Church, which held "one-third of the soil of the Catholic world," but was nevertheless being threatened by Ottoman supremacy, served as Europe's "most powerful feudal lord" (Engels 1892/2007: 28).

The feudalistic state maintained power in a number of fundamental ways. First and foremost, dominance was achieved through the "centralization of the resources of the ruling-class" (Therborn 1978: 219). As a result, the ruled, in this case the peasantry, had to face not only local members of the ruling-class, "but a formidable apparatus in which the acquisitions of that class have been pooled" (Therborn 1978: 219). For Marxist philosopher Göran Therborn (1978: 219), the state is not just a concentrated form of external power wielded over the ruled, but it also "comprises them". In other words, both peasants and lords "were subjects of the feudal king" (Therborn 1978: 219).

The state is therefore designed to be an all-encompassing social entity. Central in the pursuit of complete control the feudal state sought to be a singular power with undivided representation. A highly concentrated repressive apparatus ran by a system of courts, bailiffs, henchmen, and prisons codified and enforced the feudal state's class character.

But the development of capitalism in London led to a split in the Christian state apparatus, resulting in England breaking from Rome and the Roman Catholic Church in a series of Parliamentary acts between 1532 and 1534. For example, the 1534 Act of Supremacy declared that the King of England, Henry, was the supreme head of the Church of England. This was a clear rupture from the Roman Catholic Church's doctrine proclaiming itself to be the rightful representative of the one true God, and therefore supreme ruler of the entire world. Because this split resulted in the fracturing of the feudal ruling-class's centralized resources and thus power, at first glance it seemed to indicate an opportune moment for the Ottomans to surge ahead.

Deteriorated Conditions in the Late Feudal State

The misery plaguing fifteenth- and sixteenth-century Europe suggested that a major political split in the Christian ruling-class state was an indicator of further decline. The instability and economic crisis of the Spain from which Columbus departed was so severe that the slightest fluctuations in food prices would cause thousands more than usual to starve to death. Regularly occurring famine in the countryside would cause an influx of desperate peasants into the cities in search of relief, which would in turn trigger epidemics and thousands of more fatalities. Sanitation was virtually non-existent with human feces and discarded animal remains rotting in the streets, and massive graves of the poor laying open, festering, waiting for an unceremonious layer of turf. For the vast and desperate peasantry, it was a virtual hell on earth.

The stench of the cities was so vile it lacks a modern comparison. Not only was bathing rare, many people never bathed their entire lives. Contributing to the putrid air was the commonplace smell of those desperately clinging to life, overtaken with oozing scabs, festering wounds, decaying teeth, and deformations left by ravenous diseases such as smallpox. Lawlessness and street crime were rampant amongst the living. Food riots were frequent and often broke out into prolonged warfare, leaving vast revolutionary traditions amongst the *many* in their wake. The suppression of the Peasant War in Germany between 1524 and 1525 left more than 100,000 of the 300,000 armed peasants slaughtered.

Slower to develop than England and France, Germany had no central hub of commerce. Individual princes sought increasingly more burdensome taxes to fund their luxuries, standing armies, and costs of government, which primarily fell upon the peasantry. The knights too increased their plundering of the peasants as industry and modern artillery increased their own expenses but with little if any new sources of income. In addition to the princes and knights, the clergy too served as feudal lords exploiting their dependents just as ruthlessly. Engels (1870/2006) notes that "in addition to the rack" the clergy "applied the fear of ex-communication … to wring the last penny from their subjects" (5). Towns also exploited the peasants to fund their growing expenses. Summarizing this situation Engels concludes that "no matter whose subject the peasant was … he was treated by all as a thing, a beast of burden, and worse" (10). However, despite this crushing oppression peasants were scattered over a large geographical area making "a single general national peasant revolt," before 1524, extremely difficult, even though "many local peasant insurrections" (11) were common.

Far from progressive, Europe was governed by a series of intolerable and reactionary feuding religious ruling-classes. Not only did peasants suffer crushing impressment, but accused witches were hunted and burned alive. It was even reported that in Milan in 1476 a man was beaten, killed, and then eaten by his assailants. In Paris the religious reformist "Huguenots were killed and butchered, and their various body parts were sold on the streets" (Stannard 1992: 61). Europe was consumed by the murderous Inquisition. Those who were not in good standing with the elites, especially people believed to be un-Christian, such as the Jewish community, were either deported in masse or brutally executed in the most horrific fashion, "on the gallows, at the stake, on the rack—while others were crushed, beheaded, flayed alive, or drawn and quartered" (62). Therborn (1978) describes these pogroms as ancient mechanisms designed by feudalistic states to *displace* unresolvable contradictions. For Therborn (1978), "pogroms [and] external wars … have repeatedly served as powerful instruments with which to divert class conflict and rally the ruled behind their rulers" (235).

Colonial Expansion as Displacement

Horne's (2020) thesis that Western Europe's struggle with the Ottomans was a "precondition of the rise of plundering of the Americas and Africa" (23) exemplifies Therborn's (1978) conclusion that states will work to displace their unresolvable internal contradictions when they erupt in crises. In the sixteenth century Madrid took full advantage of the Pope sanctifying the enslavement of Muslims in the fifteenth century, as an act of war of one dominant power against another. Ultimately, Horne (2020) characterizes this as an extension of the Crusades and therefore as "a pan-European Christian campaign against non-European/non-Christians (especially in the Americas and Africa)" (23). The concentration of ruling-class power was therefore a prerequisite of Madrid's invasion and occupation of the Caribbean islands, but was transferred and extended through the process.

Written in 1510, six years after Columbus's fourth and final voyage, the Requerimiento, a declaration read to either Native Americans, or sometimes just to an empty beach, claiming Spain's religious right of conquest, offers a vivid window into the racialized class-character informing the legal creation of the colonial state, which served as the larger context that informed the worldview of Columbus. Consider the following excerpt:

> On the part of the King ... and ... Queen ...,subduers of the barbarous nations, we ... make known to you ... that ... God ... created the Heaven and the Earth ... and ... all the men of the world ... Of all these nations God our Lord gave charge to one man, called St. Peter, that he should be Lord and Superior of all the men in the world, that all should obey him, and that he should be the head of the whole human race, wherever men should live ... [including] these islands ... We ... require ... that you ... acknowledge the Church as the Ruler ... of the whole world ... If you do not do this, and maliciously make delay in it, I certify to you that, with the help of God, we shall powerfully enter into your country, and shall make war against you in all ways and manners that we can ... ; we shall take you and your wives and your children, and shall make slaves of them, and as such shall sell and dispose of them as their Highnesses may command; and we shall take away your goods, and shall do you all the mischief and damage that we can, as to vassals who do not obey, and refuse to receive their lord ... ; and we protest that the deaths and losses which shall accrue from this are your fault, and not that of their Highnesses ...

It is therefore not surprising that one of the first things Columbus reports on in his journal after he "found very many islands with large populations" was that he "took possession of them" and encountered "no opposition" (Columbus 1493/1969: 115). Not only did he take possession of the islands, but he immediately began reorienting them through renaming the places as part of the colonial process of remaking the world Catholic. Reporting on his activity,

Columbus says, "I named the first island I found 'San Salvador', in honor of our Lord and Savior who granted me this miracle. The Indians [i.e. the Arawak] call it Guanahani" (115). After going through his list of renamed islands, Columbus feels compelled to somewhat redundantly report, "I renamed them all" (115), although we do not learn all of their original names. Further orienting his gaze toward Guanahani and the other islands as a profiteer, Columbus observes that "all these islands are extremely fertile" (116) with a wide variety of birds and fruits and accessible harbors, rivers, and mountains. Columbus, momentarily orienting his gaze in such a way as to exclude from his frame the civilization already there, describes the islands as "suitable for planting crops and for raising cattle ... and for building towns and villages" (117). Bent on securing funding for subsequent voyages by any means necessary, Columbus reports on "large mines of gold and other metals" (117) that simply were not there.

When Columbus does orient his gaze toward the "inhabitants," he does so from a Catholic point of orientation and claims they have no religion, "go naked," are "as simple as animals" and some, he claims, are "born with tails" and "eat human flesh" (117–19). At the same time, he reports that they are "men of great intelligence" and "so liberal with all their possessions that no one who has not seen them would believe it" (117–18). Taking his own economic experiences as the zero point of his orientation, Columbus commented that he has "not been able to find out if they have private property" (121). However, Columbus is not referring to the sublated form of private property at the heart of capitalism, which was still largely non-existent in Spain at the time. That is, he was not referring to the form of private property, "based on the employment of others," but rather, private property that "rests on the producers' own labor" (Marx 1867/1967: 765). Regardless, this seems to have been a mere passing reflection, for Columbus was clearly not concerned if the peoples of what is now known as the Caribbean conceived of the earth as property they privately owned because he was going to use whatever force that was required to take what he wanted despite any existing claims of ownership. Remember, Columbus came armed with not only iron swords and armor, but with the desperation of a society in decline. The bellicose informing the deadly spirit or impulse of the Requermiento reflects a position of fragility not of sturdiness or strength.

Consequently, Columbus (1493/1969) concludes that he "will bring back as large a cargo as their Highnesses may command" and "as many slaves" (122) as they request. It is telling that Columbus does not see in the happiness, friendliness, and lack of want in Arawak society a solution to the social depravity of the so-called old world, but rather, a land and people to exploit and ruin. We must remember, as far as he was concerned, Columbus was facing that which represented the "Orient." That is, an adversary depicted not as "empty" but embodying "that which is 'not Europe'" and the "resources for world making" (Ahmed 2006: 114–15). The Orient, for Europeans, came to mark the horizon, the division between opposites. This is the basis from which the simple dialect of Black and white or bad and good would emerge. The word orientation, in fact, stems from the root Orient. The orientation of Columbus had therefore already been established before he washed up on the shores of what is today known as the Caribbean basin.

On his second voyage, between 1493 and 1496, accompanied by many more ships and men, Columbus was joined by the King's physician, Dr. Chanca. Further expounding upon the cannibal myth in a letter to the King (which there has never been any concrete evidence to corroborate), Chanca (1496/1969) flippantly reports that "the captain went ashore" and "visited the houses" after "the inhabitants" had "fled" upon which time he "took a little of everything" including "four or five human arm and leg bones" (133). The disregard for not only the personal space and rights of the Arawak, but of their very lives was the product of a lawlessness of an emerging capitalism defined by "terroristic energy" and "cynical recklessness" (Marx 1867/1967: 286). This recklessness is the product of a system whose sole drive is the accumulation of value. Mediated through racism the colonists' search for value oriented their disregard for Arawak life.

Throughout his journals, Columbus very casually reports on capturing "Indians" as prisoners to enslave and extract information from. The level of cruelty and bloodletting Columbus's men unleashed on the peoples of the Caribbean, numbering perhaps in the millions, is astounding. In a few short decades the Caribbean islands were depopulated from murder for sport, to being worked to death in mines and on plantations, to the devastation of small pox and other infectious diseases the invaders carried with them. Compared to the hell Columbus and his men were coming from, the populous civilizations of the Caribbean appeared heaven-like. Columbus himself referred to the islands as Edenic, but nevertheless unleashed a level of barbarity that even surpassed the world from which he came. The orientation of the Spanish nobility toward the non-Catholic world would solidify the setting of the stage for centuries of unspeakable atrocities. However, as Horne (2018; 2020) demonstrates, Madrid's religious sectarianism would prove insufficient in competing with London's turn to a militarized form of identity politics (i.e. whiteness) as a model for settler-colonialism.

However, as a late comer London benefitted greatly from not only Madrid's racialized demonization of so-called *others*, but from the brutal warfare that weakened their African and Native American targets. That is—even though the concept of whiteness was an English not a Spanish construction—Columbus came to symbolize the beginning story of US history because it discursively turns the world upside down, where the civilized becomes savagery and savagery becomes civilized. The irony, as suggested here, is that the history record actually seems to suggest the opposite is much truer: the Caribbean was peaceful, clean, and the people were without want whereas much of the old world was wretched, violent, and the people experienced all manner of perpetual want and depravity. The Spanish's atrocities against the peoples of the Caribbean were so extreme that Bartolomé De Las Casas (1552/1992), himself a slaveowner and then colonizer and eventually a Cuban plantation owner, became a staunch critic not of colonialism per se, but of the manner in which it was carried out. De Las Casas, in fact, remained a staunch supporter of Columbus believing he was chosen by God to bring Christianity to the so-called new world referring to it as a "marvelous discovery" (3).

However, De Las Casas notes that "prominent amid the aspects of this story ... are the massacres of innocent peoples, the atrocities committed against them and, among other horrific excesses, the ways in which the towns ... have been entirely cleared of their native inhabitants" (3). Of the colonists involved in committing acts of genocide De Las Cases explains how they "had become so anaesthetized to human suffering ... that they ceased to be men in any meaningful sense of the term" (3). Outraged by the atrocities De Las Casas, writing to the King and Queen of Spain, explains that because "the indigenous peoples of the region are ... so gentile, so peace-loving, so humble, and so docile" that "it would constitute a criminal neglect of my duty to remain silent about the enormous loss of life" (6).

Indeed, in a mere thirty years after Columbus's first voyage the native peoples of the Caribbean, numbering in the millions, had been nearly exterminated. With an insatiable appetite for wealth the result of this apocalyptic holocaust drove Spanish ships up and down the North American coast of what would become Florida, Georgia, South Carolina, and Virginia spreading disease in search of indigenous peoples to enslave. Stannard (1992) tells a story of Spanish ships anchoring off the coast of modern-day South Carolina in 1521 making friends with native peoples. After two weeks of building trust, 60 to 120 indigenous people were invited onboard only to be swept off to the slave plantations of Santo Domingo. Enslaved, the captives were forced to find their own food among piles of "decomposing dogs and donkeys" (101). Four years later only one of the captives was still alive. The horrors of this experience, the unbridled terrorism of being simultaneously worked and starved to death, are difficult to comprehend. The Spanish would also establish St. Augustine, Florida, in 1565 (Horne 2014), the first permanent European settlement in what would later become the United States of America.

However, English settler colonialism would come to dominate North America's eastern seaboard. Lawrence Cremin (1970) attributes English hegemony to their use of education reasoning that they "had moved farther than any other Western power toward conceiving of colonies, not as exploitative bands of transient men, but as permanent, self-sustaining communities" that came to "embrace families, churches, missions, print shops, and schools" (p. 22). While the French and the Spanish employed education in their colonial models, Cremin contends that "none … managed to develop education as extensively as the English" (23).

Gerald Horne (2018: 7) poses and answers a similar question, asking how, "at the beginning of the seventeenth century," did "the sceptered isle … a second-class power" emerge "by the beginning of the eighteenth century … the planets' reigning super power"? Rather than pointing to London's use of education Horne (2018: 7) contends, as indicated above, that "any explanation that elides slavery, colonialism, and the shards of an emerging capitalism, along with their handmaiden—white supremacy—is deficient in explanatory power." For example, Horne notes that two-thirds of all migration into the Americas between 1600 and 1700 were enslaved Africans enriching English elites. Contributing significantly here were technological developments in vessels designed for warfare enabling London to defeat the Spanish Armada. Horne (2020) expands on his exploration into the roots of whiteness or pan-Europeanism that would ultimately prove a more effective form of amassing and wielding power than Madrid's religious sectarianism. That is, whiteness brought previously warring Europeans together as one so-called *race* in North America overcoming the limitations of England's relatively small population and the monumental and persistent threat of the rebellions of the enslaved. Madrid's focus on religion, on the other hand, excluded non-Catholics from their colonial project imposing dramatic limitations on their own ambitions. If the model of colonialism was one of the most determining or significant factor in the competition for dominance between the major European powers, then education played more of a supportive rather than leading role. This is not to say that education was not important, as we will see in the next sub-section.

England's rise to global dominance was led by feudal merchants (i.e. feudalism's middle-class) who had become enriched by slavery and strengthened by the whiteness of pan-Europeanism. This rising capitalist-class had gained a foothold within England's feudal state apparatus, which "had become too narrow for its expansive power" (Engels 1892/2007: 27). Engels points out that "before feudalism could be attacked in each country," Rome's "sacred central organization … had to be destroyed" (28). The war on feudal economic arrangements waged by the rising capitalist-class "had to take on a religious disguise" (28).

In England the King and Parliament were "in insolent conflict" with the "feudal lords" (Marx 1867/1967: 718). The old nobility had been torn asunder by the feudal wars and the *new* Nobility were children of their time, "for which money was the power of all powers" (718). The rapid expansion of wool manufacturing and the rise in the price of wool in England, for Marx, account for the *new* Nobility's acts of enclosure. As a result, privileged merchants and Nobility seized hold of peasant lands and resources. These acts, in other words, were designed to expropriate the peasants from the soil, transforming them from relatively independent producers into a class of dependent and desperate wage laborers primed to become colonizers. Because of nearly constant warfare between Europeans, these soon-to-be white desperadoes were also experienced and hardened soldiers ready to complete the process of Indigenous and African subjugation started by earlier waves of Spanish colonizers. Horne (2018) therefore notes that part of what led to England's ultimate success as a colonizer was its inability to keep its subjects content at home.

In May of 1607 when the first permanent English settlement was established, which the colonists named Jamestown, Virginia, "the people they found were greatly reduced in number from what they had been before the coming of the earlier Europeans" (Stannard 1992: 102). For example, in 1586 English troops brought "disease and death throughout Virginia" (102) leaving the pock mark scars on many of the faces of the survivors to be seen by English colonists in 1607. Damage inflicted on Native American nations and confederations by earlier waves of European profiteers contributed to London's rise.

What the English called Jamestown or Fort James was part of the Powhatan Confederacy's national territory, which they called Tsenacommacah. The Powhatan speak an Algonquin-based language and their confederacy included at least thirty nations. As was the case for Native Americans throughout the continent, a central food crop of the Powhatan was corn, developed from a strain of grass around 7,000 years ago in what is today Central Mexico. The sweet smell of corn crops would have been encountered by the British colonists. The mild scent of ceremonial tobacco smoke was also common in Powhatan society. Despite ravages of European disease and slavers, the Powhatan Confederacy was still powerful in 1607 and the survival of the untrained British depended upon the *presence* of their knowledge and assistance—not their *absence*.

As a capital venture the colonial investors and governors traded the relatively cheap and abundant manufactured goods they brought from England, such as metal pots, guns, iron axes, fish hooks, and farming implements, for not only food, but for beaver and other furs, which were abundant to their Northeastern Native American hosts, but were rare and highly valuable in European markets, contributing to England's global advance. Consequently, intensified fur trapping dramatically depleted wild game populations in North America, reorienting space and forcing indigenous communities to further reorient their organizational structures and economies away from self-sufficiency and toward an approach dependent upon foreign markets. This would further shift the balance of power from North America's first nations to the English interlopers and therefore the fall of the former and the rise of the latter.

Capitalism's immediate impact on the orientation of Native American space was less about the introduction of new objects, such as domesticated animals, and more about the re-composition of indigenous objects and the enslavement of indigenous people. Perhaps the indigenous object to have the longest and most global reach was the Native American tobacco plant, enormously popular in Europe, which quickly became the focus of colonial labor as a highly lucrative cash crop. In 1613 the London Company brought its first four barrels of tobacco to London. A mere three years later 2,300 pounds of tobacco were sent, and by 1620 it had increased to 60,000 pounds (Takaki 2008).

In this way, the investors brought an idea to Tsenacommacah: the idea of producing for profit rather than necessity. However, with an abundance of land due to the genocide of English aggression combined with the devastation of European infectious diseases severely weakening Native American nations, labor was a scarcity in seventeenth-century colonial America. Those who could pay their own way to the colonies, such as government officials, clergymen, merchants, and artisans, arrived as freemen and were typically able to purchase land and become self-directed producers. The labor of this class therefore tended not to be available to tobacco growers for purchase. Free labor for purchase was a rare commodity in the colonies rendering the project of whiteness that much more important to the advancement of English colonialism. As a result, wages were as much as three times higher in the colonies compared to England.

It is therefore not surprising that between two-thirds and three-quarters of the nearly 150,000 English, Irish, and Germans who came to Virginia between 1607 and 1660 came as indentured servants. According to Eric Foner (2009a) "the majority of newcomers were young, single men from the bottom rungs of English society, who had little to lose by emigrating" (51). Not only did the vast majority of European laborers come from oppressed backgrounds and criminalized due to the means they were forced into to survive, from prostitution to petty theft, many of them were either tricked and conned into becoming servants or outright kidnapped. Because of the process of expropriating peasants from the soil in the shift from proprietorship to wage labor in England, many of these newcomers "had already moved from place to place in England. Colonial migration was in many ways an extension of the migration" (51) happening within England itself.

Whiteness in the English colonies was not just about pan-Europeanism. The mobilization of race was also an important source of divisive social control since conditions for the enslaved and the indentured were nearly identical reflecting what Horne (2020) refers to as the Ottomans's equal opportunity enslavement of Europeans, Africans, and those from the so-called Near East. Indentured servants and the enslaved alike, in London's American colonies, could "be bought and sold, could not marry without the permission of their owner, were subject to physical punishment, and saw their obligation to labor enforced by the courts" (52). Providing even more intimate details here, Takaki (2008) notes that the indentured servants "were sometimes forced to wear iron collars around their necks, and often beaten and even tortured for recalcitrance, and always required to have passes when they left their plantations" (53). The exhausting work included clearing land of trees, bushes, and roots, plowing the soil in preparation for planting, and breaking ones back and arms from "topping young plants" and "carrying heavy loads of tobacco leaves" and forced to survive on "a dreary mess made from ground Indian corn called loblolly" (54).

Colonial Repressive State Apparatus

To establish and then maintain this system of occupation and exploitation the ruling-class concentration of state power was essential. The basis of this concentration of power can be traced to "the private, informal, and sometimes voluntary efforts of Spanish and English colonists in the Caribbean and Latin America who sought to control their growing enslaved populations" (Hadden

2001: 7). The development of the colonial state, from the perspective or orientation of the colonial ruling-class, emerged out of the demands of material conditions, such as the need for slave patrols. However, slave patrols were not just about the daily repression of regulating the movement of the enslaved and countering the ever-present danger of the slave rebellion, but in the Carolinas and then Georgia especially, they doubled as a militia to counter invading Spanish forces who had colonial holdings in what they called St. Augustine Florida, nearly a century before Londoners established their Virginia colony.

The legal basis and organizational structure of slavery and slave patrols, unlike other areas of colonial law, such as regulating trade, private property, and morality, were not barrowed from existing English law. This was simply because in the area of slavery "English common law was sparse" (Hadden 2001: 8). Slavery was not legally recognized within the boundaries of England. Rather, English law dealt with slavery only in the context existing outside of its boundaries. As a result, "English courts were slow to create extensive case law relating to enslaved persons" (Hadden 2001: 8).

Fleeing the instability of Barbados gripped by perpetual anti-slavery rebellion, thousands of Bajan slave owners, with their human property in tow, settled in South Carolina in the seventeenth century. With them they brought repressive social control practices such as setting and enforcing curfews. Codified in law curfews made it illegal for the enslaved to travel outside of their master's house after sunset or before sunrise without a note or a pass from their master or overseer. This system of passes would persist until the abolition of slavery in 1865.

South Carolina's legislative assembly, like other colonies, enforced laws regulating the behavior of the enslaved, such as curfews, patrols and watches that every man between the ages of sixteen and sixty-five were required to volunteer in. Laws were also established that required slave owners to routinely inspect slave quarters for weapons, illicit gatherings, literacy materials, and so-called stolen goods. By the eighteenth century there was a shift from volunteer enforcers to appointing "colony sanctioned authority figures" (Hadden 2001: 38) to enforce slave law.

Again, an entire story of arrival had to be invented to justify apocalyptic atrocities that would be inflicted upon Native Americans and Africans through land theft, genocide, and enslavement. Such stories of justification would serve as the basis of whiteness forged to control and wield the collective power of European laborers molded into a sinister nation of white people. This is the source of modern racialization and class-bias developed and transmitted through legal and cultural institutions made possible from the concentration of ruling-class power. In the colonial context this power was concentrated through the monarchical/religious political state codifying and mandating an officially sanctioned education.

Critical Role of Education

Even though the orientation of our gaze has been focused primarily on Spain and England, Engels's brief (1870/2006) discussion of the class character of education in sixteenth-century German feudalism offers an excellent introduction to early capitalist education in England. It's also generalizable enough to help us begin understanding the form of education brought to Virginia after 1607 by British colonists. Engels begins by describing the whole of Europe's feudalistic Middle Ages as a "primitive stage of development" devoid of its former civilization. Consequently, as was also the case in England and Spain, in Germany, the clergy was the conveyor of feudalistic ideology. As a result, the clerics dominated education. However, with technological developments in printing and advances in capitalism, the church began to lose its "monopoly" on "reading and writing" as well as on "higher education" (5). As the division of labor continued to develop with the rise of the "judicial estate," many "inroads into the intellectual realm" were forged, thereby driving religious leaders from many of the most "influential offices" (5). This process of undermining the clergy's control over the educational apparatus was part of a larger revolution of the emerging merchant, bourgeois class against their feudal foes.

So critical was education to colonialism, given the unique challenges of the colonies described above, that it took on slightly different characteristics according to the uniqueness of the different colonies from Georgia to New Hampshire. But a common characteristic among all manifestations of colonial education stemmed from the fact that "North America was colonized during the first phase of Europe's age of print … when a reading public gradually came into being that … was not confined to the clerisy or the aristocracy" (Cremin 1970: 27–8). Cremin points to the revolutionary transformation—or qualitative shift—from feudalistic tendencies to more capitalistic tendencies. Cremin describes the Europeans of this time as essentially "medieval" while "standing on the threshold of modernity" (28).

One of the central reasons why Cremin points to education as a dominant factor in why England's model of colonialism became hegemonic is because access to printing meant that colonial investors no longer had to bring a whole class of expensive experts and professionals to the colonies, and instead only had to bring a stack of books and a minister who could double as a reading instructor. Cremin describes this as the partial liberation of people from the oral tradition. In other words, English capitalists took full advantage of cutting-edge technology (i.e. modern printing), which they had access to because of their leading position within a developing capitalist system.

The argument that the Scriptures should be translated into the common languages of the people as the purest path to enlightenment was not just a theological challenge to the Roman Catholic Church's practice of excluding the laboring masses from access to written religious texts. Rather, the Protestant Reformation was a religious disguise of what was really part of the capitalist-class' war on the center of feudal power (Engels 1892/2007). By the seventeenth century so-called *white* colonists were using English translations of the Bible as one of the primary texts read and studied by the primarily indentured and enslaved labor force.

When we look at the form of education brought to North America by London and the form of education that existed during the beginning stages of the capitalist era, we see a form of sublation. That is, aspects of feudal education, like feudalism more generally, were overcome yet preserved. In other words, rather than the ending of one stage and the beginning of another, sublation reflects the presence of continuity. While feudalistic education was reserved for the religious elites and was designed to reproduce the believe that social classes were preordained by God and therefore immutable, colonialist education slowly overcame this rigidity and adopted the Protestant work ethic that allowed for at least the idea of social mobility. Religious education was therefore simultaneously overcome and preserved to support an emerging capitalism funded by colonialism.

Summarizing the religious character of education in the British colonies in North America, Lawrence Cremin (1970) notes that "during the first phases of Virginia settlement … education was in the hands of the ministers, who used it both as an instrument for promoting discipline and order among the colonists and as a device for winning the loyalty of the natives" (9). In practice, education consisted of attending church twice a day to pray for deliverance from the persistent influences of the devil believed to cause mutinies and imported laborers fleeing so-called Godly society for Indian society. Colonists were taught that fleeing the colony would result in hell fire damnation in the afterlife. By the 1620s serious consideration was beginning to be given to the education of children in the colonies with a particular emphasis on teaching religion and civilization. In 1622 John Brinsley wrote a treatise, a sort of teacher education text, for the teachers of young impressionable colonial children, aimed at the colonies with resistant indigenous peoples, including Ireland and Virginia. The persistent struggle among the investor class to maintain control over colonial subjects and prevent them from abandoning or rebelling against the colony paved the way for the widespread use of popularly written "devotional literature" which addressed the "day-by-day problems of ordinary men and women" (41).

Popular in the colonies were the pedagogical works by English Historian, John Foxe, who had observed that God's reformation of the Church was led not by the sword, but by the printing press. Foxe's texts reflected an apocalyptic view of this period. Targeting the senses and emotions, Foxe's books were filled with numerous woodcuts, "many of them representing vivid scenes of torment and torture" with title pages adorned with images of "the Lord in final judgement, the world at his feet," including "sober Protestant patriarchs … in celebration … ; tonsured Catholic monks … being dragged downward by Satan into the fires" (43). Foxe had rewritten the biblical idea of a chosen people into a sort of nascent nationalism designed to bind the English together with a common purpose and destiny in a so-called untamed wilderness. The English Protestants were portrayed as heroic for overcoming "extraordinary adversity" and therefore "entrusted with carrying the word to all nations, whatever the hazards or the costs" (45). This was a "bold conception of education" deemed necessary because of the ever-present fear of lapsing into "barbarism" (45) in the colonies. Foxe's work situated in the context of the colonies contributed to London's pan-European project of whiteness.

Contributing to the pan-European project of whiteness in what would become one of the foundations of colonial education was the Dutch Christian Humanist, Desiderius Erasmus's *The Education of a Christian Prince*. Erasmus was commissioned to write this text in 1515 by Prince Charles of Burgundy. The *Christian Prince* outlines what it considered to be the just state and a guide for its creation, covering everything from "taxation, the encouragement of industry, the enactment of laws, the negotiation of treaties" (59) and so on. Prominent in the text is the insistence that the just ruler (i.e. the Christian Prince) is not just to maintain the prosperity of the state but to extend it. Within this context the role of education was "a device for maintaining public docility and order" (60).

Here we see social control as a purpose of education and what would become the police as one of the primary functions of the repressive state.

It is important to note that Erasmus, Foxe, and other bourgeois pedagogues were not the only act in town, as it were. That is, in 1516 Sir. Thomas More, a more progressive aristocrat, offered *Utopia*, advocating for a radical humane Christianity based on his vision of an ideal society that was partly informed by reports of actually existing Native American societies as well as ancient Greece. The text even argues that among the many distinct Native American societies, there are those that are more advanced in terms of their laws and social structures than can be found in Europe. More more forcefully and bluntly insisted that genuine social justice could never really be realized without the complete equalization of concrete material conditions, including every conceivable measure of standard of living and life satisfaction. More was a proponent of social equality, communal wealth and property, and democracy or popular sovereignty. While More's work offered a progressive vision, his utopian vision included slavery, revealing his own aristocratic orientation. Of course, More would be executed for treason in 1532 for refusing to break from the Roman Catholic Church and take the Oath of Supremacy recognizing Henry as Supreme Head of the Church of England.

As noted above, England's colonial architects gravitated toward a different type of curricular vision. That is, rather than look to More's view of social justice and positive view of Native Americans, the colonists turned to the belief that "the foundation of a just society lies in the union of nobility and learning" where the idea of nobility is "inherent and natural" (69) rendering *the few* the natural superiors of *the many*. This makes sense in the context of the colonies where indentured servitude and then slavery ruled the day, which necessitated a vastly more unjust ideological orientation that rigidly locked people into their social location through biological determinism.

While the education of colonial subjects was focused on the promotion of docility and obedience, the *Society for the Propagation of the Gospel in Foreign Parts* served a very similar function for the education of Native peoples. Because the subjugation of Indigenous nations in North America was not automatic or immediate, or ever really complete, London employed all manner of so-called *law and order* to facilitate this process. The society's first mission in 1702 in South Carolina was a failed and short-lived attempt to Christianize the Yamasee. The Society never attempted to Christianize the Yamasee again. Unable to subdue them through ideology (religion), the Yamasee "suddenly found themselves hunted by English slave kidnappers and cheated by English traders" (Venables

2004a: 125–6). Consequently, in 1715 the Yamasee engaged in a mass uprising that could have eliminated the entire South Carolina settlement (Horne 2014). This uprising, the so-called Yamasee War, included a complex array of alliances between and within multiple Indigenous and European forces centered around the struggle between London and Madrid over the North American colonies.

Turning to the powerful Nations of the Haudenosaunee in New York, who, in many ways, held the balance of power between the English and the French in North America before the American Revolution, the Society targeted the Mohawk as the most English friendly. In 1702 the Society sent a missionary to live among the Mohawk, but after just a year they left reporting their conversion efforts had been evaded. The failed attempt to Christianize the Mohawk was attributed to "the continued mistreatment of the Indians at the hands of the land speculators, the disreputable behavior of the military garrison at Albany" (Cremin 1970: 349) and the competition between Dutch and English merchants for access to the lucrative Haudenosaunee fur trade. In 1712 another more aggressive attempt was made to convert the Mohawk to Christianity, but ended in 1719 with few results. Additional unsuccessful efforts were made continuously until London ended its support for the Society after the American Revolution.

The Resistance

Not only did colonial education attempts fail to Christianize Native Americans, it also seemed to have questionable initial success at engendering fear within the colony's laboring classes. For example, during the winter of 1609–10, one in seven Virginia colonists deserted the colony. As a result, martial law was declared and a military form of social organization was implemented, including the establishment of "military discipline for labor" and the use of "harsh punishments, including execution, for resistance" (Linebaugh & Rediker 2000: 33). Like education, one of the primary purposes of this extreme form of rule was to keep the imported laborers and the Powhatan apart.

Linebaugh and Rediker offer a stark comparison between colonial society and Powhatan society, offering a glimpse into the appeal of the latter. While such brief comparisons risk reproducing dichotomous and simplistic thinking, it is important to note that the Powhatans had developed structures many oppressed people found appealing, as More alluded in his *Utopia*. The following differences reflect the social formations developed around different values. For example, whereas the Powhatan freely hunted, fished, gathered, and farmed without private property or alienation from their labor, nature, or each other, the colonial laborers were called into labor by the morning drum and often toiled in complete alienation as they produced cash crops for export or constructed fortifications as protection against Spanish competitors rather than producing food for consumption. Powhatan society seemed to not be burdened by social classes, a repressive state, or a military bureaucracy for warriors, which was in stark contrast to the colonies.

Another stark contrast was that both men and women in Powhatan society experienced sexual freedom, even within marriage, while sexuality was deeply repressed in Europe and within the colonies. It is also not surprising that only three reported instances of "mixed marriage" took place in seventeenth-century Virginia before the practice was officially outlawed in 1691. Europeans and Africans who fled indentured servitude and slavery for Native American societies were officially adopted and encouraged to marry within the tribe if they desired. It was also not uncommon in the seventeenth century, before the full implementation of chattel slavery, for European indentured servants and Africans, to flee to Native American societies together and marry (Foner 2009a; Takaki 2008).

The unity between the many was viewed as a challenge, or a potential challenge, to colonial rule. The whiteness that developed out of a fifteenth-century pan-Europeanism was not only instrumental in London's eclipsing of the Ottomans and Madrid, but it has been key in fostering divisiveness and mistrust within the colony's toiling classes. In other words, workers fleeing the colonies threatened the existence of the colonies—without workers there is no work, and without work there is no profit.

Colonialism, in short, transformed the Americas and the Caribbean from a place of liberty and happiness to a place of "bondage, war, scarcity, and famine" (Linebaugh & Rediker 2000: 35). It is no wonder, given this larger context, that "in search of food and a way of life that many ... found congenial, a steady stream of English settlers opted to become ... Anglo-Powhatans" (p. 34). Ahmed's (2006) conclusion that "bodies that experience being out of place might need to be oriented, to find a place where they feel comfortable and safe in the world" (158) is particularly relevant here. The relevance stems from how oppressive life in colonial America was for laborers, English, or otherwise.

However, while it made sense for the Powhatans to practice their traditional custom of adoption during the colonial era when they had a national territory and significant center of power, today the Powhatans no longer have access to their ancestral lands and their numbers are very small. In the contemporary context with a very different balance of power the Powhatans no longer allow non-Powhatans into their recovering nation. For example, on the official Powhatan Renape Nation homepage, information attributed to the late Chief Roy Crazy Horse informs people who may be able to trace their own lineage to a distant Powhatan relative to the seventeenth century, " ... might say they were 1/16384 Powhatan. Obviously, such persons would have very little claim to membership in today's Powhatan Renape Nation, although we would value their friendship and support" (Powhatan Renape Nation). The danger today, unlike in the seventeenth century, is cooptation, which can inadvertently subvert the struggle for national sovereignty and land reclamation.

But in the seventeenth century runaway settlers were captured and returned to the colonies by military force. It was common amongst those Europeans forcibly returned to the colonies (even among those who had been kidnapped to repopulate indigenous societies decimated by European warfare and disease) to only respond to their adopted Native American names, refuse to speak anything but Native American languages, only feel comfortable in indigenous cloths, and "regard ... their white saviors as barbarians and their deliverance as captivity" (Axtell 1975: 62). The Powhatan, among many other tribes, had well-established procedures for adopting new members. Adoptees, regardless of age or gender, were treated as equals in every respect, many of whom would eventually assume leadership roles in the most important aspects of the societies. Offering a window into part of the elaborate adoption process Axtell reproduces an excerpt from a speech a Powhatan chief reportedly gave on behalf of an adopted English colonist, James Smith. According to Smith's account, he was told:

> My son, you are now flesh of our flesh and bone of our bone. By the ceremony that was performed this day, every drop of white blood was washed out of your veins. You are taken into the Caughnewaga nation ... You are adopted into a great family and now received with great seriousness and solemnity in the room and place of a great man. After what has passed this day you are now one of us by an old strong law and custom. My son ... we are now under the same obligations to love, support and defend you that we are to love and to defend one another. Therefore you are to consider yourself as one of our people.
>
> (72)

Smith reports that he was at first reluctant to believe this "fine speech" but "since that time I have found that there was much sincerity in said speech; for from that day I never knew them to make any distinction between me and themselves in any respect whatever" (quoted in Axtell 1975: 72). It is no wonder why the colonial ruling-class was so threatened by the way indigeneity successfully and swiftly reoriented so many indentured colonists and enslaved Africans who were able to flee captivity. Again, the oppressiveness of colonial society drove many laborers to seek a more affirming alternative.

To strike fear in others and prevent them from doing the same, returned colonists were often executed in the most horrific fashion, from being burned alive, hanged, shot, drawn and quartered, and so on. For Linebaugh and Rediker (2000) this colonialist terrorism "created boundaries" (35). That is, it reaffirmed the orientation of the world rigidly divided between *us* and *them*, and painted white and black. The Powhatan would not accept the destruction of their world and came to the conclusion that to preserve it the Virginia colony must end. However, more than a decade before the Powhatan came to this conclusion, they tried multiple times to maintain a peaceful coexistence. A famous speech by the Powhatan leader the English called Powhatan is indicative of their orientation and desire for peace:

> I am now grown old and must soon die, and the succession must descend in order, to my brothers, Opitchapam, Opechancanough, and Kekataugh, and then to my two sisters, and their two daughters. I wish their experience was equal to mine, and that your love to us might not be less than ours to you. Why should you take by force that from us which you can have by love? Why should you destroy us who have provided you with food? What can you get by war? We can hide our provisions and fly into the woods. And then you must consequently famish by wrongdoing your friends. What is the cause of your jealousy? You see us unarmed and willing to supply your wants if you come in a friendly manner; not with swords and guns as to invade an enemy. I am not so simple as not to know that it is better to eat good meat, lie well, and sleep quietly with my women and children; to laugh and be merry with the English, and, being their friend, to have copper, hatchets, and whatever else I want, than to fly from all, to lie cold in the woods, feed upon acorns, roots and such trash, and to be so hunted that I cannot rest, eat, or sleep. In such circumstances, my men must watch, and if a twig should but break, all would cry out, 'Here comes Captain Smith.' And so, in this miserable manner to end my miserable life. And, Captain Smith, this might soon be your fate too through your rashness and advisedness. I, therefore, exhort you to peaceable councils, and above all I insist that the guns and swords, the cause of all our jealousy and uneasiness, be removed and sent away.
>
> (Powhatan 1609/1995: 111)

The final straw that pushed the Powhatan Confederacy over the edge were plans to build an Indian college designed to convert the Native peoples to Christianity. The Powhatans understood that adopting white ways would give whites a major advantage by stripping them of their culture and forcing them to deal with whites only on white terms. What is more, the colonists' numbers were growing. The encroachment on Powhatan land was therefore intensifying as was the colonists' demand on the Powhatan's food stores.

Threatening their land, culture, and food supply, Powhatan leadership decided to exterminate the aggressive, expanding Virginia colony. In 1622, Powhatan warriors, intimately familiar with colonists' routines from being their primary food vendor, simultaneously struck thirty-one locations across a 70-mile area and killed nearly 350 of a population of 1,200 (Venables 2004a: 81–2). As a result, hundreds of colonists fled to England. Cut off from their food supply, 500 additional colonists died that winter of starvation. As a result, James I, using the attack as an excuse, took over Virginia, which was the London Company's private investment. Having been operated as a private venture for its first seventeen years, Virginia "became [a] royal colony in 1624 and control transferred to the Crown appointed governor" (Urban & Wagoner 2009: 18). This led to ten years of bloody war and contributed to an already developing trans-Atlantic African slave trade.

Conclusion

In this chapter, we saw how the colonial model of development in the Caribbean informed the settler model of development in North America. However, despite attempts to limit the proportion of enslaved to free in the North American colonies, the lust for slave profits proved too intoxicating. As a result, slave rebellions and insurrections would not be limited to the Caribbean and would eventually give way to the counter-revolution of 1776. The grueling life for indentured servants and the enslaved in North America's settler colonies compelled vast numbers of laborers to flee the colonies for the surrounding Native American countries. The problem of controlling workers through the combined use of a repressive state apparatus (i.e. the police and prisons) and ideas, such as whiteness, would come to dominate education from that time on. In Chapter 3 we will continue to see these processes develop with elites on one side and the various groups of the many on the other pushing back.

3

The Trans-Atlantic Slave Trade and the Balance of Forces in the Colonies

Introduction: Connection to the previous Chapter

In Chapter 2 we saw Madrid's move west to colonize the Caribbean not a sign of strength and global leadership, as the US dominant narrative boasts, but rather a sign of internal and external vulnerability and destabilization. We saw the emergence of pan-Europeanism and whiteness as a similar sign of desperation, which would eventually propel London not only ahead of Spain, but more significantly, ahead of the powerful Ottoman Empire. We saw the concentration of ruling-class power manifest itself in the unique context of the colonies with repressive and ideological apparatuses serving the purpose of social control. We also saw that despite the mobilization of ruling-class power, the widespread resistance and insurrection in the colonies could be slowed down, but they could not be stopped.

The present chapter explores these themes in considerable more detail within the trans-Atlantic slave trade. For example, this chapter explores the role of persistent and intensifying slave rebellions as an additional factor causing the colonial ruling-class to contribute to the institutionalization of whiteness as a defensive form of power concentration. It is within this context that the slave patrols and city guards would further develop as one of the early forerunners to the modern police. We will also see the further combined development of the repressive state apparatus and education for the enslaved as mandatory ignorance. In response we see the informal education of the enslaved created and transmitted from one generation to the next with the purpose of advancing the struggle for emancipation.

Finally, the present chapter continues to map the balance of forces between competing European powers over control of the American colonies.

Critical Role of Capitalism

"That the slave trade was the very life of the colonies had, by 1700, become an almost unquestioned axiom in British practical economics" (Dubois 1896/2007: 2).

Continuing the discussion of slavery and capitalism in the American and Caribbean colonies, DuBois reminds the contemporary reader that London's (as well as Madrid's and Paris's) colonies did not and would not have an independent economic existence separate from the economies of the countries that established them as basically off-shore businesses. Even today, while individual capitalist countries have their own internal economic institutions, regulations, growth rates, etc., they do not exist independently from the larger global capitalism system. Nevertheless, nation states, mobilizing an atomized gaze, tend to portray their own economies as independent entities disconnected from the rest of the capitalist world, even while either negotiating trade deals with other countries on one hand, or threatening to or carrying out trade-related military interventions on the other. While there is just one interrelated, global, capitalist economy, it is composed of shifting and competing forces within and between capitalist states and between capitalist and socialist states. This global system is the same system that existed in the seventeenth century, just at a different place in its development.

Orienting our gaze to the European colonies of the seventeenth century, their primary purpose was to provide value or wealth to advance the development of capitalism in Europe, which was "racked by a general crisis in the international economy, the political system, and moral and intellectual life" (Genovese 1969: 23). The ability of the emerging English working-class, whose sublated tradition of resisting the deep exploitation of late feudalism enabled them to slow capitalism's internal drive to increase the rate of exploitation. This resistance limited the development of capitalism itself, which is dependent upon compounding growth. As a result, the colonies' ability to provide a lucrative source of wealth to build up London, for example, played a crucial role in the larger balance of global forces.

Genovese argues that because the "purchasing power" of the peasantry in the American colonies "remained minimal and offered a poor market for Western goods," the "most advanced capitalist countries" (e.g., England and Holland) felt compelled out of economic necessity to use slavery for "enormous economic gain" (24). Horne (2014) provides another important factor that explains why London in particular turned to the enslavement of Africans as a primary source of labor in the colonies rather than the more readily available English working-class: they "were more inclined to see the poor as a necessary resource for ensuring the prosperity of the metropolis itself, notably as a reservoir of labor that should not be squandered in colonial projects" (44). That is, a reserve-pool of labor not only offers the capitalist some flexibility in the size of their active labor force (which is necessary because of the ebb and flow of production) but it fosters competition among workers for jobs, thereby suppressing wages and effectively countering working-class collective resistance.

The colonies provided value-laden raw materials for manufacture in England, and when possible, also served as an emerging market to unload manufactured goods produced in the mother country. For example, tobacco produced in Virginia with enslaved Africans purchased by the Royal African Company (chartered by Charles II in 1672) would be processed and manufactured into consumer goods in London and unloaded in markets globally. In this way "colonialism was the midwife that assisted in the birth of European capitalism" (Loomba 2005).

Inventing Slave Law

Since there was not a substantial legal precedent in English Common Law for slavery, it had to be constructed in practice (Hadden 2001). By 1645, we find records of Africans being sold with livestock and thereby being classified as property in London's North American colony. By the 1650s, roughly 70 percent of Africans in Virginia, still a relatively small number of individuals, were living as legally constructed chattel. In 1661, the Virginia Assembly began to pass laws making slavery de jure. By 1669, the Virginia legislature defined a slave as property (Takaki 2008). The repressive state apparatus would develop along with this gradual codification of slavery. However, it was the ongoing flaring up of rebellions, such as the multi-national (i.e. ethnically diverse) Bacon's Rebellion of 1676 that propelled the colonial ruling-class to take decisive measures to ensure greater social control including segregating and dividing the laboring classes. Some have argued that one of the consequences was the shift from a reliance on European indentured servants to the enslavement of more and more Africans (Foner 2009a; Takaki 2008).

However, DuBois (1896/2007) and Horne (2014) argue that African's intense resistance to enslavement in the Caribbean was the primary factor that caused mainland colonists to attempt to limit their reliance on slavery, but "the lust for the profit Africans produced was so mesmerizing that it tended to override commonsensical judgement" (74). For example, enslaving colonists were particularly weary of any African who had spent time enslaved with the militantly rebellious Africans in Barbados or Jamaica, countries that Horne (2014) refers to as "training schools" for "revolt" (54). In other words, it was not only the unity between poor whites, Africans, and Native Americans that concerned colonists, but the intensity and persistence of rebellions against slavery. Consequently, as the slave trade and the corresponding atrocities intensified, the expanding capitalist system driving it was simultaneously creating its own gravediggers in the oppressed slaves. Clearly, the Africans celebrated in Horne's work are not passive victims without agency, but savvy tacticians who fought back and, in the process, significantly altered the balance of forces.

Another Reason for Whiteness

Horne locates the emergence of a specific codified form of whiteness around 1660. Historian Theodore Allen (2012), after pouring through countless Virginia county records, locates what he argues is the first official use of the term "white" in a 1691 Virginia law. However, a construct as ubiquitous as whiteness does not just have one cause or appear and reorient the world overnight. Taken together Horne and Allen offer additional insight into the social forces that gave way to the invention of the so-called white race. Again, rather than placing emphasis on the purpose of whiteness as primarily focused on dividing the working-class and subverting African, Native American, and European unity, as has been customary within critical pedagogy, Horne (2014) stresses its elite intention was more about forging a united European front across ethnic, class, and religious lines against "violent Africans and their indigenous comrades" (31). At the same time, whiteness would effectively remove millions of poor Europeans from the impulse in the colonies to unite across ethnic lines. Critical pedagogy's history of whiteness thesis and Horne's are therefore not mutually exclusive.

Bacon's Rebellion

Going back for a moment to Bacon's Rebellion, it is worth mentioning that it was a complex affair much more nuanced than a simple case of the exploited rising up against their exploiters, although that was certainly a part of it. European and African indentured servants and the enslaved, after having their highly abusive servitude either repeatedly extended or even made permanent (as was happing to Africans) their anger and frustration were beginning to boil. They demanded liberty and freedom from bondage. Required to defend the colony militarily, stemming from the slave patrols, most servants of all backgrounds were armed thereby making a ready-made army.

Bacon, however, was not indentured or a servant of any kind. Bacon was a moderately wealthy planter whose anger was against Governor Berkeley whose lucrative fur trade with Native Americans led him to protect indigenous national territory against the planters' insatiable appetite for new lands. As the demand and value of tobacco soared, the drive to expand their growing operations saw no limit. What is more, the wealthier and more influential planters were beginning to monopolize politics and production pushing less influential planters like Bacon out of business. Bacon's anger, initially, was directed at the Native Americans whose land he desired. After attacking Native communities, his army of 500 white and Black servants turned to Berkeley and Jamestown, which they burned to the ground before so-called *law* and *order* was restored and the uprising subdued.

Enslavement and Patrolling

Contributing to the surge in the African slave trade was the so-called Glorious Revolution of 1688, which opened up the Monarchy's monopoly to privateers. Horne (2014) refers to this move as opening the market in Africans to a form of free trade and private traders. This massive deregulation in London was a major step forward for US capitalism. As the devastation and atrocities intensified, so too did African resistance, which had already forced many colonizers in the Caribbean to flee to the mainland as Maroons were gaining ground and inflicting major casualties on the terrorism of slavery. Summarizing the African response to what was becoming a more aggressive and barbaric slave trade, Horne notes that the "increase in the slave trade also delivered deadly perils in the form of enraged Africans who could reverse the theretofore delightful fortunes of colonizers and murder them all or—as mainland settlers came to fear—ally with a European power, then murder them all" (43).

After the 1650s, we see a corresponding spike in the number of people captured in Africa and transported to America in the most unimaginable conditions. Takaki (2008) summarizes this shift, noting that "from 5 percent of the colony's population in 1675, blacks increased sharply to 25 percent by 1715 and over 40 percent by 1750" (61). The journey across the Atlantic itself was horrific and became more so the more demanding the trade in human flesh became. Offering a vivid window into this traumatizing experience, Olaudah Equiano

(1789/1997), in his slave-narrative written in 1789, situates his experience being captured, taken across the sea on a slave ship, and then enslaved, next to a vivid description of the peacefulness and ease of the West African province he was from, Eboe. Equiano reflects on the overwhelming smell upon being taken aboard a slave ship, "I received such a salutation in my nostrils as I had never experienced in my life; as that, with the loathsomeness of the stench, and crying together, I became so sick and low that I could not eat" (151). Ironically, Equiano reports that he and the other prisoners in the bowels of the slave ship believed that the savage slave traders were going to cannibalize them. Rather than being devoured outright by the slave traders, the planters would consume the enslaved piece by piece as they extracted every bit of labor they could out of them.

So desperate for and dependent upon slave labor planters, blinded by staggering profits, deemed any interference with the slave trade "grand obstruction" (DuBois 1896/2007: 3). England therefore instructed their colonial governments to encourage the trade, frowning upon, and at times even forbidding, tariffs on the trafficking of human beings. London would eventually reverse this policy as African insurrection was leveling too high a cost on London's slave trade.

DuBois's study of the repression of the slave trade beginning in the eighteenth century looks at various tendencies in the South (i.e. Georgia, South Carolina, North Carolina, Virginia, and Maryland), the middle states (i.e. New York, Pennsylvania and Delaware, and New Jersey), and in the North (i.e. New Hampshire, Massachusetts, Rhode Island, and Connecticut), what he refers to as the planting colonies, the farming colonies, and the trading colonies, respectively. Because of the soil and climate of the southern planting colonies, they would become "the chief theatre of North American slavery" and what they did impacted the future of slavery for all of the colonies. In general, DuBois concludes that "whatever opposition to the slave-trade there was in the planting colonies was based principally on the political fear of insurrection" combined with "some moral repugnance" (9).

In an attempt to limit insurrection and prevent the negation of slavery slave patrols and city guards continued to be developed. Towns and cities only sparsely began to develop in the South during the eighteenth century. Geography played a big role here as the first southern towns were created close to the coast at the base of large navigable rivers. Wilmington, North Carolina and Charlestown, South Carolina are early examples that created night watch city guards to monitor and control the movement and behavior of the enslaved. As these cities developed and industrialized, slave owners found it profitable enough to allow their slaves to permanently live far away from them. Slave communities therefore developed in such cities offering escapees a place to elude pursuers. The presence of such enclaves caused white residents to be extra nervous about the prospects of slave rebellions. Consequently, white residents frequently complained about the ineffectiveness of night watchers and city guards in enforcing laws that banned the enslaved from purchasing alcohol, gathering in unruly groups, and selling their labor as if they were freedmen.

In an attempt to restrict the circulation of ideas and information that could inspire resistance (i.e. knowledge of developing slave revolts), the enslaved were also barred from obtaining literacy skills. Reflecting on this balance of forces between the slaver and the enslaved, Genovese (1969) concludes that "a ruling-class does not grow up simply according to the tendencies inherent in its relationship to the means of production; it grows up in relationship to the specific class or classes it rules" (5). We could therefore observe that both sides of a class antagonism, such as enslaving settlers and the enslaved, never wisely act to either preserve or negate whatever class system without a thorough, up-to-date assessment of one's class adversary. Consequently, slavery might have been created by the slavers, but it was largely directed and eventually negated by the enslaved.

The specific orientation informing Genovese's dialectics directs its gaze at the point or points of impact between opposing forces internally related, consider: "the extent to which its inherent tendencies develop and the forms they take will depend on the nature of this confrontation as well as the nature of confrontations with other classes outside its immediate sphere of activity" (5). Pointing to the gap between slavery and the end of slavery, as an open and unknown future during slavery, the actions of the enslaved represent the force directly opposed the slaveowners. The orientation informing those who experienced being enslaved is therefore crucial for assessing the balance of forces and the general direction of the future as open and therefore not predetermined by any presupposed stages.

It is within this time that the dialectics of race and the concept of whiteness in particular become more central to the colonial project. Highlighting the fact that whiteness is more about privilege, sowing class division, and defeating rebellious Africans than about the bogus concept of race as a biological category, the terms "Christian," "English," and "free" became synonymous with white during this era. The effect of whiteness was the creation of white privilege, which we can understand as a bribe or the cost paid to the part of the working-class from Europe for not just siding with one's own class antagonist (i.e. the capitalist-class/the exploiters/the oppressors), but helping them subjugate and oppress non-white members of their own working-class. Of course, like all ideology, whiteness is not stable but always developing as the balance of forces and the capitalist-class's changing racial needs shift. The purpose of this history of education for the many is to celebrate the enslaved's righteous resistance and to encourage multinational unity. The point here is therefore not just historical accuracy, but to carry on the tradition of resistance through a history of education for the many.

Critical Role of Education

While official colonial education was virtually inseparable from religion, the religion developed by the enslaved themselves also served an educative function, especially since they were banned from literacy beginning around the early-to-mid eighteenth century. Summarizing the "religion of slaves" Genovese (1979) notes that it was "led by their own Black preachers." Their religion was not a simple copy of the slaveowner's Christianity, which Frederick Douglas (1845) describes as the most horrible vulgarization of Christianity designed to justify every conceivable crime against them:

> I assert most unhesitatingly, that the religion of the south is a mere covering for the most horrid crimes—a justifier of the most appalling barbarity—a sanctifier of the most hateful frauds—and a dark shelter under which the darkest, foulest, grossest, and most infernal deeds of slaveholders find the strongest protection. Were I to be again reduced to the chains of slavery, next to that enslavement, I should regard being the slave of a religious master the greatest calamity that could befall me. For of all slaveholders with whom I have ever met, religious slaveholders are the worst.
>
> (67)

In his autobiography, Douglas reflects upon the experience that taught him of the educative effect of the slavers' religion upon the slave masters themselves. That is, the orientation of slavery's religion served to reinforce a process that left the slave masters, in the eyes of the enslaved especially, devoid of any traces of humanity. The dehumanization of the slave owner, for some white, racist abolitionists from the North was astonishingly the sole reason for their rejection of slavery. Painting a picture of this dehumanization Douglas is painfully vivid:

> In August, 1832, my master attended a Methodist camp-meeting ... and there experienced religion. I indulged a faint hope that his conversion would lead him

to emancipate his slaves, and that, if he did not do this, it would, at any rate, make him more kind and humane. I was disappointed in both these respects ... If it had any effect on his character, it made him more cruel and hateful in all his ways; for I believe him to have been a much worse man after his conversion than before. Prior to his conversion, he relied upon his own depravity to shield and sustain him in his savage barbarity; but after his conversion, he found religious sanction and support for his slaveholding cruelty ... As an example, I will state one of many facts going to prove the charge. I have seen him tie up a lame young woman, and whip her with a heavy cow skin upon her naked shoulders, causing the warm red blood to drip; and, in justification of the bloody deed, he would quote this passage of Scripture—'He that knoweth his master's will, and doeth it not, shall be beaten with many stripes.' ... Master would keep this lacerated young woman tied up in this horrid situation four or five hours at a time. I have known him to tie her up early in the morning, and whip her before breakfast; leave her, go to his store, return at dinner, and whip her again, cutting her in the places already made raw with his cruel lash. The secret of master's cruelty toward 'Henny' is found in the fact of her being almost helpless. When quite a child, she fell into the fire, and burned herself horribly. Her hands were so burnt that she never got the use of them. She could do very little but bear heavy burdens. She was to master a bill of expense; and as he was a mean man, she was a constant offence to him.

(47–8)

Douglas is clear, however, that his critique of the slavers' religion did not extend to the slaves' religion. In distancing himself from the religion of the slave masters Douglas highlights its hypocrisy, which was so stark, so over-the-top, so all-encompassing; it is hard to imagine that even the slavers actually believed it:

I have ... spoken in such a tone and manner, respecting religion, as may possibly lead those unacquainted with my religious views to suppose me an opponent of all religion. To remove the liability of such misapprehension, I deem it proper to append the following brief explanation. What I have said respecting and against religion, I mean strictly to apply to the *slaveholding religion* of this land, and with no possible reference to Christianity proper; for, between the Christianity of this land, and the Christianity of Christ, I recognize the widest possible difference— so wide, that to receive the one as good, pure, and holy, is of necessity to reject the other as bad, corrupt, and wicked ... I love the pure, peaceable, and impartial Christianity of Christ: I therefore hate the corrupt, slaveholding, women-whipping, cradle-plundering, partial and hypocritical Christianity of this land. Indeed, I can see no reason, but the most deceitful one, for calling the religion of this land Christianity. I look upon it as the climax of all misnomers, the boldest of all frauds, and the grossest of all libels ... The man who wields the blood-clotted cow skin during the week fills the pulpit on Sunday, and claims to be a minister of the meek and lowly Jesus. The man who robs me of my earnings at the end of each week meets me as a class-leader on Sunday morning, to show me the way of life, and the path of salvation. He who sells my sister, for purposes of prostitution, stands forth as the pious advocate of purity. He who proclaims it a religious duty to read the Bible denies me the right of learning to read the name of the God who made me.

(101–2)

But what can we say more specifically about the religion of the enslaved? According to Genovese (1979), the Christianity practiced by slaves was based on a message of "love and mutual support" and "their own worth as Black people" (7). The Black liberation theology that emerged from slavery was necessarily infused with the commitment to the "ultimate deliverance from bondage," serving as a "bulwark against the dehumanization inherent in slavery" (7). Situating the faith of the enslaved in the cruel context of America, political prisoner and world-renowned journalist Mumia Abu-Jamal (2003) notes that "any religious practice seen to be at variance with the dominant faith was both proscribed and punished severely as paganism" (16–17). Citing a number of slave narratives reiterating the previously mentioned sentiments of Douglas (1845) regarding the Christianity of slave owners, Abu-Jamal concludes that "slaves implicitly rejected the white preacher's projection of what faith meant; slaves reinterpreted the Christian message, and by doing so, transformed the religion into a whole new perspective that spoke to their lives, their suffering, and their longing for liberation" (18).

For Abu-Jamal the faith of the enslaved was centered around "an issue that burned deep in slave consciousness each and every day of bondage: freedom" (20). This is the orientation from which the "largely illiterate, deeply oppressed" enslaved "adopted" (21) Christianity. That is, the enslaved saw themselves as the Israelites and saw "white American society" as the strange land of the "oppressive Pharaoh" (p. 21). The African freedom fighters, from Maroons in the Caribbean to North America, many of whom were women, were therefore regarded by the enslaved as their Moses, their leaders in the long struggle for freedom. Together with their leaders the enslaved longed and struggled for the Jubilee, the trumpet sounding the arrival of freedom—freedom, that is, from being "entombed in a coffin of birth-to-death bondage, not in the searing deserts of the Middle East, but in the steaming delta of Mississippi " (23). Consequently, for the enslaved, "the message of Jubilee brought hope" (28). Contributing to their struggle for liberation were tireless efforts at preserving their own humanity and self-worth, which included keeping alive their African gods hidden beneath the cover of Christian symbols.

Situated in the violence of American slavery in the South the education this religion afforded Black youth was indispensable in maintaining hope century after century. The affirmation of ones' own humanity that Black liberation theology offered was therefore indispensable for taking advantage of political opportunities to either break from slavery or defeat it. It is perhaps no coincidence that "until the nineteenth century, and even then albeit with altered content, religion provided the ideological rallying point for revolt" (Genovese 1979: 28). Having established an ideological orientation against bondage, knowledge of, for example, divisions within Spain (which controlled Florida) and divisions within the white settler-community would have been extremely valuable to be able to assess the potential for liberation in their own situation. Additional facts and analysis of how the enslaved in the Caribbean had played European powers off one another to gain autonomy from slavery in the permanent establishment of Maroon communities—usually located high-up in largely inaccessible mountain regions—would have also been highly desirable knowledge for keeping hope alive in North America.

The mandatory ignorance laws that very quickly accompanied chattel slavery in what would become the United States must be understood as an attempt to keep the enslaved ignorant of all this invaluable knowledge. Mandatory ignorance laws can therefore be further understood as a counter measure against a long tradition of the political and military sophistication of enslaved Africans facing a literal hell on earth. By attempting to keep the enslaved ignorant of contextually relevant knowledge of the larger world, the enslaving class shifted the balance of power in their favor. The desire for illiteracy certainly contributed to European slavers' practice, in theory, of avoiding the capture and taking of African Muslims "whom they regarded with fear" (Abu-Jamal 2003: 41). That is, the African Muslims transported to the Western Hemisphere tended to be literate, could speak many European languages, and played a disproportionate role in leading insurrections. This should not be surprising given their wider access to the knowledge of the enslavers. In addition, since "literacy among Europeans was a relatively rare achievement" (41) in the seventeenth and eighteenth centuries, African Muslims tended to be more accomplished than their captors. However, due to their reputation as particularly skillful workers, the enslavement of Muslims by profit-driven slavers never really abated (Horne 2020).

Attempting to restrict the importation of African Muslims was just one of the many ways the slavers positioned themselves with every conceivable advantage. For example, Harvard University, founded in 1636, and The College of William and Marry, founded in 1693, were built to advance the slave economy and the corresponding ideology of racialization, of which whiteness was a fundamental component. The purpose of this colonial form of higher education was to train the young elite men to lead and advance the capitalist economy, which included the widespread use of indentured servant and slave labor, as a more efficient form of accumulation. In this respect, Harvard trained leaders for both the church and the state. Both institutions received money from England and the colonial government of Virginia. Slavery, in other words, funded the colonial system of education, which was designed to advance slavery and deepen the subjugation of Africans.

The Resistance

Alluding to the need to turn to the voices and experiences of the enslaved themselves, Genovese (1979) notes that "nothing could be more naïve—or arrogant—than to ask why a Nat Turner did not appear on every plantation in the South, as if, from the comfort of our living rooms, we have a right to tell others … when, how, and why to risk their lives and those of their loved ones" (1). Only by understanding slavery from those who experienced it, combined with sound contextual analysis, can we begin to comprehend why slave revolts were not more frequent in North America and why the enslaved who did rebel were extra-ordinarily heroic, "even by revolutionary standards" (1). While focusing on the population ratio of enslaved to free as a primary factor the colonists consciously regulated as a preventative measure, we also looked at the creation of a repressive state apparatus, the further development of whiteness, and mandatory ignorance laws as important factors slavers employed to limit insurrection. Genovese situates the percentage of population factor in a slightly different context, offering another important vantage point.

While resistance was omnipresent, Genovese notes that outright rebellion was relatively infrequent in the South, due to many factors including the fact that the average plantation owned roughly twenty human beings, compared with the sugar-producing Caribbean where the average slaveowner owned around 200 people. Putting this in even greater context it is important to note that around half of all enslaved persons in the North American South lived on farms rather than on the much larger plantations. The plantations themselves were smaller than in the Caribbean with a quarter of enslaving fifty people or less rather than the average of two hundred found in the Caribbean. For Genovese, the significance of this resides in the conclusion that "large units provided a favorable setting within which insurrectionary movements could mature" (13). Another related factor contributing to favorable conditions for slave revolts was the ratios of Africans to whites. For example, in the Caribbean the enslaved made up as much as 80 to 90 percent of the population. In the American colonies the slave population was rarely the majority. In fact, Genovese notes that the slave trade ended in the United States nearly sixty years before slavery itself because "the southern slaveholders read the history of the Caribbean correctly and moved to end the African slave trade" (15).

The slaveholders in North America also not only had the advantage of a large armed white population employed as slave patrols, but they also had geography. That is, the unarmed enslaved were spread out over a much larger geographical area making coordination extremely difficult. The constant buying and selling of enslaved labor, or the "reshuffling of local personnel" (15), was also disruptive to long-term planning and organizing in the American colonies.

While the desperation of hunger, at particularly trying times, drove slaves to rebel, Genovese argues that "the greatest revolts" (13) were initiated during times of economic abundance due to advances in production techniques. The rage and sense of injustice stemming from dashed expectations of improved conditions was the spark, at times, that led to slave revolts. Advances in production had larger implications associated with the quantitative development of slavery that facilitated the capitalist tendency toward monopolization and concentration of the enslaved-labor force. Another important factor in determining the most opportune time to strike was the ability to assess divisions between and within the colonial and European ruling-class powers.

In Jamaica, Brazil, Haiti, and elsewhere the enslaved were able to exploit divisions between Spanish, French, English, and Dutch in their successful establishment of Maroon communities, many of which were never defeated. Genovese discusses the opportunity to gain autonomy from slavery in the American colonies noting that "during the 1730s the enmity between Spain and Britain provided favorable opportunities for the slaves in South Carolina, whom the Spanish invited to cross into Florida under assurances of freedom" (21). Experience throughout the Caribbean and South America taught the Spanish that "self-emancipated black warriors would provide a formidable border army" (21). It was within this context that the slave revolt at Stono occurred in which dozens on both sides were killed. As literacy was banned for the enslaved, there exist very few first-hand accounts of slave rebellions from the enslaved themselves. Texts that do exist, such as *The Confessions of Nat Turner*, tend to be the products of scribes. For example, George Cato, the great, great grandson of a Stono rebellion leader, narrated his story to a researcher in 1937:

> 'Yes sah! I sho' does come from dat old stock who had de misfortune to be slaves but who decide to be men, at one and de same time, and I's right proud of it. De first Cato slave we knows 'bout, was plum willin' to lay down his life for de right, as he see it. Dat is pow'ful fine for de Catoes who has come after him. My granddaddy and my daddy tell me plenty 'bout it, while we was livin' in Orangeburg County, not far from where de fightin' took place in de long ago.
>
> 'My granddaddy was a son of de son of de Stono slave commander. He say his daddy often take him over de route of de rebel slave march, dat time when dere was sho' big trouble all 'bout dat neighborhood. As it come down to me, I thinks de first Cato take a darin' chance on losin' his life, not so much for his own benefit as it was to help others. He was not lak some slaves, much 'bused by deir masters. My kinfolks not 'bused. Da[t] why, I reckons, de captain of de slaves was picked by them. Cato was teached how to read and write by his rich master.
>
> 'How it all start? Dat what I ask but nobody ever tell me how 100 slaves between de Combahee and Edisto rivers come to meet in de woods not far from de Stono River on September 9, 1739. And how they elect a leader, my kinsman, Cato, and late dat day march to Stono town, break in a warehouse, kill two white men in charge, and take all de guns and ammunition they wants. But they do it. Wid dis start, they turn South and march on.
>
> 'They work fast, coverin' 15 miles, passin' many fine plantations, and in every single case, stop, and break in de house and kill men, women, and children. Then they take what they want 'cludin' arms, clothes, liquor and food. Near de Combahee swamp, Lieutenant Governor Bull, drivin' from Beaufort to Charleston, see them and he smell a rat. Befo' he was seen by de army he detour into de big woods and stay 'til de slave rebels pass.
>
> 'Governor Bull and some planters, between de Combahee and Edisto [rivers], ride fast and spread de alarm and it wasn't long 'til de militiamen was on de trail in pursuit of de slave army. When found, many of de slaves was singin' and dancin' and Cap. Cato and some of de other leaders was cussin' at them sumpin awful. From dat day to dis, no Cato has tasted whiskey, 'less he go 'against his daddy's warnin'. Dis war last less than two days but it sho' was pow'ful hot while it last.
>
> 'I reckon it was hot, 'cause in less than two days, 21 white men, women, and chillun, and 44 Negroes, was slain. My granddaddy say dat in de woods and at

Stono, where de war start, dere was more than 100 Negroes in line. When de militia come in sight of them at Combahee swamp, de drinkin' dancin' Negroes scatter in de brush and only 44 stand deir ground.

'Commander Cato speak for de crowd. He say: 'We don't lak slavery. We start to jine de Spanish in Florida. We surrender but we not whipped yet and we is not converted.' De other 43 men say: 'Amen.' They was taken, unarmed, and hanged by de militia. Long befo' dis uprisin', de Cato slave wrote passes for slaves and do all he can to send them to freedom. He die but he die for doin' de right, as he see it.'

(Cato 1937)

Knowing about the strategic alliance that had been forged with Spain is testament to how important it was that the Stono rebels were aware of it since it was one of the details preserved for over two centuries. After Stono Africans were considered the biggest threat to the stability and viability of London's entire North American settler-colonial project—more of a threat than even Native Americans fighting to hold onto their national territory or competing Spaniards. It was within this context that the Carolina colonists were concerned about growing numbers of Portuguese-speaking Africans who could communicate with their Spanish rivals in Florida. Rather than adopt a new model of economic development to prevent further uprisings, colonists expanded and professionalized the repressive apparatus of slave patrols and city guards. This only sparked further outrage, rebellion, and repression "in an endless loop of destruction" (Horne 2014: 112).

The Stono revolt gave Carolina colonists even more incentive to expel Madrid from the continent. The larger context of why Madrid sought an alliance with the rebellious Africans "was fierce jousting between the powers over the control of the fruits of the immensely lucrative African Slave Trade" (113). In this contest London portrayed itself as the fair-skinned, Protestant master race and the Spanish as dark-skinned Catholic heathens. With this London temporarily stopped the development of its pan-European whiteness project that had propelled it ahead of the Ottoman Empire in the sixteenth century.

Day-to-Day Resistance

Beyond the less frequent collective rebellions, the day-to-day existence of enslavement engendered a culture of resistance that took many forms. For example, the push and pull struggle over the speed of labor was a normal part of the day. Overseers or slave-drivers negotiated this perpetual struggle with the whip, and even capital punishment, intent on breaking spirits and the will to be free. There were even slavers who specialized in spirit breaking. Frederick Douglas (1845), after learning to read and running a clandestine Sunday school where he taught others how to read, thereby building confidence and agency, was caught and sent away to be broken. Recounting how his spirit had in fact been broken Douglas (1845) explains:

> If at any one time of my life more than another, I was made to drink the bitterest dregs of slavery, that time was during the first six months of my stay with Mr. Covey. We were worked in all weathers. It was never too hot or too cold; it could never rain, blow, hail, or snow, too hard for us to work in the field. Work, work, work, was scarcely more the order of the day than of the night. The longest days were too short for him, and the shortest nights too long for him. I was somewhat unmanageable when I first went there, but a few months of this discipline tamed me. Mr. Covey succeeded in breaking me. I was broken in body, soul, and spirit. My natural elasticity was crushed, my intellect languished, the disposition to read departed, the cheerful spark that lingered about my eye died; the dark night of slavery closed in upon me; and behold a man transformed into a brute!
>
> (73)

Of course, Douglas's transformation into a brute would not to be permanent, and in the long run, the experience would only deepen his desire for freedom and abolition. Perhaps the most subtle and terrifying form of resistance, poisoning, was also one of the most common. Through poisoning the cruelest, the kindest of the slavers' children would inherit plantations. Similarly, by ensuring slavers' only had one son to inherit their fathers' estate, Africans could offer themselves some degree of protection against the breaking up of their own families. Because of the horror its discreteness engendered, poisoning was a highly effective counter-balance of forces.

In his nuanced analysis Genovese (1979) argues that the Haitian revolution marks the beginning of a shift in slave revolts and agency, "from attempts to secure freedom from slavery to attempts to overthrow slavery as a social system" (3). However, Genovese is clear that this general shift should be understood as a tendency rather than a hard line of division indicating a clean ideological break. In other words, eras of historical change tend to look more like torn, uneven fabric with many stops and starts rather than a clean, surgical cut separating *before* and *after*.

Many of the revolts against slavery can be understood as more or less "spontaneous acts of desperation" (3) against hunger, extreme physical abuse and torture, and all manner of depravations designed to demoralize and drain the enslaved of energy or desire to revolt. Genovese stresses the importance of remembering that slave revolts occurred within a larger global system. While the earliest of these slave revolts predate the first public appearance of the word "socialism" by more than a century, they advanced the movement for bourgeois rights such as freedom, equality, and democracy by serving as its most radical wing. Genovese argues that these insurrections foreshadow the movement against capitalism itself.

Genovese reminds us that "the slaves never constituted a blank slate" (xvi). In fact, "the successive waves of Africans brought with them as many commitments to and preconceptions of justice and legitimacy as their captors did" (xvi). Informed by a deep sense of justice "they fought tenaciously, by all available means, including the ultimate confrontation of revolt, to enforce their own view of social relations" (xvi). Situating the slave revolts within the larger global system in which they existed Genovese notes that they "cannot be understood outside the context of a developing world history within which the politics, economics, and ideology in Europe, Africa, the Americas, and Asia as well, had become inseparable" (xx).

Conclusion

The present chapter has made clear the significance of slavery in the development of capitalism. At the same time, it brings attention to the further development of what would become the modern police and the relentless resistance of those enslaved. Among the wide array of forms of resistance the clandestine tradition of informal education in the face of mandatory ignorance laws is among them.

As we will see in Chapter 4 the agency of the enslaved eventually compelled London to rethink slavery as a sustainable model of economic development. As a result, England began to consider policy directions that horrified wealthy settlers compelling them into rebellion and establishing the United States of America.

Part Two

From Counter-Revolution to People's Revolution

4

The Reactionary Character of 1776 and the Movements of the Many

Introduction: Connection to the Previous Chapter

What began as a Crown-chartered, settler-colonial venture designed to advance the British metropolis developed into the United States of America, but not automatically or inevitably as traditional narratives would suggest. Americans grow up on a narrative that paints 1776 as a collective and inevitable struggle against British tyranny and inherited power. This narrative portrays the American Revolutionary War as a progressive advancement beyond inherited power and rule by the few to elected power and rule by the many.

In this chapter we begin by examining an alternative assessment of what led to 1776. This assessment concludes that 1776 did not really emerge as a collective struggle of so-called *Americans* against an oppressive British power. Rather, the evidence suggests that 1776 was a rebellion of the few who were driven by a furious desire to prevent the end of slavery, and therefore to *prevent* a progressive advance. Within this discussion we will see that the so-called founding fathers did not seek widespread egalitarianism for the *many*, which elite settlers called *pure democracy*, but rather, economic independence for themselves.

After this discussion we turn to the economic conditions of the newly formed United States that led small farmers in Massachusetts, mostly of British and Scottish ancestry, to rebel against the state in the 1780s (known as Shay's Rebellion). Shay's Rebellion would quickly spread throughout the United States. These uprisings are important to understand because they directly led to the Constitutional Convention of 1787.

From these discussions we begin to better understand the education that was created in the post-1776 United States. The architects of this education, such as Benjamin Rush and Noah Webster, constructed a sublated form of colonial education. The religious education intended to ideologically shackle imported labor to the colonial tobacco plantations was sublated into a nationalist education designed to create consent to the new country. Rush and Webster insisted on creating history narratives that glorified so-called founding fathers such as George Washington. By ignoring essential information like the fact that he was one of the wealthiest slavers of his time, and by claiming he was humble and wise, narratives portrayed (and portray) Washington as a saintly hero of the people. In this way the religious education for social control in the colonial era was sublated into religion in education for a national context. In the process, we explore the connections between Rush's model of patriotic education and the elite's desire for a more centralized and powerful federal government unhindered by the limits of the Articles of Confederation.

The resistance highlighted here focuses on the tradition of pan-Indian alliances of the Old Northwest designed to challenge the westward expansion of settler-colonial capitalism ramping up during this era.

Taken together, these discussions shed considerable light on the orientation of the system of education developed by elite forces within the United States.

Critical Role of Capitalism

History of US education textbooks tends to point to political and ideological factors, like those associated with the Enlightenment, as the primary cause of 1776. While these narratives generally do not deny that the founding fathers of the United States were among the wealthiest of the planter and merchant settlers, they typically do not explore this as a direct factor of 1776. Horne (2014), on the other hand, identifies a number of central or primary factors that contributed to 1776, none of which are the Enlightenment. Far from a central factor, Horne demonstrates that the Enlightenment offered Protestant settlers a philosophical excuse to step aside from the raging religious war between London and Madrid and pursue clandestine trade deals with Spain and France all the while ignoring the plight and very existence of enslaved Africans. Consequently, the Enlightenment was mobilized by the "victorious rebels" to "claim the high ground" and characterize "their foes (even enslaved ones)" as "misguided counter-revolutionaries" (249). Horne's account is particularly relevant here because it, along with Shay's Rebellion explored in the next subsection, offers a more accurate orientation to understand the form of education that the founders would forge after the 1787 Constitutional Convention in Philadelphia.

Factors Leading to 1776

The most central factor leading to 1776, for Horne, was London's so-called Glorious Revolution of 1688 that permanently ended the Monarch's absolute power, which subsequently turbo-charged the development of capitalism. Driving capitalist development here was the end of the Royal African Company's (RAC) monopoly on Britain's slave trade. This opened up a free trade in Africans, which dramatically elevated the rate of exploitation of Africa and of Africans. The resulting deregulation not only lined the pockets of Britain's merchant class, but it also enriched the colonial ruling-class to such an extent that they ceased to be economically dependent on London and could conceivably break off. Further incentivizing elite settlers' desire for economic independence was the massive debt they owed London's RAC for unpaid Africans—a debt they wished to default on. Another important factor was the aforementioned secret deals American settlers were cutting with Madrid and Paris, whom London was either at war or in competition with.

As a British colony, South Carolina and even Virginia were vulnerable to Spanish attacks launched from St. Augustine, Florida, as mentioned in Chapter 3. In 1686, and again in 1687, Spanish naval detachments, heavily bolstered by African and Native American forces, surprised Carolina settlements with European-style murderous, plundering expeditions. In 1693 His Catholic Majesty offered the enslaved able to make it to St. Augustine emancipation knowing they would gladly contribute to the fighting force being amassed against their British competition in exchange for freedom. In 1737 Madrid even offered to buy enslaved persons for a sizable sum of money, thereby "incentivizing the greed of the ascending capitalists, turning slavery against itself" (89). Having had established a permanent settlement in what would become the United States, Madrid saw London as the interloper. As a result of Stono's Revolt in 1739, which is said to have been one of the bloodier of the African-led insurrections in South Carolina, Spain had "advanced further on the road to destabilizing their colonial competitor to the north" (p. 90). This contributed to the war between London and Spain from 1756 to 1763, which was a "catastrophic victory for the British" and, as a result, "emboldened their now liberated mainland colonists to revolt in 1776" (90).

So shaken by this ongoing Southern threat, London had already been forced to "re-evaluate its colonial project" and "pursue a different model of development" (87). What emerged from this reassessment in 1733 was Georgia, which was to serve as a "firewall protecting the exposed flank of the Carolinas while challenging Spanish Florida and even Cuba, all of which could change the political and economic calculus in the hemisphere" (87). The idea behind the creation of Georgia was to populate it with "white" laborers, believed to be a reliable force to fight the advancing Spanish. Fleeing religious persecution in France and Eastern Europe, Georgia was an invitation to Protestants, which had the effect of expanding the reach of whiteness beyond Englishmen. Georgia would also serve as a "catchment basin to ensnare fleeing Africans from Charlestown" (92).

However, the profitability of slavery led to the continuing arrival of thousands of enslaved Africans in South Carolina. The lure of profit was too great. Large numbers of Africans enslaved in Georgia, from London's perspective, were problematic since it is next to Florida and therefore less secure. Consequently, slavery was banned in Georgia in 1735, although the penalty for violating the ban was a fine. However, clamor for Africans amongst the investing settler class only grew. These wealthy men complained that European servants were the most deplorable of mankind who came with bad habits. What is more, situated in the white supremacist context of the colonies, it was easier for them to blend in and runaway. The investor's message was clear: they understood that it was a mistake to allow the population of Africans to get too large, but excluding them altogether was a hindrance to the profitability of their ventures.

Enslaved African's insurrections in the Caribbean were also causing London, as well as Paris and Madrid, to rethink their reliance on slavery as the center of their model of economic development, which enraged the planting class. In the Caribbean progress toward negating slavery did not come from London, Paris, or Madrid. Rather, it came from the success of Africans in their struggle against slavery. For example, in 1730, a London traveler to St. Vincent, one of Paris's Caribbean colonies, observed how the slaves' "skill in subversion" had forced the French to treat them like free people, with respect, courtesy, and allowing them a degree of economic independence. The effectiveness of African resistance and the great cost it was inflicting upon enslavers were causing London to feel economically compelled to follow the reforms Madrid and Paris were forced into by those who refused to accept enslavement. To combat the attacks launched by Madrid from St. Augustine, Florida—attacks that included large numbers of armed Africans—London was seriously considering abolishing slavery and arming the thousands of Africans enslaved in Virginia, the Carolinas, and Georgia. The enslaving class of settlers was, no doubt, enraged by the possibility of having "their" property (i.e. Africans) taken away (i.e. freed) and empowered, as they were on their own, with arms.

Mainland elite settlers therefore viewed London as unconcerned about their *need* for slavery, especially after the 1772 Summerset case, which was a major advance toward the abolition of slavery. James Summerset was an enslaved African who was purchased by Charles Stewart in Boston. Stewart brought Summerset with him to Britain in 1769. In 1771 Summerset escaped. After he was re-captured, Summerset's former godparents appealed to the court before Stewart could send him to the auction blocks in Jamaica. Lord Mansfield ruled that British common law had never officially authorized and could not authorize slavery. The court ruled that it was unlawful for Stewart to send Summerset to Jamaica against his will. Even though the ruling was limited to prohibiting removing people from England against their will, enslaved or not, it represented a major milestone in the abolitionist cause. Driven by the ceaseless insurrections of the enslaved to turn against slavery, London increasingly clashed, "sharply with the model of development on the mainland, which presupposed the despotic enslavement of Africans" (77).

Other economic factors also motivated the settler ruling-class's desire to pursue economic independence from London. That is, with continued economic development settlers wanted to establish their own factories and trade with London's most bitter rivals, Madrid and Paris. At the same time, the enslaved population in the Northeast was expanding. Explaining this trend, Horne notes that "as the number of Africans in the northeast increased, this made this region ever more similar to the southeast, uniting the two, providing both with further reason to support slavery, to resist slave revolts, and to question the trend in London to rely upon Africans to confront Madrid" (144).

As this was happening, Maroon colonies in the Caribbean were strengthening, and London was therefore turning more and more to its mainland settlements for the economic value needed to fuel its own internal development. An intensifying Rhode Island-based slave trade in the mid-eighteenth century saw an accompanying escalation in shipboard insurrections. Unlike French and Spanish holdings in the Caribbean, mainland settlers were more resistant to creating a buffer of free Africans. London was feeling like they were losing their competitive advantage to Paris and they blamed the diminishing power of the RAC since they had to compete with English free traders for the purchase of Africans.

During this time the number of Africans brought to London's mainland colonies exploded, as did their anger toward the enslaving. This in turn presented Spanish Florida with additional opportunities against their northern British rivals. Horne observes that London concluded that it was easier to wage war on

Spain, despite the enormous costs, than to curb settlers' desire for Africans or to alter their ardent anti-African sentiments. So extreme had elite settlers' anti-African sentiments developed that, ultimately, London's move toward abolition and the arming of Africans in North America drove them to revolt against the Crown, starting the "American Revolution." Summarizing this larger context Horne notes, "colonists had endured actual poisonings by the enslaved, had to squash slave revolts instigated by the Spaniards, and now confronted Africans armed by London. It is little wonder that the settlers rose as one to oust London's rule" (237).

While the orientation offered by Horne is indispensable for understanding the motivations of the elite settlers, Howard Zinn's (1980/2015) classic narrative offers an account of how 1776 was not widely popular among impoverished settlers who constituted part of the many. The next subsection offers deeper insight into this segment of settlers fundamentally at odds with wealthy merchants and enslavers in the post-1776 context. However, before moving on it is important to note that this class war was fought over soil expropriated from Native American nations. As highlighted throughout this text, Indigenous struggles for land reclamation continue to rage on today.

The Debate around Shay's Rebellion

The focus of this subsection, the yeomen uprising of 1786 popularly known as Shay's rebellion, is an event in early US history that historians have long debated. The first accounts were penned by the victors of the rebellion, the wealthy merchant Federalist supporters of a powerful, repressive, centralized state. These authors "depicted the rebels as selfish, traitorous, and largely ignorant farmers spirited on by ruthless demagogues" (Goldscheider 2015: 64). Historians writing around the end of the rebellion softened the federalist narrative, arguing that the yeomen did not necessarily lack intelligence, but rather were confused and misguided in their response to the state's unwise policy decisions in a tenuous time of instability and change. Goldscheider notes that for roughly 150 years these two slightly different perspectives formed the basis of the dominant explanation of Shay's rebellion. The narrative would begin to shift when the recognition of the yeomen's legitimate grievances and actions were more fully explored. Other narratives have challenged the position that the yeomen's uprising was about debt and foreclosures because of the inclusion of wealthy farmers without debts in the rebellion. However, the founding fathers understood the actions of the yeomen as a harbinger of what was to come in a class-based society. As a result, they responded to it as the new country's first dangerous uprising. To limit the amount and severity of future uprisings a faction of the new ruling-class sought to more centrally pool their collective power in more far-reaching repressive and ideological state apparatuses. What they successfully created was a legal structure in the form of a new Constitution and a sublated model of education for social control. David Szatmary's (1980) narrative is useful here.

Shay's Rebellion as Discontent

In his classic study, *Shay's Rebellion: The Making of an Agrarian Insurrection*, Szatmary (1980) demonstrates that the economic crisis of the post-(counter) Revolutionary War era brought New England's predominantly subsistence farm community into conflict with the regions' capitalist-class. Szatmary notes that roughly 70 percent of New England's population consisted of yeomen who tended to lack a "strong commercial orientation" (4). While their existence was remarkably similar to that of Europe's vast peasantry, a key difference was they tended to own the land they tilled due to its "relative abundance" (5)—land expropriated from indigenous nations/countries—rendering New England's yeomen particularly protective of their autonomy. Rather than living in isolation with a competitive orientation, Szatmary comments extensively on their "cooperative, community-oriented interchanges" (7). During harvest season, for example, yeomen would commonly come together to ease the burden of individual toil.

Szatmary contrasts this somewhat idealized or romanticized depiction of yeomen with the "New Englanders along the coast and in inland market towns" who, he argues, "lived in a largely commercial culture" and were therefore "market-oriented" (10). Guided by the internal logic of capital the merchants—including slave traders, shopkeepers, commercial farmers, and others—were driven by profit. In effect, Szatmary paints a dichotomy between the collective orientation of the yeomen (as well as the country artisans) and the region's emerging capitalist-class. While the depiction of these two extreme poles, collectivity on one end and individualism on the other, is surely an over simplification, the general tendency offers a larger context to begin understanding the forces that would give way to Shay's Rebellion. The dichotomy also highlights the coexistence of multiple modes of production, which offers another important challenge to stagist presentations of history. In other words, the notion of stages suggests clean breaks between different modes of production whereas a nuanced analysis uncovers a more complex, non-linear process of development.

For example, in the 1780s (and before) capitalists in the newly formed United States invested in many enterprises from cotton mills, glass works, to land. Land speculators chasing real estate were generally not interested in farming, "but intended to profit from their purchases through quick sales to incoming settlers" (11). In addition to having *their* farms targeted for real estate ventures, yeomen were drawn into the grips of capital as potential consumers of manufactured goods. Without access to cash money "merchants offered these items on short-term credit and accepted surplus farm goods on a seasonal basis for payment" (16). When the growing season's yield was low, which every grower experiences from time to time, the yeomen's debt to the merchants, as a class, individually and collectively, deepened. This tendency toward deeper and deeper debt "encouraged the production of surplus crops and inescapably drew farmers into the market economy" (16). Once ensnared in the cycle of debt, the external forces of capital became ever dominant. One by one then farmers were forced into the center of a system of commerce they could no longer keep at bay.

In times of crisis merchants exerted the power they had amassed over yeomen by demanding the repayment of loans in hard currency, which lead to waves of foreclosures. Of course, many yeomen resisted this encroachment of capital. With the penetration of market forces came a commercial culture fundamentally at odds with the culture of yeomen. Szatmary concludes that the yeomen tended to reject "competitive, acquisitive values and tenaciously clung to" (17) their traditional orientation centered around building community through cooperation. It is within this context that Szatmary contends the struggle that came to be known as Shay's Rebellion emerged. In short, "the rebellion became … a contest between two economic classes: yeomen who faced the loss of their properties, and merchants, lawyers and speculators who stood to gain from these loses" (18).

Post-War Economic Crisis

Immediately following the counter-revolution of 1776 economic and cultural pressures exerted on the yeomen intensified. That is, cut off from London's Caribbean sugar trade and related credit lines coastal merchants turned toward inland retail shopkeepers for hard currency in place of credit. Shopkeepers in turn increased their pressure on farmers to repay loans in cash rather than the customary payment in surplus crops. Consequently, many yeomen were "dragged into debtor court and threatened with the loss of their land. Others ended up in jail for unpaid debts" (Szatmary 1980: 19–20).

The counter-revolution of 1776 was, again, in part, resistance to London's attempts to limit trade with their rivals Madrid and Paris. This is significant because the United States' ability to freely trade with France and Spain after breaking from London did not go according to plans causing deepening economic crisis externalized onto the yeomen. New England merchants sought free trade policies with Spain since they were blocked from bringing their exports to Spanish markets after the war. Trading with France was hindered by credit problems. Consequently, trade with British merchants worked to "cement mercantile relations between the United States and Great Britain" (21) in the postwar era. As a result, "England supplied America with manufactured commodities such as glass, iron, and medicine on credit. In exchange, American merchants seasonally exported foodstuffs, lumber, and fish to Britain" (21). As an underdeveloped nation, the United States continued in its colonial-like role serving as an "agricultural satellite of an industrializing England" (21).

Britain also barred US vessels from entering the waters of London's Caribbean holdings. US exports had to be carried to the Caribbean by British ships. London simultaneously "encouraged the duty-free exportation of West Indian coffee, pimento, rum, sugar, and molasses to the United States" (22). Glutting the US market with European and Caribbean goods, American merchants remained economically dependent on London. We might therefore say that in the balance of forces between Washington and London, the latter pursued a policy of maximum exports and minimum imports with the former. Szatmary concludes that London's pursuit of revenge here against the elite settlers' counter-revolution was "partly achieved" (23) as a number of New England merchants were crippled, thereby intensifying the above-mentioned tendencies that contributed to the yeomen uprising. For example, US merchants who sent ships to Africa to carry African captives to the Caribbean in exchange for molasses and sugar for sale back in the United States were severely restricted. This in turn atrophied Boston's shipbuilding industry, causing much anger and frustration among associations of artisans.

As a result of British trade sanctions, the centers of Northern merchant capital like Boston were losing their hard currency. Once drained of cash money, the British merchants who had given credit to their US counterparts also went bankrupt. Consequently, exporters and creditors closed their doors to US business, refusing to execute any new transactions and demanding the repayment of past loans. As a result, the already existing economic crisis of many New England merchants devolved into unrecoverable bankruptcy. Merchants were flush with land and consumer goods, but lacked the liquid capital necessary in a cash economy (Szatmary 1980). Like all capitalist crises, US merchants were experiencing a crisis of realization. In addition to squeezing the yeomen for payment of loans, tax codes placed the majority of the tax burden on yeomen by taxing land much more heavily than transactions and stock. The resulting seizure of yeomen farms and property, as well as the tendency to imprison farmers for unpaid debts, was infuriating. Coming from a cooperative culture, yeomen responded by coming to one another's aid against the external forces of capital. Between 1784 and 1786, the farmers' orientation toward the existing political system was that it could be reformed to meet their needs.

Initially, the reformist solutions yeomen advocated for included "state-issued paper money and tender laws as panaceas for their troubles" (37). Facing the devaluation of specie (i.e. hard, coin money) farmers knew they would have more easily been able to pay their debts with soft or paper money. Even though they knew it would have dragged them further into the market economy, they were willing to compromise for immediate relief. In addition, yeomen advocated for tender laws that would legally allow them to "discharge specie debts through payments in goods" (41). But the New England capitalist-class rejected such proposals as "financially unsound and socially disruptive" and legislatures tended to cater to the wishes of this most powerful class. Having been cut off from trade with the Caribbean in the 1780s, American "wholesalers and retailers had little need of surplus crops and rejected proposals for tender laws" (46).

Professionals and merchants would turn to calls for "industry, frugality, and saving to indebted farmers" (47) seeking to win them over to their side. This represents a shift in the merchants' discourse because they rejected a similar call by Puritans in an earlier era because they needed consumers. However, by the late eighteenth century merchants believed that if they could convince yeomen to limit their consumption, they could undermine the very reason for their rebellion. The merchants' thinking here was either naïve or desperate because the economic forces acting upon the independence of yeomen had little to do with the choices of individual consumers. Nevertheless, famed pedagogue and inventor of the first American English dictionary, Noah Webster, developed educational materials from this orientation encouraging frugality hoping the educational effects would "diminish agrarian resistance to the demands of creditors and make paper money and tender laws unnecessary" (48).

Contributing to the yeomen's growing frustration was the orientation of the constitutions of many New England governments that tended to favor the elite sectors of the merchant class. For example, Massachusetts' 1780 Constitution was drafted primarily by lawyer John Adams and merchant James Bowdoin and was pushed through the state convention with what was regarded as a fraudulent two-thirds majority. The Constitution may have extended voting rights (i.e. the franchise) to most white males, but it simultaneously set monetary requirements for holding political office, which heavily favored merchants who possessed the majority of Northern capital. Merchants saw this as a necessary safeguard against the pirates of democracy or the tendency among the many to struggle for equality. Yeomen, on the other hand, complained of the merchants stacking the deck in their favor.

Ultimately, yeomen vulnerability and crisis rendered their land holdings more easily accumulated by speculators and bank capital. In other words, paper money and tender would have facilitated yeomen in shifting some of the burden of inflated debt back to the merchants. In the struggle between forces the merchants were not going to allow the balance of power to move in the yeomen's favor. Merchants and their political operatives even sublated religious arguments claiming paper money bred dishonesty and evil. Consequently, the tensions festered reaching a "stage of incipient violence by late 1786" (38). It was within this tumultuous era of class struggle that slave patrols and city guards were being more fully professionalized as paid and regularized positions resembling more and more modern police departments (Vitale 2018).

Calling themselves Regulators, by the fall of 1786, yeomen turned from peaceful methods to armed struggle to advance their proposed reforms. The aim was to regulate the courts through armed actions after legislatures made it abundantly clear that they would use their privileged positions to prevent the introduction of paper money and tender laws. In other words, yeomen, with few exceptions, finally concluded that the system was so rigged against them that the only way to survive as such was through armed revolt. This represents a qualitative shift in the yeomen's orientation. Conscious of the merchants' desire to transform them into wage laborers or tenants, a powerful call to arms echoed throughout the yeomen community to strike down the aristocrats and subvert their oppressive tendencies and aims.

The armed revolt phase of Shay's Rebellion began by groups of 500 to 1,500 farmers throughout New England seizing upon and shutting down debtor's courts and sometimes holding governors and assembly men hostage. Their desired goal was to suppress the collection of hard coin by debt collectors. By the end of the year roughly "9,000 militants or about one quarter of the 'fighting men' in rural areas had surfaced in every New State except Rhode Island" (Szatmary 1980: 59). Yeomen in Rhode Island, Szatmary speculates, had been placated after winning the struggle for paper money. Horne (2014) suggests that Rhode Island merchants may have been motivated to prevent the yeomen uprising from spreading to their state to protect their status as one of the "headquarters for the trade in Africans" (143). In other words, a yeomen rebellion in Rhode Island would surely have spread to the already rebellious spirit of enslaved Africans causing an unmanageable situation. Following a series of devastating African revolts on slave ships that had departed from Rhode Island Horne speculates that "perhaps as a result, there was significant pressure internally for Rhode Island to move toward European indentured labor" (144). If this is true, then the precedent for compromising with the yeomen in 1787 would have been preemptively established in the 1740s.

Ethnically, the majority of Shaysite Regulators reflected the English and Irish background of inland New Englanders. The majority of African American New Englanders lived in coastal, commercial regions. There were, however, African American yeomen, men with names like Moses Sash and Tobias Green, who joined the Regulators as Shaysites (Szatmary 1980: 60). Again, if the insurrection had spread to Rhode Island, then it is likely it would have spread from the predominantly white yeomen to coastal African American communities.

Bringing to life the voices of the rebelling yeomen Szatmary allows us to hear their biting indignation: "John Chapman of Uxbridge, Massachusetts, wanted to 'put a stop to those iniquitous ways of obtaining wealth, by which a set of plunderers have for years been rioting on the spoils of the industrious'" (67). While the yeomen resorted to armed struggle, their demands remained reformist. Of course, merchants and professionals, fearing the loss of even *some* of *their* wealth, exaggerated their cries claiming that the Regulators were seeking to abolish private property, all debts, and create a leveling effect through revolutionary struggle. The yeomen themselves owned private property and sought only a more equitable compromise within the system as it existed. Yeomen, in other words, did not seem to have the vision of resolving the essential contradiction.

Nevertheless, government leaders painted a picture of yeomen *recklessly* dragging society back into a *natural* state that they associated with barbarism and so-called *savage* Native Americans, thereby exposing, once again, this ruling-class's bigotry. Not only did the merchants resort to bigotry, but the very merchant class that acted in tyrannical ways against the yeomen paradoxically warned that a more equitable system would inevitably lead to the rise of tyranny. Since they believed that competition was a natural drive rather than a learned behavior, "they thought that a strong individual would eventually demonstrate superior power and rise above all others ... The resulting tyranny, based on physical compulsion rather than reason, seemed an almost inevitable consequence" (73).

In reality, the commercial ruling-class likely did not fear that the Regulators were plotting to overthrow capitalism and private property since their demands were clear and included no such calls. Rather, they feared a yeomen coup and their own fall, or partial fall, from power. Attempting to cast the Regulators in a treasonous light, the ruling-class accused the Regulators of being agents of London working to destabilize the union to facilitate restoring British rule. The yeomen adamantly denied this charge, which took attention away from their grievances. Despite the non-existence of any evidence connecting the yeomen's struggle to London, the charge served its propagandist function fueling hysteria amongst the opponents of Shaysites.

Consequently, the repressive state came running to the merchants' rescue. However, rather than compromise with the Regulators by either accepting or promising to accept their reformist demands for paper money and tender laws, the state mounted armed attacks against them. This response was not a deviation but consistent with the founding fathers' position during the American Revolutionary War. That is, while the founders sought economic self-determination for themselves, they insisted upon a subservient domestic population suppressing egalitarian impulses among the many. The merchants' and governments' violent and hysterical response to the Regulators, rather than suppressing their struggle, pushed them from reform into rebellion. Many radicalized farmers began to desire the overthrow of the government and engaged in over five months of raids on lawyers, military leaders, and inland merchants. However, the heavy casualties the yeomen endured from better trained and armed state troops hunting them down, combined with newly acquired Native American lands in what is today the mid-west (i.e. Ohio, Michigan, Indiana, etc.) they could migrate to, the raging flame of their armed struggle was dramatically reduced.

A More Centralized Repressive State

It is within this context of African and yeomen insurrection that the post-1776 American ruling-class eventually deemed it necessary to revisit the Articles of Confederation in a Constitutional Convention in 1787 in Philadelphia. Adopted by the Continental Congress in 1777 and ratified in 1781 the Articles of Confederation articulated the state apparatus as a one house Congress where each state, regardless of size, was afforded a single representative vote in federal matters. Each state retained its own sovereignty, freedom, and independence. There were no national president and no judiciary to interpret laws. George Washington did not take office until 1789, after the 1789 Constitutional Convention. The power of the one house Congress was limited to declaring war and negotiating treaties. The federal government therefore did not possess the centralized power to levy taxes and it had no real budget. The collective power of the ruling-classes in each of the thirteen states was therefore not effectively pooled, amassed, or centralized. Amending the Articles of Confederation required the unanimous consent of each of the thirteen state representatives.

In 1786 a Constitutional Convention was held in Annapolis but failed to attract representatives of all thirteen states. Plans to construct a stronger, more centralized state to more effectively control the laboring classes and enforce a national economic policy were not materialized. Merchants and slavers in Connecticut, Maryland, South Carolina, and Georgia, for example, were thriving in the postwar crisis and were therefore concerned about "the possible dangers that a stronger national government posed to their state-based power" (Szatmary 1980: 122). As the yeomen resistance to debtor courts spread to South Carolina, Virginia, and Pennsylvania the propaganda that painted the yeomen's movement as essentially anti-capitalist convinced reluctant states to embrace the calls for more completely centralizing or pooling ruling-class power through a state apparatus.

Successfully bringing all thirteen state representatives together the conveners not only amended the Articles of Confederation, but they replaced them with a new structure or apparatus outlined in a new Constitution. Rather than having just a one house Congress, two more branches were formed: an Executive or Presidential branch, and a Senate whose members were to be appointed by the President. Senators were not voted on for the first 125 years of the country through the 17th Amendment. The idea of the Senate was to create a safety valve to ensure that the ruling-class's monopoly on state power was never threatened. That is, the Senate has ultimate veto power over any law passed by the popularly elected House of Representatives. In this way, the ruling-class's power was not only pooled, but it was also protected or safeguarded from the democratic will of the masses whose yearnings were expressed by people like Daniel Shays and Nat Turner.

In addition to the two additional branches a Supreme Court was also outlined in the newly formed Constitution. The Justices would be nominated by the President and confirmed by the Senate and serve for life. Few guidelines for the Supreme Court were specified in the Constitution. While year after year school curricula rehearse the old cliché of the Supreme Court as the neutral arbiter of Constitutional justice, in reality it has served as the last line of defense for the capitalist-class subverting the possibility of a truly democratic process (Fisher 2008).

In addition to pooling ruling-class power by excluding the broadest masses from accesses real political power, the conveners also centralized control over currency. Because Rhode Island, New York, North Carolina, and Georgia had issued paper money to quell stirrings of yeomen resistance, elites in the North and South sought a federal instrument to "block paper money and tender laws" (128). Toward these ends, convention attendees proposed that individual states be prohibited from coining money, issuing bills of credit, or accepting anything but gold or silver for payment of debts.

Conveners also argued that internal unrest deterred foreign investment and therefore proposed "two types of military force" to "suppress future rural rebellions and slave insurrections" (129). That is, they proposed that the federal government be given military jurisdiction over all of the states enforced through a federally centralized militia. The intention here was "to discourage rebels from hiding in bordering states as the Shaysites had done" (130).

The yeomen objected that the new Constitution would effectively hand the power of the entire federal government over to the merchant class. They "believed that the mercantile elite would seize power through the proposed national military force" and degrade "independent farmers to tenants and wage laborers" (132–3). In the end the new Constitution "had passed by a slim margin of 187 to 168" (133).

Observing the widespread instability of the time the founders seemed to be as aware as Adam Smith (1763/1978) was that, "in cities where there is [the] most police and the greatest number of regulations concerning it, there is not always the greatest security." For Smith this can be explained by the fact that the police have no impact on the conditions that lead to so-called crime. In other words, *crime* emerges when people have "no other way of getting their subsistence but by committing robberies, and living on plunder, which occasion the greatest disorder." It is the enforcement of private property laws and the resulting poverty of the property-less, or the working-class, that leaves the greatest masses "in the most indigent circumstances" and therefore "forced to commit the most dreadful crimes."

Smith concludes that "it is not so much the police that prevents the commission of crimes" but essentially a society where people have true self-determination and their basic needs met. Since the founders were not interested in changing the class dynamics that would prevent so-called crime, they set out to create a stronger, more centralized repressive state apparatus capable of suppressing the occasional uprisings they knew would exist as long as capitalism and/or slavery were functioning. Covering all their bases, ideological forms of social control were also afforded significant attention by the eighteenth-century ruling elite.

Critical Role of Education

The anti-capitalist or anti-commercial orientation of the yeomen and the insurrectionary tendencies of newly arrived and enslaved Africans and still enslaved Africans who had become a Black nation due to their unique and especially brutal treatment played a central role in considerations of what a post-1776 education might look like in theory and in practice. However, rather than look to this evidence as the primary factors leading to the creation of what would become the system of US education, history of education survey textbooks have argued that the so-called founding fathers' actions were inspired by the emergence of new, progressive ideas (i.e. the Enlightenment). Within this narrative of progress the continuation of slavery in the new republic tends to be depicted as a contradiction rather than its very reason for being.

For example, in the second installment of his *American Education* trilogy Lawrence Cremin (1980) concludes that the American Revolution "created a *republic* more liberal and equitable than any other in history" that "provided a place of *refuge* for oppressed people everywhere" and "laid the foundations of an empire wherein liberty, science, and virtue would flourish and in due course spread throughout the world" (5).

Similarly, H. Warren Button and Eugene Provenzo (1989) argue that "the most important cause of the American Revolution was ... political ... The fundamental issue underlying the Revolution was independence, freedom from what was seen as the tyranny of King George III and Parliament" (50). Decades after Cremin (1980), Wayne Urban and Jennings Wagoner (2014) continued to advance virtually the same narrative commenting that "new currents of thought ... that eventually became known as the Enlightenment provoked momentous changes in nearly every aspect of Western society" including "politics, economics and educational theory" (55). In nearly identical terms John Rury (2013) claims that "the Revolution was influenced by the ideas of ... Enlightenment thinkers" (49). Similarly, Joel Spring (2014) argues that "political freedom was central to the American Revolution" and that "changes in thinking about schooling and freedom of ideas were part of the ideological justification of the American Revolution" (31–2).

Such strong progressive language is astonishing given the aforementioned evidence that the American Revolution was actually counter-revolutionary as it was motivated by schemes to reverse the tide toward the abolition of slavery. Suggesting that the American Revolution was informed by ideas that were so compelling by virtue of their correctness that they would eventually be self-propelled around the world is another mystification of what became US imperialism.

Of course, the deep, cruel, irony of wealthy slave owners orienting themselves as oppressed by London's unfair taxes (i.e. impressment) and victims of the Monarchy's form of inherited (i.e. biologically determined) power, and thus world leaders of the cause of liberty due to their positionality and experiences, was certainly not lost on the Black nation and Africans in America (Horne 2014). It is rather astonishing that US history texts tend not to pick up on this rather obvious observation.

That educational historians would continue to reproduce the narrative that the American Revolutionary War was a war of enlightenment is particularly striking given their own reporting on the continuity of pre and post-war forms of *unenlightened* education for social control—education, that is, designed to simultaneously reproduce and extend gender, race, and class inequalities and suppress the tendency toward rebellion through ideological manipulation. What tends to be excluded from the educational historians' frame of perception, oddly enough, is the existence of the long and active tradition of insurrection documented throughout this book—a tradition that crossed ethnic and geographical boundaries. It is precisely this tradition of working-class and oppressed resistance that offers a much more practical explanation for the form of mass schooling the ruling-class advanced in both the pre- and post-war eras. Pointing to the agrarian uprisings that led to the Constitutional Convention of 1787 historian Merrill Jensen (1976) offers a sizable statement worth quoting:

> By February 1787 the political climate had changed radically as a result of the agrarian outbursts throughout the United States. In April 1786 a paper money party, whose members were looked upon as 'Levellers' in other states, captured control of the government of Rhode Island. By February 1787, it was widely reported that the Rhode Island legislature was considering a bill for the equal distribution of all property every thirteen years. In September 1786 New Hampshire farmers surrounded the legislature at Exeter, and some of them

shouted for the abolition of debts and taxes and for the equal distribution of property. Sheriffs in Pennsylvania, Virginia, and South Carolina found it difficult and often impossible to collect taxes, and some of them in Pennsylvania were beaten up by farmers. The violence culminated dramatically in Massachusetts with the armed uprising known as Shay's Rebellion.

(178–9)

Given the seriousness of this uprising, it is no wonder the elites came together to forge a new, more centralized and repressive state structure as a defense against the impulses of the many for relief, if not liberation. Throughout the newly formed states elites came forward with their arguments for stronger centralized state control. David Daggett (1787/1981), for example, in New Haven Connecticut, in what seems to be an attempt to ramp up hysteria, argued that Daniel Shays, someone he claimed was "without abilities" and "without influence" (162), was able to shut down the government in a number of counties in Western Massachusetts. What if someone "greater than Shays ... should arise," Daggett speculates, "where are our bulwarks against the attack?" (162). Making his case for a centrally controlled repressive state apparatus Daggett cries out, "if we look up to Congress, they are chained and fettered in impotency" (162).

Benjamin Rush, who was not only a Philadelphia physician, Declaration of Independence signer, architect and philosopher of US education, but also a slave owner, played an even more central role in generating support for the Constitution as a replacement for the Articles of Confederation. Education was a fundamental piece of Rush's vision for suppressing the rebellious spirit of the many. Rush's (1787/1981) "Address to the People of the United States" is widely cited in history of education survey texts. However, educational historians tend to extract the statements on education while ignoring their relationship to the text's larger purpose. Rush's "Address" was written as a sort of justification for the more centralized form of government constructed by the highly secretive Constitutional Convention of 1787.

Rush opens his Address noting that while the American War is over, the American Revolution is ongoing. For Rush, this ongoing revolution is centered on "perfect[ing] our new form of government" and "prepar[ing] the principles, morals, and manners of our citizens, for these forms of government" (46). In setting up his argument for perfecting the form of government, which meant discarding the Articles of Confederation, Rush argues that "in our opposition to monarchy, we forgot that the temple of tyranny has two doors. We bolted one of them ... but we left the other open, by neglecting to guard against the effects of our own ignorance" (46). Rush, in other words, is dismissing the validity of the yeomen's grievances expressed in Shay's Rebellion as the result of ignorance. This was a common theme throughout the debates between 1787 and 1789. The caricature of Daniel Shays, in other words, was frequently invoked as a scare tactic by ruling-class supporters of the proposed Constitution. The claim was that if bold steps were not immediately taken, such as those outlined in what would become the US Constitution, then the ignorant masses, at any time, could "enroll themselves under the banners of some enterprising ruffian, and, at one bold stroke, annihilate all government and introduce anarchy into these states" (Wilson 1787/1976: 291).

Rush (1787/1981), however, does not stop with what he calls ignorance, but goes on arguing that "most of the present difficulties of this country arise from the weakness and other defects of our governments" (46). Responding directly to the desire not to change the structures of inequality and exploitation that had been giving way to the rebellions of the many, but to more efficiently suppress them Rush identified "the deficiency of coercive power" as an area the new Constitution would rectify. Directly responding to states like Rhode Island that had issued paper money as a concession to the yeomen demands to avoid insurrection Rush then identifies not having the exclusive power to issue paper money and regulate commerce as the next deficiency the new Constitution would overcome, thereby ensuring power would remain in the hands of the merchant and enslaving class. Centralizing sovereign power in the federal government was the next corrective measure Rush identifies. Finally, Rush argues that the leaders of government needed to have longer tenures in their posts and the new Constitution would ensure this. The Senate would appoint and possess veto power over the popularly elected Congress, and the important offices would be appointed by the President. The yeomen concluded that this new government would effectively place all the power of the state in the hands of the merchants. It is striking that history of education texts do not regard this development as significant enough for comment or reflection.

Rush, in fact, is so open about his commitments to ensuring that power remains concentrated and protected by the few that he argues the many "possess" power "only on the days of their elections," after which "it is the property of their rulers" (47). To popularize this new structure Rush proposed the creation of a federal university and a federal post office that would disseminate literature to the populace. Rush called for competent professors to teach the citizenry such as the "principles of commerce" (47). Remember, yeomen understood perfectly well that issuing paper money could give them some flexibility in paying debts thereby enabling them to retain their holdings (i.e. land/farms). Rush, on the other hand, wanted to teach the citizenry to believe that states surrendering "their power of emitting money" would serve the common good and facilitate trade. While it is not uncommon for history of education texts to mention Rush's unrealized proposal for a national university, the larger context its purpose would support tends to remain unexplored.

In the post-war era Benjamin Rush understood perfectly well that a narrative was needed that would facilitate the development of consent to the more centralized ruling-class power structure advanced at the Constitutional Convention of 1787. The continuity of a slightly readjusted narrative centered around a dichotomous dialectics of race would be fundamental. The slave-owning founding fathers whose own economic interests drove them into rebellion had to be portrayed as "exemplars of industriousness, honesty, and intelligence" and elevated to the status of "biblical heroes" (Cremin 1980: 73) to serve as the positive side of the dichotomy. Untamed immigrants, enslaved Africans, Native Americans defending their national territories, and women in general served as the negative or corrupt side of the dichotomy in the dialectics of identity. A strong centralized state was therefore portrayed as the great father and protector of all who is good and virtuous.

In the realm of European immigrants, education would serve as the mechanism through which so-called Americans, that is, white people or citizens, would be fashioned. Pointing in this general direction, Cremin concludes that "as education assumed a role in creating the American Republic, it inevitably became involved in defining the American people." Consequently, "in the minds of many, education became a subsidiary to citizenship and dependent upon it" (7). Intimately connected to the idea of citizenship was "the nature and size of the national domain," which "was a thorny question on several counts" (8). For over a century the drive to expand the national domain was driven by capitalism's need for ever larger supplies of raw materials and food-producing land. Slavery would also come to exert growing pressure on the expansionist impulse with technological innovations in production. The ensuing process of Westward expansion would come to embody an "educational imperative" as one of the central tools in extending so-called "civilization over a vast continent" (11). The expansionist intensions of the post-'76 ruling-class were deeply rooted in both the spirit of the Requirmiento and the pan-Europeanism of whiteness.

Cremin also points to the orientation of figures such as Thomas Paine as advancing a sort of universal justice represented by his anti-slavery position.

Born in England in 1737 Paine emigrated to Philadelphia in 1774 and began working as a journalist. Paine adopted and contributed to a conception of the world that was "an ordered universe set in motion by a benevolent God and inhabited by reasonable men who could know God's law and live according to its dictates" (20). For Paine God's dictates were abolitionist. In his letter, "African Slavery in America," Paine (1775) concludes,

> to go to nations with whom there is no war, who have no way provoked, without farther design of conquest, purely to catch inoffensive people, like wild beasts, for slaves, is an height of outrage against humanity and justice, that seems left by heathen nations to be practised by pretended Christians. How shameful are all attempts to colour and excuse it!

Paine's (1775) anti-slavery position must be situated in the context of the time where London's move away from slavery was more practical than moral. Understood within this frame it makes sense why Paine would point to the threat of slave revolts in his formal statement against slavery: "how just, how suitable to our crime is the punishment with which Providence threatens us? We have enslaved multitudes, and shed much innocent blood in doing it; and now are threatened with the same."

However, the orientation of Cremin's (1980) text fails to capture this primary factor driving the move toward abolition within Paine's London. Simply put, it was the agency and insurrection of Africans resisting slavery in the Caribbean and throughout the Americas that made slavery too costly for investors and planters. Benjamin Rush was also an outspoken advocate of the abolition of slavery. As a prominent figure in history of US education texts Rush's abolitionist tendencies tend to be portrayed as the product of his own progressive thought, and the fact that he held another human in bondage as a slave is explained away as a contradiction.

However, as an unflinching advocate of a centralized repressive state needed to subdue the yeomen rebellion and the constant threat of slave uprisings, his abolitionist sentiments must be understood within this context. That is, the dominant arguments against slavery made by settlers were not moral, but were rather based on the combined fear of insurrection and the need for a larger and more flexible repressive apparatus. It is therefore not surprising that Rush's (1773) position against slavery would focus on the so-called crimes of the enslaved, which he attributes not to immutable biological deficiencies of Africans, but to slavery itself: "all the vices which are charged upon the Negroes in the southern colonies and the West-Indies, such as Idleness, Treachery, Theft, and the like, are the genuine offspring of slavery, and serve as an argument to prove that they were not intended for it." Rush goes on to challenge the slavers' insistence that their cultivation of sugar in the Caribbean could not be possible without slave labor arguing, instead, that free labor is much more productive and therefore profitable. As with his philosophy of education, his position on slavery appears to be more about maintaining the rule of his class than with notions of egalitarianism, which his class had been adamantly opposed to.

Rush is widely quoted in history of education books but his ideas on education tend to be presented without much explanation. For example, Rush, along with many founding fathers, believed that children of the elite should be discouraged from studying abroad because "it is well known that our strongest prejudices in favor of our country are formed in the first twenty years of our lives" (quoted in Urban & Wagoner 2009: 67). However, Urban and Wagoner do not situate this statement in its proper historical and international context. The new American elites were attempting to gain economic independence from London but struggled even after the successful insurrection of 1776. Elites in the newly formed United States viewed the perpetuation of the tradition of studying abroad as a barrier to breaking their ongoing economic dependence on London.

In regards to the schooling of the many Rush also shared many beliefs with other founders, such as Jefferson, that the public should be taxed to fund a minimum basic education for free citizens. Cremin (1980), for example, cites Rush's insistence on the creation of a "uniform system of education" that "will render the mass of people more homogenous, and thereby fit them more easily for uniform and peaceable government" (quoted in Cremin 1980: 117). However, ignoring the way Rush, Jefferson and others were conceptualizing education as a response to the yeomen rebellion that had spread throughout the country, Cremin attributes Rush's focus on fostering homogenization to a concern with the effects of immigration. While it is true the founders sought to mold the minds of new immigrants through whiteness to fit within the newly formed United States, Cremin avoids the very real issue of the many's tendency to rebel against the abuses of the few.

Urban and Wagoner (2009), on the other hand, do report on Rush's insistence that instituting an education tax is beneficial to even those without children in school because of its assumed ability to limit rebellion. Rush argues that the benefits accrued by society in general from an educated citizenry far outweigh the costs. Rush emphasizes the savings accrued "by being able to sleep with fewer bolts and locks on his doors" (quoted in Urban & Wagoner 2009: 67). Rush elaborates on this theme discussing how a moral, Christian-based education will reduce crime and limit the need for prisons. Again, Urban and Wagoner do not comment directly on these bold statements, but rather reiterate Rush's insistence that "for freedom to exist, restraints have to be internalized by the citizenry" (67–8). The proper frame from which to understand the obsession with social control was a society out of control, that is, a society in rebellion against a ruling-class viewed as irreparably unjust. Of course, those identified to be citizens of the newly formed United States and those whose enslavement would be extended in the new republic were not the only ones targeted by the founders.

Even though Thomas Jefferson did not directly participate in the Constitutional Convention since he was in France, he contributed to the process through correspondence. While Jefferson agreed with Rush that education was indispensable for preventing future rebellions, he consistently opposed centralizing power in a federalized state apparatus. Jefferson's own comments on Shay's rebellion reflect his deep commitment to education over corporeal punishment. Many commentators have interpreted Jefferson's comments as lending support to the insurrection. However, Jefferson believed that the rebels were incorrect and uninformed in their critique of merchants and debtor courts. However, Jefferson did not advocate for capital punishment as an appropriate response to the yeomen. Rather, he used it as an opportunity to advocate for education/instruction. Referring to the rebellion Jefferson states:

> I say nothing of it's motives. They were founded in ignorance, not wickedness. God forbid we should ever be 20 years without such a rebellion. The people cannot be all, and always, well informed. The past which is wrong will be discontented in proportion to the importance of the facts they misconceive; if they remain quiet under such misconceptions it is a lethargy, the forerunner of death to the public liberty … What country can preserve its liberties if their rulers are not warned from time to time that their people preserve the spirit of resistance? Let them take arms. The remedy is to set them right as to facts, pardon and pacify them … The tree of liberty must be refreshed from time to time with the blood of patriots and tyrants. It is its natural manure.

While it is clear Jefferson agreed with Rush and the Federalists about education, he simultaneously challenges Rush's proposal to create a stronger central government. In other words, Jefferson is arguing that if education is properly executed, it would not be necessary to redistribute state power from individual states to a federal body. However, the Federalists, whose vision for the new country was based upon the creation of a powerful commercial republic with close alliance with European powers which was favored by financiers and merchants, won the debate as reflected in the original US Constitution. The Federalists, whose capitalist economic interests were antagonistically related to the many, distrusted not only the rebellious yeomen, but the working masses more generally. One of the objections of the anti-Federalists was that the Federalists did not include a Bill of Rights in the Constitution they forged. This was viewed as a serious digression since many state Constitutions did include a Bill of Rights and under the Articles of Confederation individual states retained their sovereignty and independence. Four years after the Constitutional Convention of 1787 a Bill of Rights was added as a concession won by the many.

Contrary to the Federalists Jefferson's vision for the United States lay in the westward expansion of small homesteads and slave plantations rather than maintaining commercial connections with Europe. Initially, wealthy slavers tended to have little interest in urbanization and manufacturing or anything in the interest of bankers and business leaders. Like the yeomen, they believed the emerging class of powerful capitalists threatened the new republic. However, many prominent slave holders like Jefferson would come to embrace the Federalist vision as its hegemony became secured.

Decades later, in a letter to his future son-in-law William Smith, Jefferson reiterates his position against a strong centralized government, which he refers to as taking state power away of the people. Jefferson the slave master maintains his preference for ideological control as a more effective means of domination.

> I know no safe depositary of the ultimate powers of the society but the people themselves; and if we think them not enlightened enough to exercise their control with a wholesome discretion, the remedy is not to take it from them, but to inform their discretion by education. This is the true corrective of abuses of constitutional power ... Convinced that the people are the only safe depositories of their own liberty, and that they are not safe unless enlightened to a certain degree, I have looked on our present state of liberty as a short-lived possession unless the mass of the people could be informed to a certain degree ... And say, finally, whether peace is best preserved by giving energy to the government or information to the people. This last is the most certain and the most legitimate engine of government. Educate and inform the whole mass of the people. Enable them to see that it is their interest to preserve peace and order, and they will preserve them. And it requires no very high degree of education to convince them of this. They are the only sure reliance for the preservation of our liberty.

This debate between striking the most effective balance between ruling through force versus ruling through consent is at the heart of modern policies of social control. That is, from a ruling-class point of view the question is how to most effectively maintain the essential contradiction thereby subverting the negation of the negation.

The Resistance

With the establishment of the United States land speculators could now more aggressively move to appropriate the national territories of Native American social formations. The Indigenous fight back is an important part of the long tradition of resistance. The competition between European powers is relevant here. For example, in *Conquest by Law* Lindsay Robertson (2005) explores the difficulty of London's land speculators, George Washington not the least of them, in gaining access to tribal lands west of what were the thirteen colonies due to the effectiveness of France, in alliance with several Native American nations, in keeping them east of the Allegany Mountains. Even with the end of the Seven Years' War in 1763, when the interests of Paris were expelled from North America, London determined the mountains were a necessary barrier between their colonies on the eastern seaboard to prevent additional wars with powerful indigenous nations. Colonial land speculators were therefore barred, by way of the 1763 Proclamation of King George III, from pushing west into tribal lands by designating them *Indian lands* (Robertson 2005). For elite settlers this Proclamation was nearly as controversial as the aforementioned 1772 Summerset case advancing the abolition of slavery.

The 1763 Proclamation made it nearly impossible for colonial governors, such as the governor of Virginia, Lord Dunmore, from "legally" granting lands west of the Allegany Mountains to speculators. While it was difficult for conglomerates like the Illinois Company to secure vast swaths of tribal land after 1763, a steady stream of lawless settlers all along the border from North to South squatted on and terrorized native nations. It is therefore not surprising that in 1774 Dunmore agreed to participate in a failed deal designed to circumvent the King's Proclamation to "legally" obtain vast tracks of western tribal lands (Robertson 2005). Like many land-hungry settlers Dunmore remained loyal to London and therefore "threatened to unleash armed Africans on a brewing revolt against the Crown" (Horne 2014: 211) in 1775.

The political situation was indeed complex. London's response to even their most trusted governors' attempts at undermining the 1763 Proclamation was the Quebec Act of 1774, "attaching these lands to the Province of Quebec"

(Robertson 2005: 11). For Robertson these moves pushed elite settlers to open revolt against London arguing, "Virginians took their anger to Philadelphia, where, with representatives from other aggrieved colonies, they convened the First Continental Congress. Seven months later, the colonies and Britain were at war" (11). It was certainly no secret to Indigenous peoples that Europeans had been maneuvering for centuries to wrestle control of North America.

During the American (counter)Revolutionary War so-called patriots were unable to defeat the Native American supply-base at the British held Fort Detroit. Having neither been defeated nor surrendered, after 1776, "Indians lost jurisdiction over their lands north of the Ohio River at the Treaty of Paris in 1783 when the British gave the United States political sovereignty over the area without ever consulting a single Indian ally" (Venables 2004a: 278). Even though it seems that immediately following 1783, "Congress' goal was to prevent war with Indian nations by protecting their land against state encroachment" (Berkey 1992: 195), it would not take long for the United States to recover from the war and resume its expansive impulse.

Ever since 1746 the Shawnees of present-day Ohio had formulated the idea of a "pan-Indian movement" (Venables 2004a: 236) to block and push back against white expansionism. Again in 1769 Native American nations along the Ohio River, including the Shawnee, Miami, Ottawa, and Delaware, began organizing such a confederation. However, the balance of forces between the many Native American nations, soured by centuries of interventions and manipulations of the competing European imperialists, presented an insurmountable barrier to a complete alliance.

The Shawnee would continue to lead the pan-Indian movement until the United States successfully took control of what the settlers called the Old Northwest. While the balance of forces shifted between Native American nations across North America, Indigenous efforts to forge an independent confederacy allied with European forces as a bulwark against US expansion gained momentum. As US elites prepared for the 1787 Constitutional Convention, the US Congress, in its last days under the Articles of Confederation, passed the Northwest Ordinance. The Northwest Ordinance unveiled the true intentions of the United States toward First Nations despite a series of treaties recognizing Indigenous land holdings. Among other things "the act implied that the United States would not allow Indian nations to establish an independent confederacy in the area" (22). Echoing the haunting horrors of the Requermiento the Ordinance boldly stated that Native peoples and their property would be left alone unless Congress authorized a *just* war, and ruling-class settlers were skilled fabricators of so-called *just causes*. The Ordinance itself sent a clear message to Native nations that the United States, one way or another, intended to take possession of their lands.

While the Ordinance is admired for its provisions against slavery and for the political rights it guaranteed would-be settlers, these provisions might be viewed as concessions designed to win popular support amongst a rebellious non-Indigenous population. Congress approved the Northwest Ordinance despite reports that Native Americans were opposed to any cession and were already outraged over lands ceded through the fraudulent Treaty of McIntosh in 1785. McIntosh paved the way for the Land Ordinance of the same year whereby corrupt Congressmen allied with the Ohio Company moved to obtain thousands of acres of what amounted to stolen tribal lands for pennies (Venables 2004b). These, including many other similar actions, increased tensions between the United States and Indigenous nations of the Old Northwest, including the Shawnee of present-day Ohio. Contributing to US aggressions Britain still had a foot hold in the region of present-day Detroit due to the lucrative fur trade. With the recent yeomen rebellion, the ongoing slave insurrections, and Spain "threatening to close the Mississippi River to American Trade" (32), London believed the newly formed United States would soon be a failed state allowing them to advance their position on the continent.

In September 1790, on orders from President Washington, General Harmar departed from Fort Washington near present-day Cincinnati with roughly 1,500 troops heading North toward the Miami towns with orders to engage and destroy. With rumors coming to Britain at Fort Detroit that Harmar's envoy numbered close to 10,000, the Miami fled leaving the United States left to burn five of their towns and destroy 20,000 bushels of corn. Sending a few hundred troops ahead after destroying several native towns to seek out Native warriors and suffering humiliating defeats as a result, Harmar and his troops hurried back to Fort Washington licking their wounds (Venables 2004b).

Harmar's defeat in Ohio and the subsequent fame of Miami leader Michikinikwa (i.e. Chief Little Turtle) throughout the many Native American towns in the Old Northwest caused concern in Philadelphia. Joseph Brant, a Haudenosaunee Mohawk leader and devout Christian, who led a contingent of warriors who fought on the British side during the American Revolutionary War, had strong enough diplomatic ties to mediate a successful peace treaty. Brant, speaking as a leader of one of the most dominant Native nations on the continent who had dominated the tribes of the Old Northwest for centuries, orients his discourse in way that would be familiar to the likes of Washington.

In a letter written to the US federal government in 1791 Brant argues that those among the tribes of the Old Northwest who are the "most enlightened" and willing to adopt the ways of white society are turning away from moving in this direction not because of a "defect in nature," but because it seems "to them that the white people under whatever pretense aim at their eventual destruction" (quoted in Venables 2004b: 34).

To reorient this "most enlightened" Indigenous leadership Brant argues that "they must first be convinced that [white] civilization will not place them in a worse state than the one they are in now and that must begin by a strict adherence to the dictates of justice" (p. 34). Brant argues that to establish peace the United States must give up the idea of conquering the Old Northwest and accept the fact that the Treaty of Paris was incorrect. Toward these ends, Brant insists that the United States must stop attempting to negotiate with individual tribes and accept the existence of a "United Nations" of Indians (34). Brant's pleas would be made in vain.

While Eastern politicians desired a peaceful resolution, Frontier ambitions driven by the insatiable thirst of land speculators would launch violent military expeditions into the heart of Ohio country making a new war an inevitability. Early on, Little Turtle had a number of victories against the invaders, but Brant had warned them that in the long run the United States had more wealth and numbers and would ultimately be victorious. It is worth noting, in light of the yeomen insurrection, that the "American public ... seemed to favor the Indians. Many Americans understood that the Indians were fighting only to defend their homes against white invaders" (38). But Washington had to consider the frontiersmen in the Kentucky territory. These settlers were considering seceding from the United States and joining Spain if the United States could not protect them from Native Americans defending their national territories.

Washington therefore went to work successfully pushing a reluctant Congress to authorize a third federal army, this time consisting of 5,000 professionally trained soldiers led and trained by Revolutionary War veteran, General "Mad Anthony" Wayne, far superior to the failed detachments of undisciplined frontiersmen. Washington would be setting a precedent for the United States' imperialist ambitions. At the same time pro-war statesmen went to work applying pressure to London to abandon their Northwestern posts as dictated by the 1783 Treaty of Paris thereby cutting off Little Turtle's immediate source of supplies. At the same time Congress passed a new Trade and Intercourse Act in 1793 to entice more tribes to refrain from joining Little Turtle. Ultimately, fleeing from a cunning attack orchestrated by "Mad Anthony" Wayne Little Turtle's British allies would betray them at Fort Miami forcing them to negotiate with Washington's administration (Venables 2004b). After John Jay successfully signed a treaty with London, the Native Nations of Ohio eventually signed away much of their Ohio lands in 1795 in the Treaty of Greenville. Reflecting on the betrayal of their British allies and the intentions of the Americans in the wake of Greenville Shawnee leader, Blue Jacket (1807/1995) orients his discourse toward another emerging pan-Indian alliance:

> The summer before Wayne's army came out, the English held a council with the Indians, and told them if they would turn out and unite as one man, they might surround the Americans like deer in a ring of fire and destroy them all. The Wyandot spoke further in the council. We see, he said, there is like to be war between the English and our white brethren, the Americans. Let us unite and consider the sufferings we have undergone, from interfering in the wars of the English. They have often promised to help us, and at last, when we could not withstand the army that came against us, and went to the English for refuge, the English told us, 'I cannot let you in … ' It was then we saw the British dealt treacherously with us ….The Wyandot said, I speak to you my little brother, the Shawnee at Greenville, and to you, our little brothers all around … Now send forth your speeches to all our brethren far around us, and let us unite to seek for that which shall be our eternal welfare; and unite ourselves in a band of perpetual brotherhood.
>
> (132)

Still holding sizable tracks of their lands in Northern Ohio after the Treaty of Greenville that the United States would continue to encroach upon, the movement for a pan-Indian alliance Blue Jacket pointed to would once again flare up. As we will see in Chapter 5 a Shawnee leader would take up this task and become well known in the process. His name was Tecumseh and he continues to inspire peoples movements.

This defeat of the tribes of the Old Northwest also showed President Washington that "the national government could" effectively "mobilize a large force" and thus, without hesitation, in 1794, called 15,000 soldiers together "to put down rebellious Pennsylvania frontiersmen who objected to the federal whiskey tax and had begun the so-called Whisky Rebellion" (Venables 2004b: 46).

Conclusion

Rush's insistence on creating a stronger, more centralized repressive state apparatus as a safeguard against future rebellions proved beneficial to an emerging imperialist power. Created by the wealthiest merchants and slavers, the founding fathers had no intention of eliminating the exploitation and subjugation of the many that was the cause of the ongoing rebellions, from the enslavement of the Black nation, to yeomen, to Native Americans fighting for their national territories.

Because equality would not be pursued or tolerated, plans had to be in place for suppressing occasional flair ups. In addition to state repression, and the police in particular, education would play an increasingly central role in social control. At the same time, the many would also more vigorously pursue their own visions for an education for liberation as the balance of forces would continue to drive capitals' ongoing development.

5

Monopoly Capitalism and Three Systems of Education

Introduction: Connection to the Previous Chapter

In Chapter 4 we saw how 1776 was a counter-revolution against the end of slavery accompanied by an intensification of the repressive state apparatus to manage the resulting instability. We then saw a further intensification of state repression in what came out of the 1787 Constitutional Convention as a response to Shay's Rebellion. We also saw the architects of the repressive state apparatus, such as Rush, had a larger vision for social control that included the manipulation of ideas through education.

In the present chapter we see how capitalist development gives way to ever-deepening poverty and the tendency toward monopolies. Within this context we will see yet another intensification of the repressive police state coupled with an expansion of the educational sphere.

In his discussion of the process of expropriating peasants from the soil and the feudal tradition of holding property in common, Marx (1867/1967) notes that by the nineteenth century the English working-class had forgotten this history. In other words, workers were disconnected or alienated from their stories of arrival. Marx clearly understood that the movement against exploitation must be grounded in a conscious awareness of its story of arrival.

The question of how lands being seized through the violent process of westward expansion would be developed continued to be hotly debated. That is, would new lands serve as colonies supplying older states on the eastern seaboard with raw materials and food, or would they be included as equal partners? In our discussion of the resistance we turn once again to the movement for a pan-Indian alliance emerging in the Old Northwest in an attempt to stop the capitalist-driven process of westward expansion. First, however, we turn to the struggle of the labor movement and the role of education as one of their central demands aimed at abolishing child labor. In the final subsection within the resistance we turn once again to Frederick Douglas and his struggle for literacy.

Critical Role of Capitalism

Technological revolutions in production during the nineteenth century resulted in a major surge in capitalism's ability to produce and accumulate capital leading, in the United States in particular, to a growing demand for immigrant labor hours, enslaved labor hours, and Native American lands and lands held by Mexico.

The labor-saving technology dominant in this era, the mid-nineteenth century, is the machine factory and the cotton gin. It is the beginning of the era of monopolies. Bringing attention to the significance of these developments Lenin (1916/1986) notes that monopoly is "the most important phenomena of modern capitalism" (17). We will explore these developments within the sections on education and resistance.

This expansion of capital contributed to the most profitable firms growing ever larger enabling them to lock out more and more of their competitors, which gave rise to ever-larger monopolies or trusts. As production became concentrated or controlled by fewer and fewer capitalists and enslavers, the percent of the total work force employed or owned by fewer and fewer profiteers also increased. As a result, ever larger numbers of workers and the enslaved were brought together under one roof or one planation, which not only increased productive efficiency, but also made peoples' movements and rebellions more practical. The dialectical balance of forces became more volatile as each side of the class antagonism experienced greater concentrations of power.

In other words, "the yoke of a few monopolists on the rest of the population" became "a hundred times heavier, more burdensome and intolerable" (Lenin 1916/1986: 25). Capitalism and slavery therefore led, on one hand, to some of the largest fortunes ever amassed, and on the other, to similarly unprecedented levels of poverty, suffering, and mass uprisings. The ruling elite responded with new forms of education for domination and the expansion and increased professionalization of the police state. The outcome of this dialectical struggle, which included westward expansion, was not inevitable, as we will see below. In other words, the *thing* the system sublated into was not picked from a selection of predetermined choices. Rather, as always is the case, history is the outcome of a complex array of factors influenced by competing drives and tactical choices.

The Police State Intensified

For the vast majority of immigrants and US-born whites being pulled into a growing factory system marked by low wages, long hours, and extremely unsafe working conditions, a system of common schooling was advanced as part of the efforts to counter their more militant tendencies. However, roughly a decade before the system of common schooling began to be institutionalized, beginning in Massachusetts, professionalized police departments were created in response to the same working-class uprisings common schools were designed to counter.

In 1838 Boston built a more professionalized police force. Vitale (2018) notes that "Boston's economic and political leaders needed a new police force to manage riots and the widespread social disorder associated with the working-classes" (36–7). A year before institutionalizing a professional police force it took the state militia and 800 cavalry to suppress what were called the Broad Street riots involving some 15,000 Irish immigrant workers.

Not to be outdone New York City established a professional police force in 1844 as a response to widespread labor unrest. Like Boston, NYC took in hundreds of thousands of new immigrants who were being "chewed up by rapid and often cruel industrialization, producing social upheaval and immiseration that was expressed as crime, racial and ethnic strife, and labor unrest" (Vitale 2018: 37). In 1802, 1825, and 1828, for example, white and Black dock workers went on strike carrying out militant actions and sabotage. Skilled workers in 1809, 1822, and 1829 also organized even larger strikes against the new forms of labor-saving technology displacing their jobs. From this struggle, in 1829, the first working-class party was formed, the Workingmen's Party, which demanded the workday be reduced to ten hours. Beyond the very purposeful militant work actions general rebellions flared up consistently, sometimes monthly.

The same pattern of labor unrest and rebellion in other centers of industrialization from Philadelphia to Chicago were met with similar capitalist-class responses. That is, an intensified and professionalized repressive state apparatus combined with new efforts of morality training and education. In addition to being led by political bribery and engaged in voter suppression, newly formed police departments worked to "suppress workers' organizations, meetings, and strikes" (Vitale 2018: 38).

Slave Patrols Expanded

For the enslaved the system of enforced ignorance or education denied, intensified during this period as a deadlier form of slavery led to a rise in slave rebellions

(Anderson 1988; DuBois 1896/2014; Watkins 2001). That is, as capital's demand for raw materials became increasingly insatiable with monopolization, it became more profitable in the nineteenth century to work the enslaved to death than to take care of them into old age. When insurrectionary plans were discovered, all weapons and evidence were collected and the accused plotters were rounded up, taken to local authorities and tried for slave crimes in slaveholders' court (Hadden 2001).

In the aftermath of a subverted or materialized rebellion, such as Nat Turner's rebellion of 1831, more men would be called into duty and more patrols would be set into motion. The creation of extra patrols would often focus on more intensive harassment and abuse of the enslaved through searching their houses, stealing their property, and physical assaults. It was often poor whites who were called into this service which it was reported offered them an opportunity to exercise a false sense of authority and prove their subservience to the slave-owning class (Hadden 2001).

Often, however, increasing the brutality and numbers of patrollers and patrols were thought to be an inadequate response and entire militia units were called into action. The intensified patrolling and militia supplements could last for several months after an incident (Hadden 2001).

It was also believed that increasing the awareness of patrol laws would act as a deterrent to insurrections. Consequently, after an insurrection many localities would reprint patrol laws to general consumption. There were also unsuccessful attempts to enact new laws such as laws requiring slavers to provide the names of all of the adult men they had enslaved to patrollers or to allow patrollers easier access to plantations. Hadden (2001) speculates that what prevented such measures from becoming law was the paternalistic nature of the slave economy and the unwillingness of individual slavers to allow other men to intervene in *their* property.

However, at the end of the day, "little could be done permanently to prevent slaves from rebelling" (Hadden 2001: 152).

The Reservation System

Designed for Native American youth a system of education for extinction was designed as part of the state's final solution to suppressing Indigenous resistance (see Adams 1995; Churchill 2004). As industrial capitalism expanded its need for raw materials and sources of food for a dramatically expanding immigrant-based working-class, US imperialism secured its final westward expansion through a reservation system that functioned in many ways as prison camps. Summarizing this approach Vine Deloria Jr. and Clifford Lytle (1984) note that "evolving federal policy in the 1880s was designed to strengthen the government's control over the Indian tribes as they settled on the western reservations" (28).

Subverting tribal governments, with few exceptions, the Bureau of Indian Affairs in conjunction with the court of Indian offenses guided "the overall organization of reservation councils" (Deloria & Lytle 1984: 29). Supporting this move the US Congress responded by "appropriating funds to support the Indian police and these courts" (29). The result was "a system in which efforts are made to circumvent the existing customs and leadership patterns of the reservation people" (31). Despite widespread objections from reservation people and multiple reform initiatives, reclaiming tribal sovereignty remained a subverted objective. Deloria and Lytle (1984) define a state with political sovereignty as "possessing a wide range of municipal powers ... which perform a certain and specified function" (36). Rather, what Congress was willing to concede were reforms limited to granting reservation people the power to "approve expenditures from tribal funds by the agent" (36).

Critical Role of Education

The three educational systems outlined below were all designed to subdue the many's varied responses to the way monopolization was impacting their lives. All three models have their own specialized areas of study and research within the field of the history of education. Within summative history of education textbooks for survey courses (e.g., Spring 2014; Urban & Wagoner 2009) these three systems tend to be atomized as separate and distinct. Highlighting their interconnections points to multinational struggle.

Education for a So-Called Common Schooling

Reflecting the power and strength working and oppressed people had relative to capital during the post-Second World War era, in 1976, Basic Books, a widely read US publisher that offers titles aimed at both academic and trade markets, released Bowles and Gintis's Marxist analysis of US education, *Schooling in Capitalist America*. In their book Bowles and Gintis fundamentally challenged the field of the history of US education in their assessment of the nineteenth-century common school era.

For example, the traditional narrative within the history of education presented the emergence of common schooling around the middle of the nineteenth century as a reflection of the desire of the growing working-class for a more common system of education and therefore as evidence of the flourishing of democracy. To Bowles and Gintis, however, working in the era of the Black Panther Party, the American Indian Movement, and socialist and national liberation movements around the world, such claims of nineteenth-century democracy and harmony seemed strange. In other words, the traditional story of arrival woven to explain the emergence of US common schooling appeared suspicious given the profound lack of harmony between the oppressed and the oppressors during the 1970s.

Returning to the archives, Bowles and Gintis made significant contributions to the reorientation of the history of education concluding that the elites and the business class of the nineteenth century were won over to support a system of common schooling not due to democratic or egalitarian commitments. Rather, common school crusaders such as Horace Mann successfully convinced industrialists that educated workers were more manageable compared to uneducated workers. Mann's promise was essentially to reorient how workers understand how to improve their conditions. The objective was to replace the view that better working conditions and a better life are achieved through unions and collective struggle with an individualist orientation. The notion of pulling yourself up by your bootstrap where the romanticized rugged individual who started with nothing and through their own grit, hard work, and determination achieved upward social mobility, represents the self-centered identity Mann championed. Replacing class-consciousness with an individual consciousness is the ultimate goal here.

In an 1841 report Mann pleaded to industrialists by noting the benefits of the educated worker and the drawbacks of the uneducated worker. As evidence Mann cited an industrialist, Bartlett, quoting, "the educated worker was safe and malleable, whereas the uneducated worker was dangerous and recalcitrant" (quoted in Urban & Wagoner 2009: 120). Bartlett reasoned that capitalists with great fortunes would be wise to invest in common schooling as a form of "insurance on their property ... thereby educating the whole mass of mind and constituting a police more effective than peace officers or prisons" (120). What educational historians tend to miss in this passage is the larger context in which public investment in the police had been expanding. Mann was weighing in on the policy of expanding the repressive state apparatus through the police as a response to labor unrest. Essentially, Mann was making the case that investing in the ideological state apparatus was a more productive use of resources and form of crime prevention than the police. In his report Mann concludes that the half a million dollars a year spent on the police in New York City is a waste of resources. That is, for Mann, education prevents crimes of ignorance not only through moral training but through upward social mobility.

Another common argument Mann used to appeal to capitalist sensibilities was aimed at the religious background of New England capitalists. That is, Mann spoke of capitalists as stewards of the earth, who should give back in the form of taxes to fund common schools, an act both God and mortals would favor. This later argument tends to be the one reproduced in history of education books. For example, Gerald Gutek (1970), in his book, *An Historical Introduction to American Education*, notes:

> In framing his appeal for a tax-supported system of common schools, Mann developed a theory of humane and responsible capitalism which greatly resembled the stewardship concept contained in the Protestant ethic. ... Mann saw the abuses in the ruthless capitalism of the nineteenth century, he believed in working within the system rather than against it.
>
> (56)

The role of the capitalist was therefore to consent to a tax levy for education that would socialize workers with the proper moral foundation that would preemptively subvert proletarian insurrections (Cremin 1957) rendering the investment in the police redundant. We know increasing educational attainment alone will not lower the general rate of poverty in a given society or globally. What will eliminate poverty is a socialist program where basic needs, including housing, health care, and a job with a livable wage, are guaranteed constitutional rights. However, Mann's proposal was in direct opposition to socialism's class analysis. The lawyer-turned education crusader, on the other hand, advocated for a *common* schooling because he believed that if the children of both workers and capitalists attended the same schools, workers would develop a life-long loyalty to the bosses and their rule.

Rather than advancing a working-class democracy Bowles and Gintis (1976) argue common schooling was, and remains, about mediating the contradiction between capitalism and democracy. Rather than providing a path toward a more equal society, common schooling advanced the myth of meritocracy by giving white workers equal access to education thereby shifting blame for rising levels of poverty and suffering from the system of capitalism to individual workers assumed to be lazy or somehow inferior (Ford 2018). Bowles and Gintis locate the emergence of common schooling in developments within capitalist production that rendered the feudal-like apprenticeship model of training inefficient and inadequate due to the changing labor needs of capital.

Major advances in labor-saving technologies in manufacturing greatly enhanced the efficiency in production, and the demand for laborers, which, paradoxically, tend to be accompanied by an increase in working-class poverty. Between 1820 and 1840 industrial output in the United States increased by 127 percent. Mechanization in agriculture similarly reduced the amount of time it took to harvest an acre of wheat from sixty-three hours to three hours from the mid- to late nineteenth century (Foner 2009a; Noble 1984). Thousands of farmers and farm workers were subsequently driven from their relatively recently expropriated Native American lands into urban centers to sell their labor for a wage entering the ranks of the proletariat.

At the same time, Bowles and Gintis (1976), without acknowledging Native American genocide or militarily enforced relocation to reservations, note that "an abundance of land" (158) resulted in a labor scarcity, making it difficult for capitalists to maintain a sufficient reserve pool of labor. In the nineteenth century US industrialists demand for immigrant labor therefore exploded. Between 1846 and 1856 the United States absorbed 3.1 million immigrants. Bowles and Gintis offer these factors (i.e. urbanization, immigration, and mediating the contradictions between capitalism and democracy) as the primary driving force that contributed to capitals' need for a new form of mass schooling.

While Bowles and Gintis stress the importance of immigrants fueling capitals' desire to create a common American culture, they do not explore the ideas of immigrants themselves until the imperialist era around the 1890s when they note that "schooling would Americanize immigrant groups with a dangerous penchant for European radicalism and socialism" (186). By observing that immigrants in the 1840s arrived "with few resources other than their labor power" (158), Bowles and Gintis fail to directly connect one of the most valuable resources they came with to the common schooling movement.

Paul Buhle (1987/2013), in his history of the US left, argues that US-born workers' approach to struggle in the mid-nineteenth century tended to be limited to trade union consciousness, or negotiating over the rate of exploitation. Many of the roughly 8 million German immigrants who came to the United States between 1820 and 1870, fleeing the aftermath of a failed revolution in Germany in 1848, however, carried with them Marx's class analysis and the call to seize state power and liberate the means of production from capitalism as the only way to not only limit exploitation, but to abolish it.

When the fact is brought into the frame of perception that it was within impoverished immigrant communities that Marxism and revolutionary socialism entered the United States, alluded to by Bowles and Gintis (1976), we better understand common schoolings' emphasis on creating a common American culture. Horace Mann's anti-immigrant bigotry is best explained within this context. Writing in the *Common School Journal*, Mann, making a case for the establishment of common schools, warns of the threat of what he described as ignorant immigrants destroying America:

> We have repeatedly called the attention of the government ... to the danger arising from the great influx of ignorant foreigners, and the imperious necessity of providing more and better means than now exist for their instruction ... who are now beginning to control our elections, and of course to pervert our institutions ... Nothing is to be hoped from any of the parties that are now struggling for power, for even that party which would raise the slave, is kneeling before the power from which we have twice as much to fear as from the continuance of slavery.
>
> (Mann 1852: 266–8)

Educational historians tend to emphasize Mann's anti-Catholic bigotry as the primary factor driving his anti-immigrant prejudice (Spring 2014; Urban & Wagoner 2009). However, Mann's comparison of the so-called immigrant threat with the threat of slave rebellions points to the oppressors' true fear of the many rising up in pursuit of their own liberation. It therefore seems as though it was not immigrants' so-called strange culture that so offended Mann, but their proletarian class-for-self-consciousness.

When we understand the role of slavery as a form of primitive accumulation that accumulated the necessary wealth needed to expand and develop industrial production, and in the process, fomented slave rebellions, it becomes clear why Mann compares the so-called threat of ignorant immigrants and the threat of slave rebellions as an argument intended to advance the cause of common schools.

As suggested above, particularly offensive to Mann was the analysis that "some are poor because others are rich" which he therefore viewed as "dangerous" and the product of "revolutionizers" (Bowles & Gintis 1976: 166). To counter this class-consciousness and convince workers to attend his common schools Mann required an entirely different argument tailored to his audience. That is, he could not use the same arguments to persuade labor to attend common schools that he used to convince the bosses to fund them. When addressing workers Mann focused on the promise of common schoolings' individual benefits, such as the possibility of upward social mobility (i.e. meritocracy). Mann also argued that the power of literacy could be mobilized as a weapon to prevent "the domination of capital" (Urban & Wagoner 2009: 123) over labor. The most commonly known of Mann's many arguments was his bold statement that common schooling is the great equalizer or balance wheel of society.

Education as Mandatory Ignorance

> The century of industrial expansion was slowly dawning and awakening that vast economic revolution in which American slavery was to play so prominent and fatal a role ... and ... there were ... in the South faint signs of a changing moral attitude toward slavery, which would no longer regard the system as a temporary makeshift, but rather as a permanent though perhaps unfortunate necessity. (DuBois 1896/2007: 29)

Highlighting the connection between Northern industrial development and southern slavery, DuBois notes that "the history of slavery and the slave-trade after 1820 must be read in the light of the industrial revolution" (106). For example, another crucial aspect of the rapid industrial growth of the nineteenth century was the Cotton Gin. As a piece of labor-saving technology, the Cotton Gin dramatically reduced the average amount of labor hours it took to convert a given quantity of raw cotton into a useful commodity. That is, a direct result of the labor-saving Cotton Gin was that processed cotton entered the market loaded with much less value than before the integration of the machines' effect on necessary labor time. Reducing the value of cotton in this way, combined with its natural properties compared to wool, drastically increased demand in the era of monopolization, propelling capitalism's growth and development and driving it very quickly in search of new markets.

The world's primary cotton market of the time, Britain, saw an increase in the consumption of raw cotton from 13,000 to about 3.5 million bales from 1781 to 1860 as a result of these advances (DuBois 1896/2014). Whereas wool, once harvested, could be immediately spun into thread, harvested cotton was loaded with seeds that had to be picked out, which, before the Cotton Gin, was labor-intensive. Pre-cotton gin-processed cotton was therefore loaded with much more value (i.e. labor hours) than wool rendering cotton goods, compared to woolen goods, too costly for average consumers who were workers, peasants, and the enslaved. Once technology enabled cotton to be able to compete with wool, cotton's other natural properties such as its light weight and breathability resulted in a surge in demand.

Because of the drive to develop labor-saving technologies, capitalists always have an incentive to reduce circulation time or the time between production and consumption. That is, if a capitalist had not sold all of their commodities produced with pre-cotton gin cotton before the cotton gin reduced the market value of cotton, the capitalist would not be able to recoup all of the value they had invested in pre-cotton gin commodities. Creating new or penetrating into existing consumer markets is another way capitalists reduce circulation time. Often, penetrating into existing market requires the repressive state apparatus.

For example, one of the mechanisms through which the value in cotton goods manufactured in Britain was realized was the English cannon aimed at "the finances, the morals, the industry, and political structure of China" (Marx 1853/2007: 5). Part of this war included the use of opium as a form of warfare on China's national sovereignty leading to the Opium Wars between 1839 and 1860. As a result of the instability British imperialism, and later Japanese imperialism, inflicted upon China, a major shift occurred where China no longer led the world in economic output. Western powers and Japan assumed this position during what China refers to as a century of humiliation. As a result of China's decline by 1860 the first Chinese immigrants had immigrated to California lured by the gold rush. The legacy of racist, anti-Chinese education and the community's resistance to dehumanization in the United States is an important part of a history of education for the many, although beyond the scope of this chapter (see Au, Brown, & Calderon 2016). Nevertheless, US slave cotton can be understood as one of the driving forces behind global capitalism in the nineteenth century before 1865.

As the production of cotton became increasingly profitable, the trend toward the abolition of slavery ground to a halt. DuBois (1896/2014) argues that between 1808 and 1820, driven by the fear of insurrection, the South "half wished to get rid of this troublesome and abnormal institution" (108). However, with the new profit motive as a deadly driving force, slavery was not simply carried on as it had been before. Rather, when cotton became a central part of global capitalism, the slave system shed its feudalistic tendencies, such as primarily producing use values for wealthy enslavers or adding to the consumption fund of families as individually owned slaves. In its place slave labor became more centralized in fewer and fewer hands forming a mass of labor producing surplus value directly. Because of the existence of illicit supplies of Black replacement labor, it therefore became more profitable to work the enslaved to death than to take care of them into old age. Similarly, it became more profitable to "despoil rich, new land in a few years of intensive culture, and move on to the Southwest, than to fertilize and conserve the soil" (108).

When large cotton plantations began to dominate the southern slave economy and slavers started working their human property to death with growing regularity, slave rebellions also escalated in frequency and intensity. Hence, slave patrols also increased in intensity, number, and frequency.

In addition to slave patrols the enforcement of mandatory ignorance laws as a form of social control also intensified. For example, whereas it was illegal for the enslaved to learn to read and write in the eighteenth century, the laws became more punitive and far reaching in the nineteenth century: from outlawing just the enslaved from literacy to all Black people enslaved or free; from fining teachers for teaching the enslaved, to jail time and whippings in addition to fines for teaching any Black person, enslaved or free. In 1833 a law in Georgia read:

> If any person shall teach any slave, negro, or free person of color, to read or write, either written or printed characters, or shall procure, suffer, or permit, a slave, negro, or person of color, to transact business for him in writing, such person so offending, shall be guilty of a misdemeanor.
>
> (Moree & Mitchell 2006: 35)

Common schooling for immigrants and US-born poor whites and the denial of education among enslaved Africans were therefore not separate developments but part of the same effort to subdue the many. That is, the ideological tactic was to reinforce the idea that capitalism and slavery were ruling-class favors generously bestowed on Africans and working-class whites perpetually held back because they held innate, inferior qualities unaccounted for by histories of arrival.

Education for Extinction

Capital's insatiable drive to accumulate value gives way to constant revolutions in production. The revolution in production that ushered in the era of industrial capitalism—and by the end of the nineteenth century, imperialism—immensely increased the industrialists' appetite for not only slave labor and immigrant labor, but raw materials, sources of food, land, and consumer markets. This insatiable appetite drove the centralized repressive state apparatus made possible at the 1787 Constitutional Convention westward into so-called *Indian territory*.

Rapid expansion undermined the carefully worked-out constitutional relationship between the United States and Native American nations, shocking the latter. Hundreds of thousands of Native peoples were killed through the long marches of forced removals and massacres.

Westward expansionism savagely opened up millions upon millions of acres of land stolen from Native American nations for settlement and exploitation.

In addition to the use of the repressive state to subvert indigenous sovereignty, Indian boarding schools were designed to eliminate Native American nations by turning Native peoples into American workers. Richard Pratt, the military officer who designed these schools, argued that while it is "sad" when "Indians" are slaughtered by the US military, it is "far sadder" when they stagnate under the treaty system and remain isolated on reservations—isolated, that is, from "the best of our civilization."

Advancing a form of cultural racism against biological racism, Pratt argues that Native peoples, like all people, are born a blank slate rendering the so-called "savage born" not inevitably a "savage." Making this point Pratt notes, "transfer the savage-born infant to the surroundings of civilization, and he will grow to possess a civilized language and habit" (Pratt 1892).

The Eurocentric bigotry does not end here. Pratt continues arguing that those stolen from Africa and brought to America were more fortunate than Africans still in Africa since slavery took them out of the "savage" surroundings of Africa and put them in close proximity to the "higher race."

The Resistance

The Wage Slaves

It is important to note that the orientation of organized labor in early nineteenth-century Britain, the birthplace of modern capitalism, did not view education as the remedy to their problems of wages and time of labor. Making this point John Mitchell (1903), who began mining coal when he was fifteen and became president of the United Miners of America in 1898, notes, "the panacea of the laboring class was sought not in the use of the ballot or in free education, but in a universal strike of all the workers" (39). However, capital's ability to maintain its hegemony, despite working-class resistance, shifted labor's tactical orientation.

Consequently, organized labor in the United States began viewing free universal education as "a step toward the emancipation and elevation of their class" (70). Education would therefore be included as one of labors' demands. After the implementation of Horace Mann's Common Schooling, organized labor viewed it as a victory even though, in practice, it tended to serve the interests of capital. Nevertheless, public education, along with increasing wages and reducing the hours of labor, was emphasized by labor as necessary components of a fulfilling life. Summarizing the orientation of workers' organizations during this era Mitchell notes that "the shortening of the working day ... stands for freedom from toil at the time when it becomes most exacting, nerve wearing, and dangerous; still further, it stands for leisure, recreation, education, and family life" (120).

Mitchell (1903) argues, "if trade unionism had rendered no other service to humanity, it would have justified its existence by its efforts on behalf of working women and children" (131). The most obvious connection between working women and children is the teaching profession, which had been feminized early on using the sexism of US society to reduce the cost of teacher labor. Conscious of their own exploitation and lack of political rights (women did not win the right to vote until 1919) teachers in Chicago "threw their fortunes in with their fellow-workers and became affiliated with the Chicago Federation of Labor" (135). As a result, in 1897 teachers started the Chicago Federation of Teachers. Such efforts not only provided teachers with an organizational mechanism to defend their own interests against a predominantly, if not exclusively, male leadership, but also gave them a means by which to fight for the educational rights of working-class children.

Outlining the devastating situation for hundreds of thousands of child laborers in nineteenth-century industrial America, ruined by labor unsuited for their age, Mitchell offers a summary worth quoting at length:

> It is hard to reconcile the humanity and vaunted intelligence of this era with the wholesale employment of children in industry. Childhood should be a period of growth and education. It should be the stage in which the man is trained for future efforts and future work. With each advance in civilization, with each improvement of mankind, the period of childhood should be extended in order that the men and women of the next generation shall be mature and developed ... Apart from the particular and special evils of the system as it exists today, the policy of extracting work from children and exploiting their slow-growing strength is utterly vicious and entirely self-destructive.
>
> (136)

Mitchell goes on to argue that if we were talking about a society gripped with such deep poverty that it had to put young children to work for self-preservation, that could perhaps be understandable. However, in capitalist societies like the United States with a class of millionaires and billionaires child labor is unacceptable. Through the leadership of the unions and socialists workers put pressure on the state to both fund education and enact laws prohibiting child labor.

However, enforcement was difficult since the super profits of child labor incentivized authorities to look the other way. Union leaders were aware of this situation and continued to advocate for the rights of some of the most vulnerable children—including immigrant children and the children of immigrants. As the organization of workers active on the factory floor, in the mines, and in various shops, the activity of trade unions themselves resulted in "the number of children engaged in manufacturing" "gradually reduced" (139). Concluding his remarks on child labor and education Mitchell forcefully contends that "no permanent progress can be attained until all workmen and all well-intentioned members of society are united in a determined effort to protect children and to guarantee to them a happy, healthy and useful existence" (141).

Understanding that in an industrial, urban context public education represents the institution capable of ensuring the youth are properly assisted in their cognitive development, unions were not indifferent to the political implications of education. Conscious of the power of labor through organization unions sought to exert influence. Orienting his vision of union influence toward education Mitchell offers the following, "in the great field of education" union "influence should make itself felt; for the schools of the city should not in any case be antagonistic to the principles of organized labor" (211). Mitchell possessed a vision of education with a transformative purpose, consider:

> If the time should come when there are millions of workingmen acting together in common upon a boycott approved of by all, the power of the organized workmen ... will be infinitely increased. The attainment of such a strategic position by the workmen is a matter, however, of slow growth and is the result of their education to the full comprehension of the ideals of trade organization.
> (298)

Mitchell seems to be pointing to an education for class consciousness capable of facilitating the process of shifting the balance of forces to the side of labor. At the same time, however, Mitchell called for a harmonious relationship between labor and capital. Since coal miners tended to be more revolutionary at this time

Mitchell was critiqued for his reformism. As a result, Mitchell resigned from his position as president of the United Mine Workers of America in 1908.

The Indigenous

Before the implementation of Indian boarding schools, which included various forms of resistance including running away and refusing to quit speaking Native languages, Native nations were also resisting westward expansion more generally. The tradition of forging pan-Indian alliances in the Old Northwest would continue into the nineteenth century. As expansionists in the US Congress advocated for the conquest of Florida, Canada, and all lands west of the Mississippi, "a Shawnee named Tecumseh was attempting to unite Indians for another courageous stand against the whites" (Venables 2004b: 49).

The Treaty of Greenville began to be encroached upon by US President John Adams. In 1800 Adams scandalously created the Indiana Territory and appointed the racist expansionist William Henry Harrison as its governor. Following Adams President Thomas Jefferson would continue to plot against Native sovereignty. In a series of letters to Governor Harrison, Jefferson outlined ways he believed Native Americans could be lured into insurmountable debt and forced to sell off their lands out of desperation. After acquiring a vast territory west of the Mississippi from the French in 1803 (i.e. the Louisiana Purchase), Jefferson began entertaining the possibility of forcing the tribes of the Old Northwest to these trans-Mississippi lands.

Whereas Tecumseh had experienced some success in his movement for a pan-Indian alliance within his own region, his campaign had been less successful with Native American Nations to the west and to the South. The policy direction of President Jefferson, however, "forced Indian peoples to consider Tecumseh's pan-Indian movement as the singular option to total capitulation to US expansion" (54).

However, while Tecumseh was away recruiting in 1809 Jefferson, drawing on the example of the Cherokee in Tennessee, was busy attempting to convince leaders of the Wyandot and other tribes that it was better to accept US conquest and adopt capitalist conceptions of individual property and US laws than to succumb to a dishonest British ally. Drawing on their knowledge of capitalist conceptions of adding value to land through labor, Wyandot leaders responded to Jefferson explaining why they were not interested in ceding their lands explaining, "the reason why" we "like this land so well" is because "we have made valuable improvements thereon, which have cost" us "both labor and expenses" (quoted in Venables 2004b: 57).

While Jefferson's attempts at convincing Native peoples to passively accept conquest and voluntarily assimilate were ineffective, Harrison's attempts at subversion included the common tactic of using alcohol and bribes to get indigenous leaders to sign away vast tracts of land. For example, leaders representing the Potawatomies, Delawares, and Miamis, motivated by a desire to avoid war, agreed to a meeting at Fort Wayne Indiana with Harrison in 1809. After successfully convincing them to get drunk and accept bribes Harrison succeeded in persuading them "to sign away about 3 million acres of Indian land, including some hunting grounds of the Shawnee who were not represented at the treaty" (58). At the insistence of the Fort Wayne delegates Harrison also negotiated treaties with the Weas and Kickapoos in the same year. Among the treaty signers was the influential Miami leader Little Turtle, whose role in fighting the US expansionists in the 1790s was significant. Aware of growing US power, by 1809, Little Turtle was convinced that accepting US conquest was the only way to survive. Little Turtle therefore represented a major challenge to Tecumseh and the movement for a pan-Indian alliance.

Venables argues that after the Fort Wayne treaty Tecumseh reoriented his political discourse from advocating for an international pan-Indian confederation where various tribes came together in defense of their own individual national territories, to an ideology that had emerged among several Seneca and Delaware prophets from the mid-to-late 1700s. That is, the idea that the land commonly known as North America today, as one large mass, belongs not to individual separate tribes each owning a piece, but it belongs to all Native Americans collectively. As a result of this shift, "Tecumseh ... focused Indian attention on the concept that every Indian nation had a stake in what happened to every Indian because the land belonged to all Indians, the gift of the Creator" (59).

In 1810 Tecumseh had gathered about 1,000 warriors at the Shawnee town, Tippacanoe, ready to repel US encroachment, by force if necessary. Making one last effort to win him over Harrison arranged a meeting with Tecumseh. Tecumseh, to no avail, is reported to have told Harrison that the land was never "divided, but belongs to all ... Sell a country! Why not sell the air, the clouds and the great sea?" (quoted in Venavles 2004b: 60).

Each side having failed to win the other over, Harrison prepared for war. Nearly two months after his meeting with Tecumseh, Harrison asked the Indiana territorial legislature if "one of the fairest portions of the globe" would "remain in a state of nature, the haunt of a few wretched savages, when it seems destined, by the Creator, to give support to a large population, and to be the sea of civilization, of science, and true religion" (61). Tecumseh, however, did not want war and ramped up his efforts to recruit other tribes in the Old Northwest to his side visiting Ohio, Indiana, Michigan, and Canada in the fall of 1810. In 1811, continuing his campaign for a pan-Indian alliance, Tecumseh spoke to a large group of Choctaws, Chickasaws, Cherokees, Creeks, Osage, and Iowa, in Tennessee making his case to "unite in one common cause against a common foe" (64).

Tecumseh stressed how "the whites are already nearly a match for us all united" and pointed to how the once-powerful tribes of the Eastern seaboard succumbed to the English invaders due to their "vain hope of alone defending their ancient possessions" (64). Drawing on this past history to inform the present Tecumseh spoke to the tribes arguing that "soon your mighty forest trees … will be cut down to fence in the land which the white intruders dare to call their own" and "our annihilation … is at hand unless we unite" (64). Making a comparison to the enslavement of Africans Tecumseh warns that if they are overrun by the whites they could very well be subjected to a similar fate asking, "how long will it be before they tie us to a post and whip us, and make us work for them in the corn fields as they do them?" (64). Challenging his audience to embrace their agency as a dialectical force Tecumseh then asks, "shall we wait for that moment or shall we die fighting before submitting to such ignominy?" (64).

After Tecumseh's moving speech, a Choctaw leader, Pushmataha, spoke on behalf of peace taking a firm position against Tecumseh. Pushmataha argued that while Tecumseh's account might have been true for the Shawnee, it was not true for the Choctaw arguing that they had established a peaceful and mutually beneficial trading relationship with their white neighbors. The Choctaw, on an extremely close vote, would eventually side with Pushmataha and Tecumseh would continue on his journey heading east to the Creeks, his southern relatives (Tecumseh's mother was a Creek-Cherokee). Frustrated and desperate Tecumseh's speech to over 5,000 Creeks was a reflection of his understanding of the danger posed by Washington, "back whence they [the whites] came, upon a trail of blood, they must be driven" (67).

Tecumseh would continue to travel east and successfully gained a strong following among the Seminole, who had many similar experiences as the Shawnee. However, the Cherokees, the Osages, and others refused to see themselves as threatened and "continued to believe that longstanding animosities between Indian nations were of greater importance than unity" (67). Ultimately,

Tecumseh's efforts at unity building were not successful and it only took a couple of decades before his predictions would come true and the Choctaws and others were forced to give up their lands and violently driven at gun point to the poverty and depression of Oklahoma. Tecumseh too would be killed in battle fighting in alliance with the British against the United States in the War of 1812. Tecumseh's confederacy would die with him and in a few short decades the Native peoples of the Old Northwest would be forced out of their country.

The Enslaved

While many escaped Black people, adopted by indigenous nations, would fight alongside Tecumseh, many more would struggle from within the chains of captivity. For example, the resistance against mandatory ignorance laws was one way to push for freedom while still being enslaved. Tactics included clandestine efforts at learning to read and write. Frederick Douglas (1845) famously documents his successful road to literacy while enslaved. Since literacy rates among the enslaved ranged around 5 percent at the time of emancipation in 1865, Douglas's story was unique. His ability to translate his experiences into a book is an even more rare feat. Turning to Douglas's words here to tell the story is therefore justified.

> I lived in Master Hugh's family about seven years. During this time, I succeeded in learning to read and write. In accomplishing this, I was compelled to resort to various stratagems. I had no regular teacher. My mistress, who had kindly commenced to instruct me, had, in compliance with the advice and direction of her husband, not only ceased to instruct, but had set her face against my being instructed by anyone else. It is due, however, to my mistress to say of her, that she did not adopt this course of treatment immediately. She at first lacked the depravity indispensable to shutting me up in mental darkness. It was at least necessary for her to have some training in the exercise of irresponsible power, to make her equal to the task of treating me as though I were a brute.
>
> My mistress was, as I have said, a kind and tender-hearted woman; and in the simplicity of her soul she commenced, when I first went to live with her, to treat me as she supposed one human being ought to treat another. In entering upon the duties of a slaveholder, she did not seem to perceive that I sustained to her the relation of a mere chattel, and that for her to treat me as a human being was not only wrong, but dangerously so. Slavery proved as injurious to her as it did to me. When I went there, she was a pious, warm, and tender-hearted woman. There was no sorrow or suffering for which she had not a tear. She had bread

for the hungry, clothes for the naked, and comfort for every mourner that came within her reach. Slavery soon proved its ability to divest her of these heavenly qualities. Under its influence, the tender heart became stone, and the lamblike disposition gave way to one of tiger-like fierceness. The first step in her downward course was in her ceasing to instruct me. She now commenced to practice her husband's precepts. She finally became even more violent in her opposition than her husband himself. She was not satisfied with simply doing as well as he had commanded; she seemed anxious to do better. Nothing seemed to make her angrier than to see me with a newspaper. She seemed to think that here lay the danger. I have had her rush at me with a face made all up of fury, and snatch from me a newspaper, in a manner that fully revealed her apprehension. She was an apt woman; and a little experience soon demonstrated, to her satisfaction, that education and slavery were incompatible with each other.

From this time I was most narrowly watched. If I was in a separate room any considerable length of time, I was sure to be suspected of having a book, and was at once called to give an account of myself. All this, however, was too late. The first step had been taken. Mistress, in teaching me the alphabet, had given me the inch, and no precaution could prevent me from taking the ell.

The plan which I adopted, and the one by which I was most successful, was that of making friends of all the little white boys whom I met in the street. As many of these as I could, I converted into teachers. With their kindly aid, obtained at different times and in different places, I finally succeeded in learning to read. When I was sent of errands, I always took my book with me, and by going one part of my errand quickly, I found time to get a lesson before my return. I used also to carry bread with me, enough of which was always in the house, and to which I was always welcome; for I was much better off in this regard than many of the poor white children in our neighborhood. This bread I used to bestow upon the hungry little urchins, who, in return, would give me that more valuable bread of knowledge. I am strongly tempted to give the names of two or three of those little boys, as a testimonial of the gratitude and affection I bear them; but prudence forbids;—not that it would injure me, but it might embarrass them; for it is almost an unpardonable offence to teach slaves to read in this Christian country. It is enough to say of the dear little fellows, that they lived on Philpot Street, very near Durgin and Bailey's ship- yard. I used to talk this matter of slavery over with them. I would sometimes say to them, I wished I could be as free as they would be when they got to be men. 'You will be free as soon as you are twenty-one, but I am a slave for life! Have not I as good a right to be free as you have?' These words used to trouble them; they would express for me the liveliest sympathy, and console me with the hope that something would occur by which I might be free.

(32–4)

Douglas's account of his quest to read offers critical insight into the terrorizing experience of being enslaved. Like a great number of people enslaved Douglas was not only shuffled around between various owners, but he also spent a lot time alone, forced to endure the terrorism of slavery without the comfort and love of others facing the same situation. One can only imagine how strong the impulse was to resist such a cruel system.

Conclusion

As we saw in this chapter the experiences of the immigrant working-class, the enslaved Black people, and Native Americans in the Old Northwest were all intimately interrelated despite being treated by historians as separate and unrelated. The machine factory and the cotton gin would more closely merge the trajectory of capitalism with slavery and simultaneously lead to the intensification of exploitation and degradation of both workers and the enslaved. As the United States continued to shift from an agricultural-based economy to an industrialized capitalism, the drive to colonize Native American lands to the west proportionally intensified.

The various forms of education and the repressive state, specially fitted for each unique context, further illustrate the similar ways in which the capitalist ruling-class has worked to dominate the many.

During this era traditions of resistance would be further developed from a focus on education for liberation, to teacher unions, to orientations of unity and coalition building among the oppressed. We now turn to an exploration of the African American movement for public education in the post-Civil War era. From this point on the term "African American" will be used in reference to citizens of African descent since the abolition of slavery opened the door for the 14th amendment of 1868 universalizing citizenship to all persons born within US territory.

6

African American Agency and the US Civil War

Introduction: Connection to the Previous Chapter

In Chapter 5 we saw the expansion of the ideological and repressive state apparatuses with the rise of the machine factory, the cotton gin, and westward expansion. We also saw the agency of the many fighting back against the intensification of capitalism.

The present chapter first explores the developments within capitalism that would give way to the Civil War and the eventual abolition of slavery and the planter class. According to DuBois (1935/1992), "with the Civil War, the planters died as a class" (54). With the victory over their former captors, public education, ran and conceptualized by African-Americans, found space to grow. However, the terrorist energy of the slave patrols would be sublated in the post-Civil War era. Finally, the ongoing tradition of resistance is examined as new contradictions emerged in the ruins of slavery.

Critical Role of Capitalism

On the one hand, the enormous and ceaseless stream of men, year after year driven upon America, leaves behind a stationary sediment in the east of the United States, the wave of immigration from Europe throwing men on the labor-market there more rapidly than the wave of emigration westwards can wash them away. On the other hand, the American Civil War brought in its train a colossal national debt, and, with it, pressure of taxes, the rise of the vilest financial aristocracy, the squandering of a huge part of the public land on speculative companies for the exploitation of railways, mines, etc., in brief, the most rapid centralization of capital. The great republic has, therefore, ceased to be the promised land for emigrant laborers. Capitalistic production advances there with great strides, even though the lowering of wages and the dependence of the wage-worker are yet far from being brought down to the normal European level.

(Marx 1867/1967: 773)

The final era of chattel slavery in the United States coincided with the more complete development of monopolies giving way to finance capital. As the sums of capital required for the operation of large-scale production ballooned, the model of the family-owned company would be replaced by a new structure, the joint-stock ownership model. Because production required large capital inputs, banks went from modest middlemen to the most dominant owners and investors. As a result, banking and industrial capital would come together forming a new center of capitalist power, finance capital. Whereas industrial capitalists and banking capitalists had previously been competitors, under finance capital they were integrated as a more powerful force (Becker 2015).

Financing the Civil War dramatically accelerated this process. Before the Civil War slavers had been crying that banks were making "the North an even greater financial dictator of the South" (DuBois 1935/1992: 38). Contributing to the slavers' declining position, for DuBois (1935/1992), was their feudal-like culture rendering them ignorant and disconnected from, and hostile to, technological developments in production. The only response to the development of labor-saving technology offered by Southern elite slavers, outside of the cotton gin, was doubling down on the insistence of the efficiency of enslaved labor despite all contrary evidence. Increasingly disconnected from the rapidly expanding modern capitalist world, the response of the slavers was to attempt to survive by lobbying for more slave territories.

For example, the so-called Missouri Compromise of 1820 allowed Missouri to enter the union as a slave state partially repealing "the first Constitutional Congress of 1789–90" that "had legally excluded slavery from all Territories of the republic northwest of the Ohio" (Marx 1861/2007: 283). However, the Kansas-Nebraska Bill of 1854 repealed this mandate placing the decision as to whether or not slavery should be introduced into particular Territories to settlers. As a result of this Bill, "every geographical and legal limit to the extension of slavery in the Territories was removed" (283). If this were not enough the US Supreme Court's 1857 Dred Scott decision tore down even the weak political barrier to slavery in the Kansas-Nebraska Bill ruling that "every American citizen possesses the right to take with him into any Territory any property recognized by the Constitution" (284) including people held against their will through slavery.

At issue was a struggle over lands seized from Tecumseh and the tribes of the Old Northwest and beyond. Southern slavers sought to expand slavery into these new Territories whereas Northern bankers and settlers sought to expand modern capitalism and the so-called free-soil movement. The Republican Party emerged in this context campaigning around a number of key issues centered around not conceding any new Territory to slavery, advocating instead, for so-called *free colonization*. With the election of Lincoln, the Republican Party's first president, the South "took this victory as a pretext for drawing the sword from the scabbard" (290).

Despite Lincoln being far from an abolitionist, in response to his election, "new patrol groups and 'Minute Man' volunteer organizations sprang up across the South" (Hadden 2001: 172). Intensifying the role of the repressive state these white supremacist volunteers not only assisted patrols and harassed whites they suspected were radicals and abolitionists, they also agitated for secession.

A War of Conquest Subverted

Ultimately, enraged by possible limitations on the expansion of slavery placed on new Territories, southern slavers would engage in not a defensive war, but a war of conquest designed to push North and crush their northern capitalist competitors and transform the United States into a country of slavery (Marx 1861/2007). Alluding to this conclusion Gerald Horne (2014) observes that "defenders of the so-called Confederate States of America were far from bonkers when they argued passionately that their revolt was consistent with the animating and driving spirit of 1776" and that "1861 was an extension of 1776" (x–249). The slave patrols would continue to expand during the first years of the Civil War. For example, in 1861 patrols doubled in North Carolina (Hadden 2001).

The enslaved, of course, would take advantage of every opportunity to redirect the war against slavery itself. Consequently, when the South attacked the North, they unintentionally freed the enslaved. At the same time, when the North retaliated and invaded the South, they came as unintentional emancipators. While Marx (1861/2007) argues the South was not really seeking to break up the Union but to transform it into a slave oligarchy, DuBois (1935/1992) demonstrates that the goal of the North was to preserve the Union as it was.

In his work DuBois challenges the two primary theses regarding the views and actions of the enslaved during the Civil War. The first position assumed that "the Negro did nothing but faithfully serve his master until emancipation was thrust upon him" (57). The other position was that the enslaved fled slavery to the safety of the Northern army as soon as it appeared. Both positions excluded from the frame of perception the calculus of the enslaved.

That is, accustomed to living under southern terrorism African Americans would patiently wait assessing the changing political situation as the Civil War unfolded. Initially, there was nothing that would lead the enslaved to believe the Northern army was a force of liberation, and fleeing one group of oppressors to another made little sense. At the same time, the enslaved were not going to revolt against a Southern plantocracy whose power was on the rise. But once it was clear the Northern army was unable or unwilling to return fugitive slaves to Southern slavers whose victory was uncertain, they engaged in what DuBois calls a "general strike" and offered their labor to the Union army. For DuBois "this withdrawal and bestowal of … labor decided the war" (57). DuBois thereby challenges the dominant narrative that credits Lincoln with freeing the enslaved through his Emancipation Proclamation of 1863. Rather, despite Lincoln's persistent protests that the Civil War was not a war against slavery, by 1862:

> Lincoln faced the truth, front forward; and that truth was not simply that Negroes ought to be free; it was that thousands of them were already free, and that either the power which slaves put into the hands of the South was to be taken from it, or the North could not win the war. Either the Negro was to be allowed to fight, or the draft itself would not bring enough white men into the army to keep up the war.
>
> (82)

The Southern plantocracy's chances of winning the war relied on the labor of the enslaved to grow food and cash crops enabling white males to fight. As the war dragged on and the Southern army became increasingly desperate for soldiers, they lowered the draft age on one side to seventeen and extending it on the other to fifty. As a result, the pool of potential slave patrollers nearly completely diminished (Hadden 2001). With no effective repressive apparatus to hold the system in place, African Americans removed themselves from slavery.

This unofficial end of slavery was critical because the Northern army had no such advantage. The fighting force in the North was also the laboring force. Raising an army therefore took labor away from producing food and other necessaries. While the racist narrative suggested that the enslaved fled slavery to escape labor, DuBois argued it was particular conditions of labor that were rejected. African Americans sought "land to work" and to "see and own the results of their toil" (67). What was sought was "honesty in treatment and education" (67).

Coinciding with the establishment of educational commissions and other efforts during the war and during Reconstruction, the former slavers began ramping up efforts to induce white supremacist attitudes within the poor whites to foment divisiveness. Despite these efforts thousands of poor whites followed fleeing African Americans into the Union Army camps. After the war Reconstruction promised a hopeful future for the recently emancipated.

Defining Freedom

Defining exactly what freedom meant would be hotly debated before Reconstruction's abrupt and premature termination. For example, could freedom really be realized within the limits of a capitalist system? For many who had recently been enslaved, the answer was no.

Illustrating this point General Sherman's famous March to the Sea tens of thousands of former enslaved refugees followed behind offering labor assistance. Unsure of the fate of these masses Sherman heeded the advice of leaders among them to distribute abandoned plantation lands to the refugees. In January 1865 Sherman allocated thousands of 40-acre plots from abandoned islands along the Carolina and northern Florida coast. Lincoln made a commitment to seek Congressional legislation to make freedmen's land titles permanent (Holt 1995).

However, after Lincoln's assassination and southern-born Vice President Andrew Johnson took office, he pardoned former rebels and restored their property. As a result, freedmen either had to face eviction or agree to work for their former masters as share croppers. For these refugees, freedom meant self-determination and independence which required direct access to the means of production (i.e. land). Being forced into a form of economic dependency as either a share cropper or a wage laborer, to the *slave*, did not feel much different from actual slavery and therefore could hardly be called freedom. In response, former slave Henry Bram, writing on "behalf" (quoted in Holt 1995: 25) of a people's committee the refugees had formed, penned a letter to the General charged with carrying out the decision, General Howard, outlining their position and demands. Because of the significance of the letter and the indispensable voice it offers, the entire letter is reproduced below:

> General, It Is with painful Hearts that we the Committee address you, we Have thoroughly considered the order which you wished us to Sign, we wish we could do so but cannot feel our rights Safe If we do so,

General we want Homestead's; we were promised Homestead's by the government,[2] If It does not carry out the promises Its agents made to us, If the government Having concluded to befriend Its late enemies and to neglect to observe the principles of common faith between Its self and us Its allies In the war you said was over, now takes away from them all right to the soil they stand upon save such as they can get by again working for *your* late and their *all time enemies*.–If the government does so we are left In a more unpleasant condition than our former

we are at the mercy of those who are combined to prevent us from getting land enough to lay our Fathers bones upon. We Have property In Horses, cattle, carriages, & articles of furniture, but we are landless and Homeless, from the Homes we Have lived In In the past we can only do one of three things Step Into the public *road or the sea* or remain on them working as in former time and subject to their will as then. We cannot resist It In any way without being driven out Homeless upon the road.

You will see this Is not the condition of really freemen

You ask us to forgive the land owners of our Island, you only lost your right arm. In war and might forgive them. The man who tied me to a tree & gave me 39 lashes & who stripped and flogged my mother & my sister & who will not let me stay In His empty Hut except I will do His planting & be Satisfied with His price & who combines with others to keep away land from me well knowing I would not Have anything to do with Him If I Had land of my own.–that man, I cannot well forgive. Does It look as If He Has forgiven me, seeing How He tries to keep me in a condition of Helplessness

General, we cannot remain Here In such condition and If the government permits them to come back we ask It to Help us to reach land where we shall not be slaves nor compelled to work for those who would treat us as such

we Have not been treacherous, we Have not for selfish motives allied to us those who suffered like us from a common enemy & then Having gained *our* purpose left our allies in their Hands There Is no rights secured to us there Is no law likely to be made which our Hands can reach. The state will make laws that we shall not be able to Hold land even If we pay for It Landless, Homeless. Vote less. we can only pray to god & Hope for *His Help, your Influence & assistance* with consideration of esteem your Obt Servts.

(24–5)

In response to this letter and the freedmen's demands, which clearly lays out the conditions for freedom from the point of view of a community with direct experience having all of their freedoms systematically denied, the United States responded by telling them that they were talking too much, asking for too much, and that they were confused. The refugees were told that they had to accept the fact that freedom was not going to be easy and like others who were not rich, they would have to accept the conditions of poverty and make the best of it. They were not reminded that the wealth of the rich is produced by the poor, a fact they knew all too well from slavery. Instead, the refugees were reminded that their working time would belong to the purchaser of it, not them. They were counseled not to travel North in search of better conditions for they would only find life even more unbearable.

DuBois (1935/1992) summarizes this war against Reconstruction as "a determined effort to reduce black labor as nearly as possible to a condition of unlimited exploitation and build a new class of capitalists on its foundation" (670). Like the spirit of Columbus, DuBois notes that the post-Civil War South was defined by profound lawlessness and white terrorism. Somewhat successfully wielding whiteness as a weapon to subdue the primarily white and Black Southern many "the white laborer joined the white landholder and capitalist and beat the black laborer into subjection through secret organizations and the rise of a new doctrine of race hatred" (p. 670).

Patrols Linger On

Hadden (2001) reports that because union troops occupying Southern states after the war were often just as racist as Southern whites, it was not uncommon for them to allow and even assist in continuing former patrolling practices. Flocking to Southern cities from rural areas African Americans began to be the target of the former pass system imposed by Union forces seeking so-called law and order. Often delegated to white Southern police forces eager to return to what they knew as normal, the African American community protested petitioning the president and reaching out to receptive Northern newspapers. Eventually, Southern state constitutions were rewritten abolishing slavery and the codes that allowed for the patrols.

In response Southern states passed a series of laws called Black Codes. The laws were written to enforce "labor contracts" in addition to "prohibiting vagrancy" and relegating African Americans to "agricultural pursuits" as well as controlling their "movements" (Hadden 2001: 198). The laws placed the power of enforcement in the hands of "county or voluntary militia units, much like slave patrols of old" (Hadden 2001: 198). Such militia and groups would serve the function of the police. This history reveals that like the Northern ruling-class, the Southern ruling-class understood that without the pooling of their power wielded through a repressive apparatus, the laws of their unjust system would not hold.

Sensing they were losing control Congress eventually stepped in. The Reconstruction Act of 1867 declared no legal government existed in the South. The Civil Rights Act was passed in addition to the ratification of the 14th Amendment guaranteeing equal protection. Undeterred, white Southern terrorism would persist finding expression in groups like the Ku Klux Klan.

Despite the most difficult circumstances including the persistent threat of white terror African Americans would push forward leading the charge bringing progressive reforms to the South including public education.

Critical Role of Education

The relevance of DuBois's work on Reconstruction-era education is ongoing. For example, William Watkins (2001) situates his *The White Architects of Black Education* as a "continuation" (3) rather than a departure or challenge to DuBois. Watkins (2001), without discounting or denying the agency of African Americans in the South, explores more deeply the orientation of Northern white missionaries DuBois mentions. *A History of Education for the Many*, however, is more interested in the African American-led movement for common schooling than unwanted outside intervention.

DuBois dispels the myth that education was a gift brought from Northern missionaries during Reconstruction. Northern allies and the Freedman's Bureau, while they lasted, rather than taking the lead, assisted African American efforts. What follows is a brief review of this history.

Roughly 95 percent of African Americans could not read or write at the close of the Civil War as a result of enforced mandatory ignorance laws. After the Civil War southern racists argued that African Americans could not learn and investing resources toward such efforts was therefore wasteful. The contradictions were too obvious that if African Americans could not learn, then mandatory ignorance laws would never have been necessary.

Abolitionists and religious philanthropists would play a supportive role. While outside help was important, DuBois is unambiguous in his insistence that "public education for all at public expense, was, in the South, a Negro idea" (638).

When DuBois says "for all," he truly means *for all*. That is, DuBois documents how it was not only Africans who were illiterate before 1865, but most poor whites were also not trained in the skills of reading and writing. Two primary factors, for DuBois, account for the illiteracy of Southern poor whites. First, the slavocracy and other property owners believed that educating poor whites would make it more difficult to control them. The other reason for the lack of educational opportunities for poor whites was that they tended not to demand schooling and accepted their subordination to Southern elites. The hope they possessed for escaping their situation, before the Civil War, resided within the belief, however far-fetched, that they too might one day become a slave owner.

It was African Americans, not impoverished whites, who perceived the "connection between knowledge and power" and who saw education as a "stepping stone" (641) to a more complete liberation in a post-1865 context. Searching for an answer for why the formerly enslaved appeared to be more politically sophisticated and forward thinking compared to poor whites, DuBois speculates that "perhaps the very fact that so many of them had seen the wealthy slaveholders at close range, and knew the extent of ignorance and inefficiency among them, led to that extraordinary mass demand on the part of the black laboring class for education" (p. 641). Simply put, African Americans had a unique perspective based on their uniquely dreadful experiences.

After reviewing the history of African American efforts at establishing schools before 1861, DuBois turns to the post-Civil War context. Winning a major victory for education in 1865 public schools in South Carolina opened their doors "to all children without distinction of color" and that "twenty-five of the forty-two teachers were" (p. 643) African American.

Even after the system General Banks organized in 1864 "was suspended in Louisiana by military order" (p. 644), African Americans collected more than 10,000 signatures pledging their willingness to pay a special tax to keep the schools for their children open.

African American educational endeavors continued after the war despite the persistence of the repressive state apparatus. For example, in Savanah African American leaders took special interest in recruiting teachers from within the Black community. Struggling to find buildings that could serve as schools former slave marts were converted into schools. Within a few short months the community had opened several schools in Savanah and were actively educating more than 500 students—students of all ages.

In 1866 African Americans in Georgia organized the Georgia Educational Association whose purpose was to encourage the Black community throughout the South to embrace the importance of education in the struggle for liberation. By 1867 it was reported that 191 day schools and 45 night schools had been created through the South. While these efforts received some Northern assistance

DuBois reports that ninety-six of these schools were supported partially or entirely by the Black community. In addition, fifty-seven of the buildings the schools were housed in were owned by individual African Americans.

DuBois is also offering a window into the larger context to understand the ineffectiveness of many Freedman's Aid Societies who sent so-called friends South, many of whom had the same racist views as Southerners. Consequently, DuBois notes that many of these aid workers were willing to distribute food and clothing, but were unwilling to "cooperate in any movement looking toward the education of the Negro" (646). Making this point Anderson (1988) notes that "most northern missionaries went south with the preconceived idea that the slave regime was so brutal and dehumanizing that blacks were little more than uncivilized victims who needed to be taught the values and rules of civil society" (6). Consequently, many missionaries were surprised when they learned about the educational efforts African Americans had established. So convinced of their mission, many missionaries could not accept the fact that they were wrong.

Northern philanthropists who did go South to lend their assistance tended to be severely ridiculed by Southern whites who, DuBois reports, were adamantly opposed to the education of African Americans. Their objections were so strong that the state violence of the patrols was often mobilized to burn down schools and terrorize both pupils and teachers, Black and white. Some schools simply closed under threat of violence.

Assisted by financial appropriations and educators from the Freedman's Bureau by 1870 the education system had spread throughout the South with 4,239 schools, 9,307 teachers, and educating nearly 250,000 students. Despite these impressive numbers only about one-tenth of African American children in the South were being educated.

This progress from mandatory ignorance did not end here. The African American push for free common school was so widespread and effective that in states such as South Carolina Constitutions were amended to mention education for the first time. In addition, a comprehensive system was outlined drawing on what was the latest or most cutting-edge educational theory and practice. The educational system expanded rapidly in South Carolina. By 1870 there were roughly 16,000 African American students and 11,000 white students attending these multinational or integrated schools. While there were still hostility and violence directed toward such efforts, advancements were being made.

While it was more difficult to establish public education systems further South and inland, progress was nevertheless being made. For example, whites in Georgia were unable to stop the educational tide. In 1870, on the 100th anniversary of an act passed by the Georgian legislature making it a penal offensive to teach Africans to read or write, Georgia passed legislation establishing a state board of education, a school commissioner, and an education fund.

One notable obstacle to the movement for common schooling in the South was white people who refused to pay education taxes. The new educational systems were therefore in constant financial difficulty. As noted, African Americans sacrificed as much as they could to keep the schools afloat, but having just won their emancipation, they were starting without savings or inherited property to draw from. Another barrier was the diversion of funds earmarked for education.

On the issue of segregation, African Americans tended to favor integrated schools for reasons of efficiency and democracy. Forcing a segregated system on the states nearly doubled the education costs since it amounted to creating two separate systems. Situated in a white supremacist context it was African American children who would suffer only receiving one-half to one-tenth the funding as white children (DuBois 1935/1992).

However, this rocky road to progress was subverted when the Reconstruction government was overthrown in 1877. Commentators mournfully reflected that Reconstruction efforts, had they not been cut short, would have provided Southern states with a world-class education system due to the determination and forward-thinking of African Americans.

After Reconstruction many of the most competent African American teachers "were dismissed at once, and their places filled with intolerant Confederates" (644). What saved African American education, despite this major setback, "was not enlightened Southern opinion," but the mission of Northern philanthropists to establish a system of "Negro colleges" (665).

Nevertheless, by 1879 a system of nearly one hundred teacher colleges and high schools had been established with the primary purpose of training a generation of Black teachers. In the face of the repressive apparatus HBCUs "soon saw a higher mission" (665). That is, they began training leaders not just for education, but for the struggle against white terrorism. Summarizing the long-lasting impact of the brief era of Reconstruction, DuBois is worth quoting:

> Had it not been for the Negro school and college, the Negro would, to all intents and purposes, have been driven back to slavery. His economic foothold in land and capital was too slight in ten years of turmoil to effect any defense or stability. His Reconstruction leadership had come from Negroes educated in the North ... and philanthropic teachers. The counter-revolution of 1876 drove most of these, save the teachers, away. But already, through establishing public

schools and private colleges, and by organizing the Negro church, the Negro had acquired enough leadership and knowledge to thwart the worst designs of the new slave drivers. They avoided the mistake of trying to meet force by force. They bent to the storm of beating, lynching, and murder, and kept their souls in spite of public and private insult of every description; they built an inner culture which the world recognizes in spite of the fact that it is still half-strangled and inarticulate.

(667)

This summary captures the essence of DuBois's challenge, which is not just that the enslaved defeated slavery, but, generally speaking, the slaver's attempts at dehumanization were subverted.

The Resistance

In the history of education it is common knowledge that W. E. B. DuBois and Booker T. Washington represent two distinct agendas for African American education. The Northern-born and Harvard-educated DuBois advocated for a critical, anti-racist education. Washington, on the other hand, was born into slavery and advanced an accommodationist model of vocational education for African Americans.

For example, DuBois critiques Washington for encouraging the Black community to focus on vocational education and work rather than politics in exchange for basic education and due process in his famous Atlanta speech. DuBois ridicules Washington's Atlanta speech referring to it as an unnecessary compromise. The result of the compromise, for DuBois, was that millions of African Americans were led to stop voting for a generation. Critical of Washington for enabling African Americans to sabotage their own political power, DuBois argues the white South was left with extraordinary political influence with devastating results. However, by 1890 segregation had been legalized in the South and lynching and white terrorism were at their peak when Washington delivered his Atlanta speech. This is not to say that Washington's position was or was not justified, but it is important to consider the larger context.

Scholars of African American literature, Henry Loouis Gates Jr. and Nellie Y. McKay (1997), argue that he "suggested the best way to ensure progress and peace in the South was for whites to respect the blacks' desire for improved economic opportunities and for blacks to respect the whites desire for social separation of the races" (488). It is easy to critique Washington from either the outside looking in or from the present looking back on the past unfamiliar with the seriousness and lawlessness of white terrorism.

Booker T. Washington's (1901/2004) autobiography, *Up from Slavery*, offers an invaluable window into the struggle for education from the perspective of someone born into slavery. The work reflects the political savviness celebrated by DuBois.

Washington was candid about the work admitting that it was written to appeal to a broader white audience for whom he depended on financial contributions and political support for the Tuskegee Institute, which he ran for several decades. Gates and McKay (1997) explain *Up from Slavery* as a political maneuver that was part of a larger survival strategy written in a non-revolutionary, reactionary time. For Gates and McKay, "the overall impression that Washington's style left on his white readers—that of an almost saintly self-forgetfulness balanced by a businesslike worldliness in the art of getting things done—went a long way toward creating the myth of the Tuskegeean as the Moses of his people" (489).

Along with DuBois other critics of Washington argue he downplayed the horrors of slavery to such an extent that he left whites with the impression that slavery was not that bad and that it actually taught African Americans the skills of self-reliance and hard work. Supporters of Washington's revisionism welcome it "as a rejoinder to the long-standing assumption among whites that under slavery black people suffered a disabling demoralization that left them unfit for any role in freedom except that of a ward of the state" (490).

Conclusion

The struggle for liberation during the Civil War and Reconstruction would only intensify as the repressive state apparatus in the South gained momentum after 1890 in the Jim Crow era outlined in Chapter 7.

7

From Monopoly Capitalism to US Imperialism

Introduction: Connection to the Previous Chapter

In Chapter 6 we saw the complex struggle between class forces within the Civil War, contributing to the development of monopoly capitalism. We also saw African Americans win the struggle to end slavery and compel the state to institute many significant gains such as voting rights and education. In the present chapter we see the state push back against these gains with *Plessy v. Ferguson* signaling the beginning of the Jim Crow era. First, we explore how the repressive state apparatus served the interests of capital during the post-Civil War economic crisis by expanding beyond the boundaries of North America transforming into US imperialism. Contributing to this era of conservative reaction the deepening corporate influence over schooling in the context of labor militancy is examined. Finally, German socialist immigrants and the Marxist class analysis they brought to an otherwise reformist US labor movement is investigated.

Critical Role of Capitalism

After the premature ending of Reconstruction a period of reaction emerged subverting the gains African Americans had won during the Civil War facilitating a new era of capitalist expansion. For example, the 14th Amendment of 1868, declaring all persons born or naturalized in the United States are citizens adopted to protect the rights of the formerly enslaved, had been coopted by 1886. The Supreme Court accepted the argument that corporations are persons with money and property protected by the 14th Amendment.

By 1896 the Supreme Court gave its seal of approval for a new era of Jim Crow racism in *Plessy v. Ferguson* ruling that a system of separate but equal segregation was constitutional. The bourgeois state therefore gave its official approval of racist terror that would hold in place a racially divided working class and the extreme exploitation of African American labor.

If this were not enough between 1890 and 1906, every Southern state passed laws, such as poll taxes and literacy tests, designed to limit the voting power of the African American community. The result was the undermining of the 15th Amendment that had banned race-based voting qualifications. Enforcing this new era of extreme racialized disenfranchisement was the white terrorism of the repressive state apparatus (i.e. the police) and the public lynching of thousands of African Americans carried out with near-total impunity by the Ku Klux Klan (KKK).

Symbolically signaling the re-oppression of the African American community was the construction of monuments to Confederate Generals. Making their intention crystal clear is the fact that they were erected throughout the South, and especially in African American communities. Monuments are intended to embody a community's ideas and values. Communities that build monuments are making a statement to others, to those both within and outside of their community, about which ideals are to be honored.

The monuments also contributed to a form of historical revisionism. The progressive role of African Americans in the Civil War was an inconvenient truth. To remove the crucial role of Black lives the war was retold as a family quarrel between equally correct white brothers in which African Americans played an insignificant role. In this retelling Reconstruction is depicted as a regrettable period of "Negro rule" imposed upon the South by a vindictive North. The objective here was to justify the persecution of Black lives.

In the South the Civil War was no longer about the expansion of slavery, but about states' rights. In the North the Civil War was re-written from being a war that was transformed by the enslaved into a war to end slavery to only ever being about Lincoln's desire for "union preservation." Excluded here are the voices of half a million or more African Americans who withdrew their enslaved labor from plantations and fought in the Civil War not to preserve the union, but to end slavery.

It is within this context of state-enforced racist conservative reaction that capitalism would grow more powerful furthering the development of monopolies into capitalist imperialism. As we will see below at the center of imperialist capitalism is the role of an increasingly smaller and smaller number of larger and larger banks.

US Imperialism

Lenin (1916/1986) defines the pre-monopoly function of banks as "middlemen" facilitating payments and transforming "inactive money capital into active, that is, into capital yielding a profit." In addition, such banks "collect all kinds of money revenues and place them at the disposal of the capitalist-class" (30). As banking capital became more concentrated in the United States toward the end of the nineteenth century and the number of banks grew smaller, they began to dominate all the money capital of all the capitalists, the means of production, and raw materials. Lenin argues that this concentration of banking capital "is one of the fundamental processes in the growth of capitalism into capitalist imperialism" (30). In other words, this process transformed "thousands and thousands of scattered economic enterprises into a single national capitalist, and then into a world capitalist economy" (33).

As a result, a few banks began to direct the flow of capital determining which enterprises were funded and which were to be dissolved. Exerting their control over industry banks either placed their own representatives on corporation's boards of directors or simply assumed the position of chairman.

Between the few banks that "remain at the head of all capitalist economy" there emerges a "tendency toward monopolist agreements, towards a *bank trust*" (39). In 1916 the two bankers at the helm of this trust in the United States were John D. Rockefeller and J. P. Morgan. By the end of the nineteenth century these two capitalists held more money and gold than the treasury department rendering their political power over the bourgeois state insurmountable. For example, during the financial panic of 1893 the US Treasury was forced to borrow $50 million from Morgan under extortionist terms to prevent an economic collapse. In the windfall from the US Supreme Court ruling corporations had the rights of persons the annual profits of Rockefeller's Standard Oil Company tripled from $15 to $45 million between 1886 and 1899 (Prins 2014).

The hegemony of finance capital manifests itself in the predominance of the financial oligarchy and of "a small number of financially 'powerful' states" or countries (57) dominating the global capitalist economy. By 1910 Britain, France, Germany, and the United States owned nearly 80 percent of all finance capital. As a result, the rest of the world was the "debtor" and "tributary" of these four "international banker countries" (59).

Central to the construction of this international system is the transition from the export of *goods* having primacy to the export of *capital* taking center stage.

In the United States, despite the existence of vast fortunes, workers after the Civil War, especially African Americans, remained impoverished and in want of their most basic needs.

One of the central economic forces underpinning imperialism is directly related to the export of capital, debt. The imperialist countries, in this context, are the usurer states relegating the overwhelming majority to the status of debtor states. The finance capitalists issue loans and the navies of their respective countries serve the function of bailiff or rent collector.

Making another crucial observation regarding imperialism's impact on immigration trends Lenin observes that emigration from imperialist countries declines whereas immigration into imperialist countries from debtor countries where wages are substantially lower increases. For example, while "emigration from Britain to the US began to decline sharply after 1884 with the rise of British imperialism, emigration from Germany reached the highest point between 1881 and 1890" (100).

State Police and Militant Labor

As the struggle between the swelling ranks of organized/unionized labor in the United States and finance capital intensified after the Civil War, the repressive needs of capitalists outgrew the existing system of local police departments. One of the centers of labor militancy at the outset of the twentieth century in the United States was in Pennsylvania. Owners looked to state leaders for help beating back workers who authorized privatized police forces, such as the Coal and Iron Police, under the direct supervision of the capitalist bosses. Countless atrocities were committed by these hired thugs including the Anthracite Massacre of 1897 where nineteen unarmed miners were killed and thirty-two others were wounded.

It became clear that the privatized forces were not just suppressing work actions, but were causing more instability, which, ultimately, is not good for business. Capitalists needed a more sustainable form of repression. The solution was the creation of state police forces. In 1905 Pennsylvania was the first state to roll out a state-wide police department.

Imperialism had created the model for the Pennsylvania State Police. The justifications for imperialism, it is important to note, were racist. Eric Foner (2009b) argues that proponents of US expansionism reasoned that because *Americans* had "demonstrated their special aptitude for liberty and self-government … Anglo-Saxons should now spread their institutions and values to 'inferior races' throughout the world" (626). With this attitude the Philippine Constabulary was used by the United States to maintain their imperialist occupation.

The Philippines became a testing ground for the latest police technologies and techniques. Filipinos resented the racist US occupation and resisted it building anti-colonial organizations and movements. The national police developed strategies to monitor and disrupt the struggle for independence. Their tactics were brought back to the United States to counter labor and their progressive organizations (Vitale 2018).

Pennsylvania copied that racist model and continued the work of the privatized police but with more legitimacy and authority as an official state apparatus.

Critical Role of Education

As competition gave way to monopoly capitalism and then outright imperialism, US industrialists (i.e. finance capital) asserted deeper control over schooling, which included the racist rewriting of the history of the Civil War. It is within the context of KKK terrorism, US imperialism, labor militancy, and intensified police repression that industrialists and the state began promoting a more aggressive "unifying patriotism" (Foner 2009b: 627). Herbert Kliebard (2004) describes Northern schools in the late nineteenth century as "joyless and dreary places" (6). Schools were so hated by children that studies found they overwhelmingly "preferred the often-grueling factory labor to the monotony, humiliation, and even sheer cruelty that they experienced in school" (Kliebard 2004: 6). While education was designed to foster consent and patriotism, its harshness often produced the opposite effect contributing to, rather than suppressing, labor militancy.

Corporate Education Reform

The corporate takeover of urban school boards in the 1890s was one of the mechanisms through which racist, capitalist interests moved to push back against the progressive gains in policy and working-class consciousness made during the Civil War. Corporate propaganda asserted that large community-based school boards were corrupt and that concentrating political power in smaller boards composed of *successful* men operating like modern capitalist board of directors would be more efficient and beneficial.

While the call for efficiency, especially after the economic crisis of 1893, was a consistent rationale for a more stratified education system that effectively functioned to reproduce social inequalities, "quite often the schools on the corporate model cost considerably more than the ones they replaced" (132). Common schooling, or a single system, in other words, tended to be more cost-effective than creating a system for the working-class and a separate system for a professional class.

However, having control over media outlets, such as magazines and radio, corporate interests were able to control the narrative inventing problems they magically had the solution for. Contributing to their success corporate interests were able to advance slogans such as *get schools out of politics* as an effective tactic to "squelch opposition" (133). The corporate reformers could paint their own approach as unbiased and neutral and the working-class agenda as political and corrupt.

The corporate model included a remade vision for the superintendent. No longer functioning as a relatively powerless district-wide teacher mentor, the newly empowered superintendents and their staff would reshape the schools based on suggestions and directions from corporate-oriented school boards. The corporate managers who had taken a direct interest in schooling, reports Tyack (1974), ridiculed conceptions of not only democratic community-control, but democratic conceptions of common schooling in favor of social efficiency or class, gender, and race-based systems of tracking. Effectively countering the working-class solidarity that developed during the Civil War as white and Black soldiers fought shoulder to shoulder against slavery, corporate education suggested that racially mediated social class reflected a natural hierarchy of intelligence and education should therefore reflect this so-called *reality*.

For many education reformers, "it was clear that the way to run a school system was the way to run a railroad ... or a bank" (142). Tyack points out that the value of corporations "jumped from $170 million in 1897 ... to more than $20 billion in 1904" (143). Because "many of the same men who supported the centralization of schools had helped to ... build the trusts," it was only logical that "the same corporate model of expert, centralized administration would serve other organizations equally well" (143).

However, the national movement for centralization, while it differed slightly from city to city, drew opponents from "those who had a political or occupational stake in the system or who viewed the reformers as snobbish intruders" (148). In some cities proponents of centralization were opposed by teachers who felt their professional authority was directly under attack. More commonly, argues Tyack, were "lower-class or middle-class ethnic groups such as the Irish" who "spoke out against the 'aristocratic' premises of the reformers" (148).

The Resistance

While anti-racist European immigrant socialists flocked to the Civil War to help defeat slavery, in *Marxism in the United States: A History of the American Left*, Paul Buhle (1987/2013) outlines their contributions to the socialist movement in the post-war era. What militant immigrants brought to the US left emerged from their unique orientation as European-trained socialists situated within a very different US context that was marked by the hateful bigotry of nativism and the specific scapegoating of foreign-born radicals.

Buhle suggests that European-born socialists, compared to US-born white socialists, more concretely understood that transforming the capitalist relations of production required a strategy that was "rooted in the real lives of the workers" including attention to their "cultural inheritance" and diverse nationalities (19). The deep divisiveness of US capitalist culture, before and after the Civil War, rooted in nativism, white supremacy, misogyny, and xenophobia, was a major barrier to maintaining and advancing unity among *the many*—a unity indispensable for building a labor movement with an orientation wide enough to reach beyond the reformism of trade union consciousness.

Summarizing the advantage of finance capital in the struggle between the balance of forces in the United States, Buhle explains how "the power of expansive American capitalism, its apologists' head-start over any immigrants in defining class ideologies (except its own) as 'alien' and undesirable, made Socialist politics a difficult proposition" (24). Given the many challenges faced by organized labor coupled with the extreme conditions they were forced to endure, from unsafe working conditions, housing not fit for humans, to below subsistence wages, Buhle argues workers could not afford to get caught up in sectarian feuds, but such tensions nevertheless surfaced. In other words, Europeans who "saw democracy in class and Socialist terms" and Americans who "saw class and Socialism in democratic terms" (23) were often too far apart politically to come together in any meaningful way.

The "principle actors" of the new socialism that would emerge in the post-Civil War context, outside of African Americans, emerged from the many "immigrant ghettoes" (24) throughout much of the United States. While whiteness was an abstract possibility for potential upward mobility, especially for the children of immigrants, holding on to a community's cultural inheritance "helped to maintain resilience against economic and social adversity among those who lacked other resources" (25). This was especially true of unskilled Eastern European immigrants for whom socialist ideas were part of what they brought to the United States. Even for skilled artisan immigrants, especially Germans known for their radical socialism, American life was becoming more desperate as advances in labor-saving technologies were throwing them out of work. Coming from the failed peasant revolution of 1848 German immigrants tended to be instinctively abolitionist in the pre-Civil War context, and anti-racist after the Civil War.

Buhle highlights Adolf Douai, himself what they called a Forty-Eighter, "had written travel books for a German audience about American customs, edited an Abolitionist newspaper in Texas, penned a political novel, and earned his salary as a distinguished progressive pedagogue" (28–9). Contributing to the socialist movement in the United States for the remainder of his life he worked as an editor for a German language socialist daily until he died in 1888. Douai was part of a strong tradition of German socialist intellectuals working in the United States within the tradition of building international solidarity among all oppressed nationalities from African Americans to Irish.

Even though the slave-owning class had been permanently abolished as a result of African American agency during the Civil War, when Southern elites reasserted their hegemony and prematurely ended Reconstruction, German socialist immigrants refocused their organizing efforts to the international context. Their desire was to establish connections with the center of Europe's radical labor movement, but since they were outsiders in the United States, they were not accepted as legitimately representing the US working-class. What is more, German socialist immigrants tended to have a revolutionary orientation viewing the US electoral political system much the same way as the yeomen insurrectionists did in 1789, but even more critically. That is, they understood that the US Constitution was created to ensure that political power would forever remain in the hands of the capitalists.

These German immigrants saw electoral politics as both practically and politically obsolete. Consequently, German socialists in the United States tended to distrust reformers and found it difficult to connect with US socialists who had not broken from the electoral system. Rather than retreat from the broadest masses of workers, as German socialists in the United States tended to do, revolutionaries like Lenin argued socialists should join their movements. Only by being with the working-class can activists support the people, make friends, and prove the correctness of their ideas through their practice.

German socialists, embracing their reputation in the United States as having an "intellectual monopoly on socialism" (41), retreated from the mass mobilizations of unskilled industrial unions to the smaller trade unions. For example, combined with the widespread distribution of a German-language socialist weekly, they successfully organized the Brewery Workers Union. This German-based union was composed of many immigrants who carried with them their union cards from the old country. Their tactics included an organizational model based on "egalitarian industrial unionism, socialist leadership, and mass boycotts against offending brewers" (41). The Brewery Workers Union won many concessions and provided an example emulated later by industrial unions. Informed by an all-encompassing orientation the revolutionaries established German-language socialist schools for children and a wide range of cultural activities to more fully engage the community.

The next wave of German immigrants, peaking in the 1880s, were even more seasoned socialist organizers. They were critical of the insular nature of the German socialist tendency they found in the United States.

Conclusion

This chapter introduces the era of capitalist imperialism. With the rise of imperialism we saw the intensification of state repression and labor militancy. We also saw the ritualization of patriotic practices in schools and the ineffectiveness of a form of schooling hated by children. Contributing to the state's reaction were German immigrants who emerged as leaders in radical socialism spear heading developments in trade unions and organizing German-language schools. We now turn to the Russian revolution of 1917 considering its deep influence on education and peoples' movements in the United States.

8

The Russian Revolution and a New Era in Educational Theory

Introduction: Connection to the Previous Chapter

In Chapter 7 we saw the more complete development of imperialism. In the present chapter, we will see how the First World War was a significant factor that led to the 1917 Russian Revolution. Whereas Chapter 7 examines the stifling impact of capitalism on public education, in this chapter we see that out of the Russian revolutionary context progressive advances in educational theory emerge that continue to be influential internationally. These educational advances are examined next to the behaviorist approaches that the US political establishment used to subvert the progressive influence of the work of John Dewey.

Critical Role of Capitalism

The 1917 Russian Revolution

"The Russian Revolution of 1917 was a turning-point in history" and might very well have been "the greatest event of the twentieth century" (Carr 1979: 1). The Russian Revolution signaled a shift in the orientation of Europe's oppressed away from the West, away from the United States which had become dominated by a crushingly oppressive industrial aristocracy, toward the East's inspiring red dawn (Buhle 1987/2013). The Bolshevik Revolution would have an immediate impact on the hearts and minds of working-class people not only in Europe, but throughout the world and in the United States in particular. In response, US capitalists would double down on their efforts to suppress working-class organization. After turning to a brief discussion of the Russian Revolution, we will explore Lenin's influences on workers in the United States and the state's repressive response.

Leading up to the 1917 Revolution were a number of related factors stemming from the global development of capitalism. In the 1890s industrialization began to make inroads into the Russian economy that was still primarily a peasant economy. Facilitating this process was the transformation of Russia's single colony, Turkestan, into a center for the production of cotton (Lenin 1916/1986). As a result, a more efficient and profitable textile trust was formed where "the processes of cotton production and manufacturing" were "concentrated in the hands of one set of owners" (80). With the concentration of capital in monopolies come growing poverty and suffering among the producers.

At the same time, this process was heavily dependent on foreign capital, which means even more of the value created by the country's cotton producers (i.e. workers and peasants) would be estranged from them. That is, wealth was being accumulated in the hands of an emerging capitalist-class and it was being extracted from Russia by larger, more powerful foreign imperialists. Industrialization therefore resulted in the development of a Russian proletariat or working-class. The emerging proletariat had begun to engage in strikes and were pushing back against the foreign and domestic forces of exploitation even before the end of the nineteenth century.

However, the proletariat was a small percent of the population. Peasants were the numerical majority and the rural economy was stagnating at the turn of the century leading to deteriorating conditions including widespread hunger. The primary party of the peasants was the Social-Revolutionary Party that had a long and violent history of engaging in acts of terrorism followed by extreme state repression.

The peasant forces were one of the three prongs of the first, unsuccessful, Russian Revolution, the revolution of 1905. This first revolution was also "a revolt of bourgeois liberals and constitutionalists against an arbitrary and antiquated aristocracy" (Carr 1979: 2). The third element of this first general insurrection was workers outraged by the violent repression by the tsar against labor actions. Carr notes that because these three elements were not organized together, they were easily suppressed. The result of 1905 was a compromise, a Provisional Government under the authority of the Duma. It was a form of *dual power*, a term coined to describe an ambiguous situation where both the few and the many held formal power. The factors that led to 1917 were similar to those of 1905 with the added burden of the First World War. As peasants were being pulled into battle and out of their fields, hunger and suffering among them only escalated.

Whereas 1905 had been described as a bourgeois revolution, Lenin, keenly tuned into the mood of the masses, objected to such a characterization and framed it as the first stage or dress-rehearsal of the bloodless 1917 revolution.

The new revolutionary state, the All Russian Congress, unanimously adopted a number of decrees including two proposed by Lenin. The first was to encourage the imperialist countries to negotiate an end to the First World War calling on class-conscious workers in those countries to help end the conflict. The other decree proposed by Lenin was to adopt in full the peasant-led Socialist Revolutionary's proposal for agrarian land reform even though it differed significantly from the Bolshevik's plan for state ownership. This decree was intended to foster solidarity between the peasants and the proletariat, which was successful.

In 1918 at the third All-Russian Congress of Soviets the republic's new name was adopted, the Union of Soviet Socialist Republics (USSR). It was also proclaimed that the Soviet Union, by definition, was a federation of freely associated free nations. Unlike the imperialist countries that seek to expand their sphere of influence imposing their will on other countries, any notion of a foreign policy outside of supporting progressive forces in other countries was foreign to USSR thinking (Carr 1979).

Communism in the United States

The influence of the Russian Revolution on working people in the United States was significant. Buhle (1987/2013) notes that because of "the rampant racism, xenophobia and anti-labor attitudes" in the United States "the light from the East" (121) was needed. The US socialist movement, for Buhle, had many important lessons to learn such as how to build broad coalitions between progressive groups with slightly different perspectives. For example, Buhle argues a common mistake made by US socialists was the rejection of feminism as a middle-class movement unrelated to the struggle of working-class and oppressed people. As a result, the US socialist movement's rejection of feminism was alienating to Finish immigrants who had long supported women's suffrage.

State repression certainly hindered the socialist movement from learning and developing political maturity. For example, much of the radical press was shut down limiting communication and the development of ideas, tactics, and strategies.

Struggling to reorient the fractured, undisciplined movement, national socialist leaders began to encourage what was at first an "uncertain relationship between revolutionary politics and ethnic culture" (129). The party provided much-needed services to immigrant communities such as labor-defense, party materials in immigrant languages, and English-language spokespeople, contacts, and interpreters. Consequently, socialist influence grew among immigrant communities and flourished as a result. European immigrants were not the only driving force within the US socialist movement. African Americans, coming from a long tradition of resistance, also found great appeal in the movement.

In *A Black Communist in the Freedom Struggle*, Harry Haywood (2012) takes his readers on a journey of how he came to view socialism as the most effective path to liberation. In the process Haywood would challenge both the escapism of Marcus Garvey's Black nationalist "back to Africa" movement and the stultifying colorblindness of the "pure proletarian" line of many white socialists.

Directly influenced by the Soviet Union Haywood came to argue that Black nationalism was a legitimate desire for millions of African Americans. In the absence of a program advocating Black nationalism, Haywood argued that the movement would continue to be unable to mobilize the tremendous revolutionary potential of African Americans. Summarizing this line Haywood noted that "our slogan for the US Black rebellion therefore must be the 'right of self-determination in the South, with full equality throughout the country,' to be won through the revolutionary alliance with politically conscious white workers against the common enemy—U.S. imperialism" (143).

While the socialist movement's own errors certainly contributed to its demise, other writers point to state repression as the primary factor. It is probably safe to conclude that the workers' movements suffered both internal and external challenges, but the overwhelming force of state repression prevented the movement from developing political maturity.

State Repression in the United States

After the Bolshevik Revolution the US federal government turned to legislative and extra-legal means to stop workers from organizing against oppression and exploitation. One of the first pieces of legislation against political dissidents in the United States was the Espionage Act of 1917. The Espionage Act made it illegal to engage in public speech or writing that could be interpreted as potentially injurious to the United States or beneficial to a foreign nation. The language defining the so-called crimes is vague enough and the punishments specific and severe enough to have created a chilling effect. Given the seriousness of the Espionage Act's language it is worth quoting at length:

> Sec. 2. (a) Whoever, with intent or reason to believe that it is to be used to the injury of the United States or to the advantage of a foreign nation, communicates, delivers, or transmits, or attempts to, or aids or induces another to, communicate, deliver, or transmit, to any foreign government, or to any faction or party or military or naval force within a foreign country, whether recognized or unrecognized by the United States, or to any representative, officer, agent, employee, subject, or citizen thereof, either directly or indirectly, any document, writing, code book, signal book, sketch, photograph, photographic negative, blue print, plan, map, model, note, instrument, appliance, or information relating to the national defense, shall be punished by imprisonment for not more than twenty years: *Provided*, That whoever shall violate the provisions of subsection (a) of this section in time of war shall be punished by death or by imprisonment for not more than thirty years.
>
> (U.S. Congress 1917: 2)

A year later the same Congress extended the Espionage Act with the Sedition Act of 1918 outlawing speech itself. That is, speech or opinions deemed to make the US government or its involvement in the First World War appear to be negative were effectively outlawed and punishable by imprisonment or death. Speech deemed to be disloyal, profane, scurrilous, or abusive toward the United States, its flag, or its military was also criminalized. While the Espionage Act is still law and has recently been mobilized by Presidents Obama and Trump to prosecute so-called leakers, the Sedition Act was repealed after the First World War and those prosecuted under its provisions were cleared of all charges and records. However, the war on political dissent was far from over.

The Smith Act of 1940 (i.e. the Alien Registration Act) extended the Espionage Act. The Smith Act made it illegal to advocate for the violent overthrow of the government or to belong to any group that was assumed to, such as socialists, communists, and anarchists. The Communist Control Act of 1954 effectively outlawed the Communist Party suspending the citizenship rights of CPUSA members. Perhaps because the Act has remained dormant and because the US Supreme Court has never ruled on its constitutionality, it remains law. Long before the Communist Control Act of 1954 the Communist Party USA was targeted for *special attention* when it emerged in 1919.

In 1920 a massive purge was initiated leading to thousands of arrests across the country, which resulted in hundreds of deportations for the crime of being affiliated with communism or even for attempting to bail a suspected communist out of jail (Churchill & Vander Wall 1990). Making this purge materially feasible was Attorney General Mitchell Palmer's 1919 appeal to Congress for a half a million dollars to "fight radicalism" (quoted in Churchill & Vander Wall 1990: 34). As a result, Congress appropriated special funds to prosecute those deemed to be political radicals through the creation of the General Intelligence Division (GID) within the Justice Department. This began the official era of the federal government actively collecting information on progressive organizations, especially those suspected of having a connection to the international working-class movement, which the Soviet Union was its center of gravity.

More than just collecting information, the GID raided the offices of labor unions without ever presenting any evidence of criminal activity. Without warrants of any kind the GID arrested roughly 10,000 workers around the country illegally deporting hundreds to the Soviet Union. Progressive workers were outrageously slandered by federal agents, and without any evidence, accused them of harboring secret plots to use terrorism to create a revolution. For workers, these accusations were ridiculous.

The arrests were so pervasive that the detention facilities in many urban areas were completely overwhelmed. Being a member of the Communist Party was enough to not only get you arrested and deported, but for those who had become US citizens, even denaturalized. While the state was accusing progressives of being terrorists, the GID was creating real terror in immigrant communities. These illegal acts were eventually stopped in 1920 by US District Judge George Anderson (Churchill & Vander Wall 1990). However, the damage had been done and by the mid-1920s immigrant communities, like African American and Native American communities, were still living in terror and coping with trauma. The evidence was in the sharp decline in socialist and Communist Party's membership. In 1919 the Communist Party had close to 30,000 members and by 1920 it had shrunk to around 10,000.

Critical Role of Education

Educational Theory in the United States

While the federal government was rounding up suspected radicals and passing laws criminalizing political dissent, by the 1920s behaviorist educational theory was taking hold in the system of public education. After the economic crisis of

1893 and the resulting poverty, the progressive movement in education gained traction with figures like John Dewey leading the way. Dewey was highly critical of traditional teacher-centered models of education based on rote learning and memorization. Rejecting the assumption that education is neutral Dewey argued that education is always political and a function of the society.

Dewey consistently argued that traditional education contributed to social problems and the perpetuation of an unjust society. Claiming to be neutral transmitters of knowledge schools tended to reproduce class inequalities by funneling students into occupational paths based on their social class backgrounds. In the process, schools failed to help students develop their own interests and skills situated in a social, and therefore collective, context. Dewey reasoned that knowledge is always collective, and central to each generation's pursuit of democracy and liberation. The solution, for Dewey, was a common student-centered approach that focused on the particularities of each student understood in the context of the collective. In this way, students will become intrinsically motivated and engaged in school and committed to pursuing a just and democratic society. Dewey's work was highly influential among educators.

However, after the Russian Revolution of 1917 the more prescriptive behaviorist traditional model of education outlined by psychologists such as Edward Thorndike (1910) began to be championed by school boards and superintendents despite objections from teachers and their unions.

Behaviorist principles, with the collective power and influence of ruling-class forces behind them, were "applied directly to educational settings" (Boyanton 2010: 49). Behaviorism was appealing to the corporate-dominated superintendents because it was based on the false assumption that the mind is machine-like rendering individuals fully programable. Believing that "the behavior of the masses" can be determined by "external conditioning" this model asserted that "the primary responsibility of education is to control student behavior" based upon "predetermined outcomes" (Malott 2011: 24–9).

Educational psychologists such as Edward Thorndike, drawing on the work of Pavlov and others, claimed it was possible "to uncover the laws of behavior" and forge an "effective pedagogy of behavior modification" (27). Thorndike's conclusions were based on the assumption that intelligence is a well-defined property and therefore absolutely knowable, measurable, and subject to external manipulation. The educational significance of the measurability of intelligence, for Thorndike (1910), is that it leads to the "knowledge of what human beings are" enabling educational leaders and educators to "choose the best means for changing them for the better" (3).

Contributing to racialization and white supremacy Thorndike argued that some differences between individuals, such as mental ability or cognition, were due to what he called *remote ancestry*. By this he meant that the more a group has remained isolated and can therefore trace its lineage back within that same group, the more a distinct race they will be. The more distinct, the more unique physical and mental qualities they will possess. Summarizing this point Thorndike reasons, "an individual may thus, by original nature, possess certain racial mental tendencies. His position on the scale for any mental trait may be due in part to his membership in a certain race" (51).

At the same time Thorndike advanced a racialized approach, he also argued that human behavior is as predictable, mechanical, and malleable as a machine, which relies on a static, reducible, unchanging conception of the world. In other words, Thorndike is arguing that on one hand human behavior is racialized and unchanging, and on the other, it is completely changeable.

Situated in the context of a world with an emerging, infectious center of working-class power in the Soviet Union Dewey's transformative student-centered educational theory was too potentially dangerous to go unchallenged. Dewey's core principles, nevertheless, continue to hold considerable weight amongst classroom teachers and in the field of education more generally.

The Resistance

Educational Theory in the Soviet Union

While education in the United States was being reoriented with behaviorist commitments and principles, a new era of educational innovation was taking hold in the Soviet Union. Leading these efforts was a young researcher named Lev Vygotsky.

The name *Lev Semionovich Vygotsky* (1896–1934) is commonplace in the field of education. Ask any teacher or professor of education about Vygotsky and chances are they will at least recall the name from their child development or educational psychology classes. As is the case with so many progressive thinkers, much of his works' most revolutionary references and implications had been stripped away in English translations for the US context. Wayne Au (2007), for example, has brought attention to the way Lenin had been systematically purged from Vygotsky's work more than a decade ago. Au's article was significant because it brought the Marxist dialectics behind Vygotsky's work to the field of education in the United States.

Vygotsky was born in 1896 to a Jewish family in the town of Orsha, Belarus, which, at the time, was part of the Russian Empire. Coming from a Jewish family in Tsarist Russia meant being subjected to a lifetime of discrimination. Jewish people lived in restricted territories, were subject to strict quotas for university entrance, and were excluded from certain occupations. These restrictions nearly blocked Vygotsky's admittance to university despite his youthful brilliance. His experiences with anti-Jewish bigotry undoubtedly influenced his work. For example, Vygotsky was highly critical of conceptions of the mind that treated the development of cognitive processes as purely *internal,* unaffected by the surrounding world. As we will see, Vygotsky demonstrated that as the child develops cognitive processes are increasingly mediated, and often limited, by cultural, social, and economic factors.

Vygotsky's contributions to educational psychology stemmed not just from his own insights and from the field of psychology, but from the Marxist tradition, Lenin in particular, and from the inspiration of his environment: Revolutionary Russia. Replacing a stagist, predetermined, purely biological view of cognitive development with dialectics is part of Vygotsky's contribution. Vygotsky, in other words, discredited the belief that child thought evolves through fixed, natural, separate, and unrelated stages.

Cognitive development is not simply a matter of biological predeterminations, but is mediated by social factors. Consequently, as society changes quantitatively within a system or qualitatively between systems through revolution, cognitive development also changes. This is what it means to say that Vygotsky's dialectical theory of development is historical. Because references to Marx and Lenin had been purged from English translations of Vygotsky's work, the fact that his approach is both dialectical and historical in its core is largely unknown, especially in the United States.

Cognitive development, in other words, is not necessarily about an individuals' inherent potential. Rather, cognitive development is about the *general* potential of specific classes, which is an expression of historical processes. To get more specific, it is an expression of a society's particular technologies, discourses, signs, tools, and modes of production. Uncovering these processes points toward the historically determined and changing nature of cognitive processes.

These insights were deeply influenced and inspired by the Bolshevik Revolution, which coincided with Vygotsky's graduation from Moscow University in 1917. The Revolution transformed many disciplines and opened up new realms of inquiry and opportunities for young, formerly oppressed and marginalized scholars such as Vygotsky.

The Bolshevik leadership heavily emphasized education after the revolution, since the predominantly peasant feudalistic social formation promoted a conservative, reactionary ideology. Lenin (1919/2019) sums this up in his address to the *First All-Russian Congress on Adult Education*. He emphasizes the working-class and peasantry's thirst for knowledge, noting "how heavy the task of re-educating the masses was, the task of organization and instruction, spreading knowledge, combating that heritage of ignorance, primitiveness, barbarism and savagery that we took over" (24).

Working in this exciting time of qualitative change, Vygotsky was taken by the potential of socialism to elevate the general potential of cognitive development. Situating Vygotsky's contributions in this larger context, renowned Vygotskian scholar James Wertsch (1985) informs his audience that "Vygotsky and his followers devoted every hour of their lives to making certain that the new socialist state, the first grand experiment based on Marxist-Leninist principles, would succeed" (10).

Vygotsky's project was dedicated to remaking psychology in Marxist terms in order to overcome the practical problems inherited from tsarist Russia, including illiteracy and the oppression of national and gender minorities.

Some of Vygotsky's (1986) most central conceptions of mind were based on Lenin's philosophical notebooks. For example, Vygotsky draws on Lenin's distinction between "primitive idealism" from Hegelian idealism. This distinction allowed Vygotsky to demonstrate that a particular society's general level of development is not biologically determined or fixed but is historically determined and therefore transformable. It brought the hope and optimism of transformation to the field of psychology. Whereas primitive idealism attempts to universalize a particular being, which Lenin calls "stupid" and "childish," Hegelian idealism distinguishes an object from the idea of the object. Such insights were fundamental in challenging decontextualized, racialized conceptions of mind used to justify the oppression of national minorities.

Vygotsky developed a complex conception of the "mind in society" that explores the dialectical relationship between thought and imagination as unity and contradiction. For Vygotsky, thought emerges from an engagement with the concrete world. Imagination is a sort of sublated thought that begins to appear in young children when they cannot fulfill their immediate desires. When this occurs:

> [T]he preschool child enters an imaginary, illusory world in which the unrealizable desires can be realized, and this world is what we call play.

Imagination is a new psychological process for the child; it is not present in the consciousness of the very young child ... Like all functions of consciousness, it originally arises from action ... [I]magination in adolescence and school children is play without action.

(Vygotsky 1978: 93)

While the development of imagination seems to be a consistent aspect of human cognitive development, as sublated thought, it is the negation of the thought of "the very young child," and is therefore contradictory.

However, like development more generally, the sublation of early childhood thought and the emergence of imagination is not immediate but develops quantitatively by degree, bit by bit. Vygotsky argues this is because "there is such intimate fusion between meaning and what is seen" (p. 97). For example, young children have difficulty repeating the phrase, "'Tanya is standing up' when Tanya is sitting in front of" (p. 97) them.

The presence of imagination as a unique human quality is the basis of our ability to engage the world reflectively rather than purely instinctively. This powerful quality accounts for the wide variance in cultures and is the basis for history. It also makes possible misinformation, bigotry, domination, as well as resistance.

This discussion on thought and imagination reflects how Vygotsky was taken by Lenin's observation that the distinction between objects and the idea of them is vulnerable to being consumed by an always latent element of fantasy, as ideas can never mirror, with complete exactness, the objects they intend to represent. There is always a gap between reality and representation. For Vygotsky, attending to the gap between objects and the ideas they intend to represent is fundamentally connected to the process of navigating the gap between what *is* and what *can be*.

This is particularly significant for challenging decontextualized and racialized conceptions of mind because there is a tendency in capitalist schooling to attribute students' actual level of development with innate or biological factors ignoring the ways unequal and highly segregated educational systems produce unequal outcomes. Challenging racist biological determinism Vygotskian researchers have consistently found that students' actual developmental levels rarely correlate to their potential development. In other words, what students can do on their own, their *independent activity*, does not necessarily correlate to what they can achieve with a teacher, peer, or other leader. This is where the *zone of their proximal development* comes into play.

Vygotsky named the gap between what *is* and what *can be* the "zone of proximal development" (ZPD) and created a whole educational theory around it. Like social formations, individual children or learners have historically determined levels of development in particular subjects or domains that can be assessed through appropriate testing instruments. Based on their actual level, learners have an immediate developmental potential in each domain. The difference between actual and potential is the ZPD. According to Vygotsky (1986):

> The zone of proximal development defines those functions that have not yet matured but are in the process of maturation, functions that can mature tomorrow but are currently in an embryonic state. These functions could be termed the 'buds' or 'flowers' of development rather than the 'fruits' of development.
>
> (p. 86)

Vygotsky referred to potential developmental levels as "buds or flowers" rather than "fruits" because they are in the process of coming into being and therefore not yet fully ripe. However, the process of coming into being is not predetermined. No one can know in advance what form the developed function will take.

The ZPD represents the gap between an existing level of development and what can be achieved with the help of more capable or differently situated peers. For example, two children may test at the same math level, so their actual level of development is identical. However, when they are pushed with examples, questions, and demonstrations, one may achieve a potential developmental level significantly different than the other. That is, even if their actual levels of development are the same, their zones of proximal development are not. For Vygotsky, such scenarios point to the complex, non-linear nature of the relationship between instruction, development, and history.

Vygotskian researchers have long pointed out that things like arithmetic systems and their uses are not natural or universal but are specific to socio-historical contexts (McNamee 1990). The ZPD, consequently, can only be understood if the historically specific context is accounted for. As contexts change, ZPDs also transform.

It is important to stress that the content of this gap between ability and potential isn't predetermined, which is what makes it a gap and not a lack or deficiency. This is particularly important as a challenge to capitalist schooling that tends to define that which deviates from some normative standard as a lack or deficiency. Rather than Spanish-speaking, for example, we are confronted with the discourse of the *non*-English-speaking or English as a *second* language. The emphasis, in capitalist normative discourse, is on what is *not* rather than on what *is*.

While Lenin was conscious of the changing roles of activists at different stages in the dialectical process toward social transformation, Vygotsky too was attuned to the changing significance of multiple interacting factors in human cognitive processes. In laying the theoretical groundwork for his revolutionary approach to educational psychology Vygotsky took up the task of challenging the world's leading educational psychologist of the day, Jean Piaget (1896–1980) of Switzerland.

Significantly, Vygotsky draws heavily on Lenin in his challenge to Piaget. For example, in *Thought and Language*, Vygotsky (1986) reproduces a long quote from Lenin where he argues that Hegel's insistence that people's thought produces their activity must be "inverted." That is, Lenin argues that it is the endless repetition a million times over of people's activity (i.e. the labor act) that produces consciousness.

Similarly, Vygotsky notes that "it was Piaget himself who clearly demonstrated that the logic of action precedes the logic of thought, and yet he insists that thinking is separated from reality" (53). Piaget demonstrated that action precedes thought by observing that children playing together understand each other despite how unclear their language is because it is accompanied by gesture and mimicry, the beginning of action. Consequently, Piaget questions whether children truly understand each other through speaking/language without acting, yet in theory he puts thought before action.

Sounding remarkably like Marx in his use of metaphor, Vygotsky summarizes the inadequacy of Piaget's formulation: "if the function of thinking is to reflect upon reality, this actionless thinking appears as a parade of phantoms and a chorus of shadows rather than the real thinking of a child" (53). Having established the dynamic relationship between mind and society, Vygotsky took social formation as the ultimate determining factor influencing the dynamic development of human personalities and consciousness.

Producing his major works during the transition from an underdeveloped peasant-based economy to socialism, Vygotsky was deeply interested in the socialist alteration of humanity. It was the intellectually exciting and creative context of the Soviet Union that Vygotsky found himself in, combined with the work and example of Lenin, that offered the concrete context from which Piaget's formulation unveiled itself to Vygotsky as incorrect.

Throughout Vygotsky's body of work he insists that at "moments of revolutionary dislocation the nature of development changes" (Wertsch 1985: 19). This is key because it once more emphasizes that the gap between *what is* and *what can be* isn't predetermined.

Vygotsky defined transition points in development in terms of changes in mediation. A fundamental feature of Vygotsky's genetic analysis is that he did not assume one can account for all phases of development by using a "single set of explanatory principles" (19).

Rather, Vygotsky emphasized,

> At certain points in the emergence of a psychological process new forms of development and new explanatory principles enter the picture. At these points ... there is a 'change in the very type of development' and so the principles which alone had previously been capable of explaining development can no longer do so. Rather, a new set of principles must be incorporated into the overall explanatory framework, resulting in its reorganization.
>
> (19–20)

At certain points there is a fundamental reorganization of the forces of development. This occurs naturally as language and social interactions become more and more prominent mediators in child development through the years. The character of social mediators impacting the development of human personalities also undergoes significant alteration with the transition from capitalism/feudalism to socialism.

Conclusion

The events in Russia in 1917, as outlined in this chapter, dramatically shifted the balance of global forces. Working and oppressed people all over the world gained new hope and inspiration for one day too successfully liberating themselves from oppression and capitalist exploitation. The US capitalist-class political establishment was so determined to stop the will of the many; they attacked the people legislatively, educationally, and physically. Meanwhile, major advances in education would blossom in the Soviet Union.

Part Three

Rise and Fall of a Global Proletarian Counter-Weight

9

The Great Depression and the Mood of the Many

Introduction: Connection to the Previous Chapter

In Chapter 8 we saw the world-shifting impact of the Russian Revolution. We saw the impact on the progressive movement in the United States and the resulting state repression. We saw the move to behaviorism in US education and the intensification of patriotism in both mainstream schools and Indian boarding schools. We also saw Native Americans mobilizing the legacy and vision of Tecumseh as well. In this chapter we explore the causes of the Depression of the 1930s and the crises' effect of moving more and more working people to turn to the Soviet Union and socialism.

Critical Role of Capitalism

The *Great Depression* of the 1930s had a colossal impact on educators, education, and the movements of the many. Workers responded to the depression by joining unions. It turned out to be the biggest labor drive in US history. Unions, united together through the Congress of Industrial Organizations (CIO), became not just an economic force but a political force that successfully petitioned the federal government to do something for the mass of people. The New Deal was the outcome, including the minimum wage and social security. As a result, the United States was more equal after the Great Depression than before it. This was made possible by increasing the taxes on the capitalist class.

Economic crises are extraordinarily complex events. Starting from this premise Harvey concludes that "crises are not singular events" (x) and, as such, have complex stories of arrival. Individual crises, nonetheless, do have "obvious triggers" (x). The triggers that account for the Depression of the 1930s are typically attributed to individual acts such as reckless speculation causing the New York Stock Exchange to crash in 1929. As a result, the story proceeds, the economy, which was already in a slump, plummeted. Consumer confidence deteriorated contributing to the economic slowdown. That panic resulted in the broadest masses rushing to their banks to withdraw their deposits.

The problem is that a big part of how banks fund and profit from capitalist enterprises is by taking deposits from nearly every employed person and business in the economy and paying them almost no interest on their deposits. The banks then turn around and lend that money at roughly 1 percent interest and loan it out at 15 percent or 20 percent interest. In an economic crisis, like the Great Depression, when thousands of businesses begin to fail and go bankrupt, workers rush to the banks to withdraw their deposits. However, when lenders want their money back en mass, the banks are not able to pay because they had lent virtually every Nickle of it out. Because businesses were failing, banks would never be able to return deposited money.

The ripple effect caused many businesses to shut down leading to widespread unemployment and poverty. This explanation suggests that such economic crises are the result of bad decisions. Orienting the 1930s Depression in this way suggests that future crises can be avoided if people make better decisions and implement proper regulations to limit reckless behavior. The Banking Act of 1933 was the capstone of New Deal legislation. It required banks to keep a portion of deposited money as insurance in the event of another banking panic. In effect the regulation restricted the percent of deposited money banks were permitted to lend out (Prins 2014; Foner 2009b).

Since banks would be restricted in terms of their investments, Congress, in an emergency session, allocated resources to bail out failing enterprises and banks. To attempt to further stimulate the economy the Roosevelt administration also severed the link between the country's currency and its gold reserves. Consequently, the Federal Reserve could issue and pump more currency into circulation than was reflected in the country's reserves of gold to further stimulate investment and economic activity. Finally, through the Banking Act the Federal Deposit Insurance Corporation was created to insure the deposits of individuals.

If crises are not just the result of reckless behavior, what is it about capitalism itself that causes them? Even though Frederick Engels (1892/2007) does not offer a general theory of crises, he does note that "since 1825, when the first general crisis broke out, the whole industrial and commercial world ... are thrown out of joint about once every ten years" (83). If there is something about capitalism itself, something about its internal logic, that causes it to go into crisis about every ten years, then the sparks that set them off are not primarily the choices of individual capitalists, investors, financiers, or consumers.

Marxist scholar David Harvey (2014) brings us a little closer to these sparks or triggers of capitalist cyclical crises. Harvey notes that "all crises are crises of realization and result in the devaluation of capital" (85). What does this mean? The most commonly known place where *realization* manifests itself is in the final phase of production when commodities are sold and capitalists *realize* the value within them. Finished commodities are loaded with value: the value of the raw materials the commodities are made from, the value of the machines transferred to the raw materials bit by bit, and the new value added to the raw materials through the labor act. As long as this value—value embodied within commodities—stays immobilized within completed products, it cannot function as capital, and is therefore temporarily *negated* as such. Once the commodity is sold on the market, its value becomes available for circulation, for movement, for productive use.

What this points to is the drive to increase the "velocity" of the "circulation of capital, because to do so is to increase both the sum of values produced and the rate of profit" (86). The desired goal here is to reduce the turnover time. That is, the time it takes for money capital to pass through all its phases of production returning again to money capital, but augmented or increased according to the particular rate of profit, which, for the laborer, is the rate of exploitation. There is an inherent volatility here since the security and wellbeing of the seller of labor power are dependent upon the ability to sell one's labor which is dependent upon the constant movement of capital.

However, since the 1893 crisis US capitalism was supposed to have solved the problem of prosperity, and therefore circulation, once and for all time. Paul Mattick (1978), offering a much more realistic depiction, begins by noting that the 1930s crisis was actually a continuation of the 1893 crisis, which had been temporarily suspended or displaced by the First World War. As a result of the First World War, Mattick reasons, the United States went from being a debtor to a creditor state. The rise of the US capitalist state apparatus had a fundamentally transformative impact on international relations, since it enabled the United States to lean more on not only colonies but smaller imperialist powers to maintain its own internal circulation or realization.

The expansion of US production during the First World War was designed to sustain a global war. The so-called roaring 1920s were built off of the momentum generated during the First World War. However, the United States would eventually join Europe and succumb to the postwar conditions negatively impacting realization. Europe itself contributed to this downturn since its own crisis limited its ability to consume manufactured goods hurting US industry. Referring to the United States in the 1920s Mattick concludes that "a state of prosperity cannot be maintained in isolation from the rest of the world" (118). When one part of the globally integrated world suffers, circulation/realization impacts the totality.

When the US economy began its rapid descent into crisis in 1929, Europe's Depression also deepened. Harvey (2014) refers to this Depression as it manifested itself within the United States as "the deflationary crisis of the 1930s" (136), which means prices dropped dramatically. A steep drop in prices equates to the value within products never being realized, thereby further disincentivizing investment leaving even more capital idle and destroyed. Contributing to deflation were major technological advancements in labor-saving technologies, which increased production leading to overproduction. That is, too many goods on the market can lead to overproduction and devaluation. This does not imply too much production in terms of what is necessary to meet human need, but too much production in terms of capitalist profitability.

Summarizing the absurdity of this aspect of capitalism in the context of a crisis Engels (1892/2007) notes that "the mass of the workers are in want of the means of subsistence because they have produced too much means of subsistence" (84). Equally outrageous, the Roosevelt administration, attempting to get capital moving again through a series of inflation-inducing reforms, such as the Agricultural Adjustment Administration, worked to increase farm prices by reducing crop production. Situated in the midst of the Depression marked by widespread hunger, it seems counter-intuitive that the state would extend lines of credit to farmers for not producing food as a solution to an economic crisis causing hunger. According to Mattick (1978), "it is a curious situation, indeed, when a general abundance of foodstuffs finds its accompaniment in starvation, even among the food producers, and when no other solution offers itself but the reduction of production and the destruction of un-salable food products" (131). Paying farmers not to farm was also supposed to counter the movement of small growers fleeing to cities in search of work. However, such policies actually had the opposite effect as landowners drove idle tenants and sharecroppers from the soil in order to hoard government subsidies for themselves.

Labor-saving technologies contributed to this crisis in another way. If profit can only be produced by exploiting labor hours, then the capitalist has an interest in setting as many labor hours into motion at the same time as possible. Labor-saving technology, over time, has the effect of reducing the number of labor hours needed to convert a given amount of raw material into useful products. If less labor hours are set into motion over time, then the capitalist's rate of profit will fall. To counteract this tendency the capitalist will employ such tactics as speeding up the machines and reducing the price of labor even while its social value remains relatively consistent. In other words, while the cost of staying alive stays the same, the price one is able to exchange for his or her labor is reduced. The result is deepening poverty and workers' decreased ability to consume the necessaries of existence, thereby negatively effecting the movement of capital or realization and circulation. However, few regulatory measures were implemented within the first few years of the Depression leaving conditions for the many to deteriorate.

Roosevelt's advisors eventually admitted that there was no invisible hand guiding the market toward equilibrium, nor had there ever been. To remain capitalist, they argued, the economy, invoking the language of socialism, must be *planned* (Mattick 1978). A crucial aspect of this planning, supported by the National Industrial Recovery Act (NRA), and enacted through the passing of the National Labor Relations Act, was guaranteeing workers' right to collective bargaining. The rationale was that unions tended to elevate wages, create safe working conditions, and suppress capital's tendency to extend the length of the work day, which were all deemed necessary to subvert capitalism's self-destruction. Unions, in other words, were understood to be a fundamental component of saving capitalism from itself.

Since individual capitalists were driven by the laws of capitalist accumulation forcing them to forever seek ways to counter the tendency toward the falling rate of profit on the backs of laborers, leading them, for the most part, to only be able to see their own narrow, atomized self-interests, these regulations had to be imposed and enforced externally by the state. However, in practice, the drive of capital was too great and the NRA codes were largely undermined by the dominance of finance capital. As conditions for working people deteriorated during the 1930s, radical workers' movements would spread in both the South (Kelley 2015) and in the North (Naison 2005). The repressive state apparatus would therefore come to play a more pronounced role as well. Rather than including a separate section on the repressive state apparatus, it will be incorporated within the remainder of the chapter.

Critical Role of Education

A number of educators would challenge progressive education to view the crisis of capitalism not as the result of bad decisions of individuals but as systemic. One of the most well-known educators to adopt a systemic analysis was Columbia University professor George Counts. Counts pushed educators to take a more purposeful and militant stand against capitalism, which we explore in the final subsection of this chapter, the resistance. Before considering the pedagogical concerns and challenges raised by Counts, more macro-level organizational approaches to building the working-class movement are interrogated through the role of teacher unions. What follows is therefore a brief outline of how teacher unions were relating to the rise of the socialist movement in the United States in the midst of the 1930s Depression.

Chicago

As the crisis of realization deepened and hundreds of thousands of production workers lost their jobs, scores of public-sector workers, including teachers, were too often not paid. Thousands of students walked out of Chicago's public schools on April 5, 1933, because teachers had not been paid for six months. Many teachers engaged in a one-day, informal strike by calling in sick. Masses of those who did go to work joined the student's protest. In the following weeks groups of 20,000 or more students, parents, and educators regularly marched through the streets of downtown Chicago demanding justice for teachers. The situation was so volatile that "on more than one occasion over 3,000 teachers battled with police as they rioted in the city's banks" (Lyons 2006: 19).

By 1937 the Chicago public school teachers had organized themselves into the Chicago Teachers' Union (CTU). With more than two-thirds of teachers joining the organization the CTU quickly became the country's largest teachers' union. However, membership in teacher unions nation-wide remained relatively low. Educational historians tend to attribute this to the more conservative middle-class composition of teachers and the fact that teachers viewed themselves as professionals and therefore more closely aligned with management than with the working-class.

The National Economic League was formed in 1932 committed to scaling back on education expenditures. Former US Presidents Herbert Hoover and Calvin Coolidge were even on its advisory council lending further weight to its anti-public education agenda. Placing the resulting budget cuts in perspective, teachers in most major cities experienced 4 to 10 percent salary reductions. In Chicago teachers were still facing a 25 percent salary contraction in 1937. Given these deteriorating conditions teachers (and students) were facing, it is not surprising that their political orientations were also shifting.

Between the 1920s and 1930s studies on teachers' political views found that they had moved from conservative and pro-capitalist to as many as 80 percent believing that socializing the means of production was preferable to private ownership (Lyons 2006). However, this shift did not necessarily coincide with a dramatic move away from confidence in the Democratic Party's ability to institute progressive reforms that would relieve their suffering. For example, in 1932 only .064 percent of teachers voted for the socialist presidential candidate, Norman Thomas. Buhle (1987/2013) contends that because Thomas's critique of capitalism was more moralistic than scientific, he was "more influential among young YMCA staff workers than industrial workers" (147). Nevertheless, the number of teachers who voted socialist in 1936 increased to roughly 6 percent (Lyons 2006). While this is small, it is a dramatic increase from little more than a half of a percent. While teachers seemed to increasingly believe that the crisis in realization was systemic, it did not, for whatever reason, translate into voting for socialist candidates.

Similarly, Buhle (1987/2013), referring to the working-class in general, concludes that while "the Wall Street crash seemed almost like a biblical confirmation of the Party Line," it did not translate into mass militant action. Even among the most militant segments of the working-class found especially in NYC's European immigrant ethnic enclaves, mass militancy was not the norm, according to Buhle. For Buhle, this was because workers were "mortally wounded by industrial lay-offs" (143). Consequently, "the Party's new-found popularity did not usually translate into mass recruitment" (143). Similarly, Mark Naison (2005), in his study of communism in Harlem during the Depression, finds similar difficulties in bringing working-class African Americans into the mass movement.

From Harlem to Birmingham

The legacy of white supremacy proved a troublesome obstacle for building a mass, diverse working-class movement. For example, in the years preceding the Depression African American and Afro-Caribbean socialists in Harlem "had little contact with rank and file Communists in the white neighborhoods of Harlem" (Naison 2005: 10). Part of the difficulty was language barriers since the German, Italian, Swedish, and Jewish immigrants were non-English speakers. Naison also argues that part of the problem was a lack of desire on the part of the European immigrants and the racial trauma carried by Harlem's predominantly Southern-born African American community.

In contrast to the North, in Birmingham and throughout Alabama and the region in the 1930s, the Communist Party was a "working-class black organization"

(Kelley 2015: xxviii). The primary obstacle to radical mass mobilization seemed to be the violence and terrorism of the police, company-owned militias, and racist groups like the KKK, which were often composed of the same individuals (Kelley 2015). State repression was so pronounced that Kelley notes that many outsiders "might think" it "inconceivable in a democratic country" (xxviii). To be affiliated with the radical left in 1930s Alabama "was to face the possibility of imprisonment, beatings, kidnapping, and even death" (xxix). Southern labor militants often campaigned to defund the police arguing "it would not only free money for municipal relief projects but reduce antilabor repression and police brutality" (61). The radical labor movement, out of shear necessity given the deep poverty, nevertheless survived and thrived in this inhospitable context.

The Southern ruling establishment was even opposed to a common system of basic education for African American youth because they view it as "a powerful distraction for their school-aged laborers" (Anderson 1988: 150). Seeking a better future for their children through education African Americans began migrating North around 1917. The political establishment eventually made concessions in order to keep African Americans in the South and available as labor. Consequently, "by the mid-1930s, black elementary schools, though still far from excellent, had been transformed into a viable system of universal education" (152). However, as was the case during Reconstruction, African Americans had to raise hundreds of thousands of dollars to keep their schools open and functioning. Even in the midst of the Depression this practice continued. Anderson notes that these self-imposed education taxes were "particularly painful for black southerners" who barely earned "what was required for bare subsistence" (173).

Whereas Naison (2005) argues European and white radicals were slow to organize with African Americans in NYC, this may not have been the case in the South. Kelley (2015) argues that in the South race relations between working-class whites and African Americans were more "fluid" and "complex" (xxix) than historians have suggested. Those who did travel to the South were often driven out by the police and the KKK. For example, NYC-born Boris Israel gained notoriety in Memphis for organizing several unemployed demonstrations and successfully defending an African American man in court. Eventually the police and the KKK forced Israel to retreat to Chicago.

From Chicago to NYC

Back in Chicago, teachers, radicalized by desperation, began joining radical marches and doing battle with the police. Lyons (2006) takes a quote from a teacher's diary that reflects the internal turmoil she had to wrestle with before bringing herself to join the rebellion. Not wanting to make a spectacle of herself she finally concluded, "Nevertheless I am trampling down my pride ... and I too perhaps shall soon join the more radical elements of the teaching force ... Tomorrow I shall parade. I've come to it at last. I loath the idea, but the public must be awakened. I feel a little like Joan of Arc" (quoted in Lyons 2006: 26–7). The more militant organization this teacher would eventually join was the Volunteer Emergency Committee (VEC).

The VEC was created by Chicago teachers designed to unite teachers across their various specialized unions to more effectively "obtain regular payment of their salaries" (25). However, the orientation of the VEC, while militant, was counter-revolutionary and actively anti-communist. So committed to an anti-communist agenda the VEC consciously tried to keep communists and radicals out of their rallies and meetings. The leader of VEC, a 32-year-old physical fitness teacher, John Fewkes, was a particularly passionate anti-communist. Fewkes participated in the expulsion of communist-oriented American Federation of Teachers (AFT) locals in New York.

The expelled locals had been the "most forceful in fighting to improve schools in Harlem and had supported NAACP efforts to equalize teacher salaries in the South" (Naison 2005: 310). It was the African American teachers (among other professional intellectuals) who had joined the expelled AFT locals that the Harlem branch of the Communist Party was most successful in recruiting rather than the more numerous working-class African Americans.

NYC's AFT-affiliated Teachers Union (TU), Local 5, would experience a struggle for power between the Communist Party and the American Communist Opposition (ACO). This was during the Communist Party's tactical use of dual-unionism, which is a strategy for winning political power by developing a union or political organization parallel to an existing union and therefore competing with it for the same potential members. The TU was organized by a group of teachers in 1916 becoming NYC's first teacher union. In its first year of existence it received a charter from the AFT becoming AFT Local 5. Clarence Taylor's (2011) *Reds at the Blackboard: Communism, Civil Rights, and the New York City Teachers Union* explores this struggle for power. The balance of these forces would manifest itself in two competing opposition caucuses or dual-unions: the Rank and File, associated with the Communist Party, and the Progressive Group of the ACO.

At issue was everything from salary, working conditions, union democracy, to the degree of member inclusiveness. That is, those in favor of white-collar unionism argued that including part-time teachers, substitutes, unemployed teachers, private school teachers, and "teachers hired under the New Deal's Work Projects Administration" (11) would degrade the union's professionalism. The Rank and File communists, on the other hand, favored an industrial union model that was inclusive of all categories of teachers. Their assessment was that the industrial model was more effective for the struggle for higher wages and pensions and better health care and working conditions.

Taylor (2011) notes that the communist teachers within the union ineffectively called on their colleagues to abandon the idea that they were professionals and accept the fact they were exploited workers sharing an objective, common class interest and class enemy with the working-class in general. Despite their small numbers and defeats, the radical teachers were able to form a caucus relying on disruptive tactics at public meetings to call out union leadership. Because of their relative ineffectiveness and irrelevancy, according to Taylor, their academic freedom and freedom of speech were not suppressed.

However, by the time the full destructive force of the Depression set in, much of this would change, and their message began to find a wider audience among teachers. By 1932 the communist teachers' caucus, the Rank and File caucus, had become the largest and most powerful force within the Teachers' Union. Reflecting their growth in 1932 the first member of the Rank and File caucus, Isidore Begun, began serving on the TU's executive board.

Whereas the union leadership in the main advocated for working with management and viewing the Board of Education as a neutral body, the communists saw the other side of the bargaining table as capitalist-class collaborators contributing to the oppression and exploitation of the working-class. Rank and File members therefore advocated for more militant approaches such as organizing mass actions and general strikes.

The communists' decision to battle their own union leadership by challenging the compromises they were negotiating with New York's mayor, LaGuardia, as unnecessarily accepting of further reductions in teacher's wages, proved to be effective. By 1934 the Rank and File caucus had several more members on the TU's executive board. The communist's tactics also allowed them to focus on recruitment. Communist leaders advocated for lowering union dues to make membership affordable to unemployed and substitute teachers. Rank and File teachers also argued that the union must defend and fight for students as well. Nearly 100 new members applied by 1934. Continuing to win members over to their side was a necessary component of building a mass movement. Despite the ongoing disruptions from state repression and other reactionary capitalist-supporting forces, the radical teachers were making significant advances.

Taylor (2011) argues that the Rank and File's Classroom Teacher Group (CTG) was their most effective mass organizing vehicle. The CTG was reportedly a well-disciplined force successful at converting teachers over to a communist orientation in terms of addressing education issues. Focused on bread and butter concerns, the CTG spoke directly to teachers and unemployed teachers. Union leaders were worried that the agenda of the Rank and File would result in the growing numbers of unemployed teachers taking over the union completely.

Embracing an international orientation Rank and File also adopted an anti-war/anti-imperialist platform. In 1934 Rank and File introduced a motion for the union to petition President Roosevelt to not spend the nearly 500 million dollars earmarked for armaments, and use it, instead, to address the growing crisis in education. Rank and File is also on record for successfully getting a motion passed for the federal government to not make Armistice Day a school holiday because it would take away from promoting peace. The communist caucus also called for the establishment of an anti-war committee in the union, and to send a representative to an international, communist antiwar conference. Loyalty oaths were also strongly critiqued for repressing teacher's ability to engage in free and open inquiry.

The administration would continue to strike back leveling many charges against both left-of-center caucuses, the Progressive Group and the Rank and File through a Joint Committee report. Among the complaints were disruption, spreading communist propaganda, disparaging the reputation of administrators, accusing the Board of Education of political bribery and fraud, and subverting an atmosphere of goodwill and harmony. A Grievance Committee was established to handle the complaints coming in against the caucuses. The goal, however, was to purge the radical caucuses completely. While the Committee portrayed the caucuses as inherently disruptive, the caucuses charged the administration with acting as a special interest group concerned only with holding onto power. The Grievance Committee also charged the two permanent caucuses, each of which had their own executive committees and secretaries, as being at such odds with each other that they threatened the very existence of the union. What is more, the two opposition caucus groups were accused of attempting to use the union to overthrow capitalism. The Grievance Committee recommended that an elected delegates assembly was formed to replace the cumbersome membership meetings. They also suggested the assembly had a chair person endowed with the power to suspend any disruptive delegate.

The opposition groups responded with their own Executive Board Minority Report, which the Grievance Committee did not allow them to present at the next meeting. The caucuses charged the Committee with being undemocratic and anti-communist, using red-scare tactics to thwart the will of the people. The administration sought the expulsion of six opposition members but could not get the necessary three-quarters of the membership's vote. This was a clear win for the opposition signaling a true radical presence in the union. The schism would continue to intensify within the TU, Local 5 of the AFT. The national AFT leadership even unsuccessfully tried to expel communist members of the TU. Eventually, the social democratic forces would break from the union forming the Teachers Guild.

This was certainly a lively time within teachers' unions, but the situation would only continue to intensify. In 1935 when FDR signed the National Recovery Act granting workers the legal right to organize unions and collectively bargain, union membership swelled. In response, progressive organizations changed their tactics and began working more directly within the AFT and other large unions. As capitalist states, including Germany and Italy, desperately began turning to fascism in response to labor militancy, radicals and progressives within US teacher unions would follow the international tactic of building a popular anti-fascist front. The TU would publicly endorse a united front against fascism by 1935.

During this time of popular front activism, coupled with a more social justice-oriented New Deal "American communists were transformed from a persecuted pariah into a semi-legitimate left-of-center force within national politics" (Buhle 1987/2013: 145). Buhle argues that the anti-fascist, popular front orientation attracted a considerable amount of support from the more progressive-leaning factions of the Democratic Party establishment. For the Democrats the communists were able to "rally constituents and bring out working-class and ethnic voters" (145). For the larger industrial unions, the communists were able to organize and discipline masses of workers.

As a result of these factors communists and their allies were able to play leading roles in the country's largest unions. By the end of the 1930s the Communist Party in the United States had roughly 40,000 members. With their growing numbers and increasingly mainstream appeal, it is no wonder that Roosevelt would authorize the Federal Bureau of the Department of Justice to monitor the activities of communists and socialists. The FBI subsequently illegally monitored Communist Party meetings. But the Bureau's activities went beyond investigating. So-called "educational" materials were reportedly fabricated and leaked to appropriate channels designed to turn liberal, religious, and union elements against the communists and their popular front (Churchill & Vander Wall 1990).

The FBI's efforts were aided by the confusion and controversy that ensued in 1939 after Moscow signed a nonaggression pact with Nazi Germany. Even though this pact was strategically necessary for the struggling Soviet Union to buy time to develop armaments before being invaded by Nazis forces, it was manipulated to portray the communists as either opportunistic or fascist sympathizers. Consequently, it became increasingly difficult for communists to remain even on the margins of the mainstream politics in the United States.

Despite working tirelessly on behalf of teachers' working conditions, union democracy, and for improved wages, the growing anti-communism led to Local 5 having its AFT charter revoked by 1941. According to Taylor (2011), "the TU was expelled from the New York City Central Trades and Labor Council, the AFT, and later the Congress of Industrial Organizations (CIO), and it was banned from the school system in 1950 because of its Communist connections" (48). Progressive Columbia University professor George Counts was elected president of the AFT in 1940 after running on an anti-communist platform. Counts warned teachers of communist infiltration and authoritarianism. However, as we will see below, this overt anti-communism represented a decisive break from his previous more sympathetic orientation.

The Resistance

In the late 1920s a group of progressive educators at Columbia University, including John Dewey, George Counts, and others, were engaged in a comprehensive examination of the widespread changes that US education had undergone as a result of the development of an industrialized capitalist economy. "When the Depression struck," writes Lawrence Cremin (1980), this group of educators "saw themselves uniquely equipped—and uniquely responsible—for working out a social and educational agenda that would address itself to the needs of an America in crisis" (188). What might be considered as their manifesto came from George Counts (1932) in a pamphlet called *Dare the School Build a New social Order?* Counts' statement is said to have "electrified the teaching profession" (Cremin 1980: 188).

Dare the School is broken up into three parts that were originally presented as speeches. Educational historian Wayne Urban (1978) describes these speeches as an attempt to "alert educators to the crisis and challenge of the economic Depression of the 1930s" and to "sketch an educational and political response to that calamity" (v). Urban notes that Counts's words were unusually passionate and bold for an academic audience likely expecting something "dispassionate" or "loaded with platitudes" despite the obvious fact that the times "called for boldness" (vi). Even though the challenge Counts (1932) posed to educators was, at times, quite harsh, the Progressive Education Association responded by suspending "the remainder of the business of the convention in order instead to ponder and react to Counts' ideas" (Urban 1978: vi). This, of course, is legendary. The fact that a group of professional educators, who tend to pride themselves on their organizational prowess and ability to create and complete an agenda, would voluntarily forfeit their program to engage in a spontaneous and undefined process is remarkable and likely unprecedented.

While *Dare the Schools* was uncompromising in its challenge to what Counts (1932) regarded as the naïve optimism of educators, the text maintains a degree of revolutionary optimism grounded in the belief that "the Depression provided an opportunity to implement educational and socio-economic change in America" (vi). Counts's insistence that systemic change was needed was a response to the widespread poverty, hunger, unemployment, and general immiseration of the Depression. In the decade preceding the Depression, Counts conducted major study after major study, each one documenting with precision how "the school was one of many American institutions that did not work for the ordinary citizen but functioned instead to maintain class distinctions" (Urban 1978: vii). For example, Urban notes how Counts "documented the failure of public high schools to reduce significantly the unequal distribution of wealth and privilege" (vii). In another study, Counts "demonstrated that school boards were controlled completely by the upper classes" (vii). Finally, Counts "chronicled the struggle of Chicago's teachers and citizens to free their schools from economic domination by elites" (vii).

Counts's insistence on systemic changes was inspired by his knowledge of the deep inequality that was not the product of individual choices but was the product of the internal logic of capitalism itself. Having made several trips to the Soviet Union to study the Bolshevik's widespread initiatives to "democratize" the country's "social, cultural, and economic life," and "assigning to education a crucial role in that process" (viii), was also very influential on Counts. Moved by what he observed and learned in the Soviet Union Counts (1931) wrote a book dedicated to the subject, *The Soviet Challenge to America*. In his work Counts draws special attention to the two diametrically opposed systems in the United States and the Soviet Union. Whereas the United States was gripped by poverty, hunger, unemployment, and the extreme wastefulness of capitalism, the Soviet Union, on the other hand, was marked by a commitment to social justice, revolutionary optimism, passionate determination, and a rationally planned economy. Counts was particularly impressed by the Soviet Union's planning attributing it to the great innovation and success of their education system, which was playing a leading role in the progressive development of the new society.

While Counts was unique among US observers for his focus on central planning, other educators in the United States marveled at Soviet teachers gravitating toward "progressive methods, such as encouraging pupils to see the teacher as a peer rather than an authority, fostering pupil self-government, rejecting traditional methods of instruction, and eliminating boundaries between classrooms and society" (Ewing 2006: 43). In practice, eliminating the boundaries between school and society and democratizing the teacher/student relationship meant that education was not just intellectually and philosophically rigorous, but it was equally focused on making schools practically relevant in terms of building a just society.

While education was being defunded in much of the Depression-stricken US system (especially outside of the South), through rigorous and coordinated planning, education expanded dramatically in the Soviet Union. For example, in just one decade the enrollment of elementary-aged children grew from 14 to 31 million pupils (Ewing 2006). Even though the Soviet Union had a long way to go in terms of training teachers and elevating the level of instruction, Counts (1931) nevertheless marveled at the great strides in elevating the literacy rate and instilling a sense of hope.

So impressive were the Soviet achievements, moving a relatively underdeveloped, peasant-based society to new levels of skill and consciousness in a few short decades, Counts regards them as unprecedented on a world-historical scale (Ewing 2006). It is therefore not surprising that Counts would come to view the Soviet system as a model to be followed globally, especially in the Depression-ridden United States.

Whereas the United States would not have a permanent federal, Cabinet-level Secretary and Department of Education until the Carter Administration in 1977, the Soviet Union had established a Soviet Commissariat of Education that had taken the initiative setting immediate goals for universal education. Even though real progress was being made toward this goal, Ewing argues there was a gap between what was desired and what could be achieved given the limitations of insufficient training and a lack of resources.

Reporting positively on what he observed in the Soviet Union earned Counts the reputation of being a communist. The publication of *Dare the Schools* contributed to this reputation. Even though he never advocates for socialism or communism in the text, he does advocate for the basic tenants of socialism, including planning, as the solution to the 1930s Depression, as we will see in greater detail below. While Counts never identified as a communist or socialist, he did believe they should be heard. He therefore published socialist articles in his journal, *The Social Frontier*. Interestingly enough, in the 1930s and 1940s, Counts led an effort to expel communists from the AFT for their presumed authoritarianism (Urban 1978). Given these nuances, we can turn to a brief review of *Dare the School*.

Counts's Challenge

In his statement, addressed to progressive educators, Counts begins by identifying a contradiction. That is, Counts notes that Americans tend to have a blind faith in education's ability to fix every conceivable social problem from poverty to racism. However, the Depression was immediately preceded by an unprecedented expansion in education. If education was truly a panacea, then the 1930s Depression would have either never occurred or it would have been quickly resolved since the silver bullet was in abundance. Rather than functioning as an agent of change, Counts concludes that schools, like the rest of society, were being impacted and shaped by the same systemic forces at the heart of capitalism. This was a wakeup call to the optimism of educators believing they were having a positive impact by the shear fact of their existence.

However, just because education was playing, at best, a passive role, it did not mean that it could not play a more active role in overcoming the serious challenges the Depression presented. Counts challenged educators to deal more concretely with the material reality of the working-class, and to make that context a central part of their curriculum. Only by joining the struggles of the many could teachers become authentic leaders. Teachers would have to accept this challenge regardless of the personal sacrifices they would have to make. Counts makes powerful use of metaphor here calling teachers to action commenting that "authentic leaders are never found breathing that rarefied atmosphere lying above the dust and smoke of battle" (4).

Counts identified a sort of vulgarized approach to progressive education as a barrier to his challenge. That is, the most popular current among curricular progressives was an extreme form of child-centeredness committed to allowing the child to grow and develop according to its own internal logic unimpeded by the interventions of educators. Counts, we might say, had identified another form of atomization. The progressive educator was so worried about infringing upon the rights of the child that they were unable to see how the child does not exist in a vacuum, but comes to school loaded with the same capitalist content the larger society is saturated in.

If education was going to play a progressive role, in other words, then educators had to become comfortable and committed to challenging students to engage with controversial ideas. Rather than promoting specific reforms to capitalist society, Counts argues that schools should advance a guiding vision highlighting the possibilities for a future beyond capitalism.

By avoiding anything that could be interpreted as an imposition on the child, progressive educators were contributing to the disconnection between education and the "serious activities of adults" (17). Counts rejected the assumption that this disconnect was an unavoidable consequence of the growing complexity of industrial society. Rather, Counts contends that it is "the product of a society that is moved by no great commanding ideals and is consequently victimized by the most terrible form of human madness—the struggle for private gain" (17). That is, capitalist-controlled schooling ensured that students would not develop a critical analysis of capitalism and its historical trajectory.

If teachers were to overcome these deficiencies Counts argued that they must "deliberately reach for power and then make the most of their conquest" (28). While Counts identifies unions as an important source of power, he argues that real power comes from the ability to win the support of the masses. Counts reiterates the urgency of his challenge over and over noting that they live in revolutionary times. Challenging teachers to think of democracy outside of the limitations of the ballot box Counts states that "the most genuine expression of democracy in the United States has little to do with our political institutions" (40–1).

Pointing toward systemic or revolutionary change Counts asks: who should "control the machine" (43)? That is, "in whose interests and for what purposes are the vast material riches, the unrivaled industrial equipment, and the science and technology of the nation to be used?" (43). For Counts, the answer was obvious: the means of production must be in the hands of the producers to benefit the many. He argued that if the productive apparatus should remain in the hands of the few, already deplorable conditions for the many would likely get worse.

The heart of the matter, for Counts, was "fairly obvious," which he summarized as the "fact that America is the scene of an irreconcilable conflict between two opposing forces" (44), namely, labor and capital. Without revolutionary change,

Counts alluded, the United States would just be one more powerful country acting as a bully at home and abroad to the great detriment of the many.

Conclusion

The 1930s crisis of realization led many educators and activists from Chicago to Birmingham to reject the assumption that the Depression was not the result of individual behavior but was systemic to capitalism itself. Ruling-class forces would respond with yet another intensification of state repression. Ironically, it would take the Second World War and the near self-destruction of capitalism itself for capitalism to recover from the Great Depression. As we will see in Chapter 10 the era of mass education following the Second World War would be followed by an era of mass incarceration as the repressive state continued to intensify.

10

From Mass Education to Mass Incarceration

Introduction: Connection to the Previous Chapter

In Chapter 9 we saw the systemic crisis of realization and the mobilization of teachers and activists in response. In the present chapter we explore the expansion of education in the post-Second World War era as capitalism's labor needs shifted with the continued development of labor-saving technologies, which coincided with the emergence of a new era in mass mobilizations spearheaded by the African American Civil Rights movement and its leaders. New crises of realization develop as the labor-saving technologies eventually render large segments of the US working-class redundant.

Unlike previous manifestations of racism designed to either justify the super-exploitation of slavery or maintain a form of the plantation system through prisoner-leasing schemes after Reconstruction, the particular form of "super-predator" anti-Blackness of the post-Second World War mass incarceration era was a response to Black workers especially being expelled from production as a by-product of automation (Puryear 2012). Racist incarceration during Jim Crow functioned to hold African Americans in the South to labor, whereas mass incarceration contemporarily operates to facilitate the removal of the African American community from the labor process. A community not valued for its ability to labor, within the logic of the social universe of capital, is a community discarded and devalued.

In this way racism has not only been preserved from previous eras of forced labor, but it has been preserved in an altered, more heinous form (i.e. sublated). It is within this context of rapid technological development and machines replacing workers that we have seen a shift from investing in human development (i.e. education) to investing in digitalization and the prison industrial complex.

Critical Role of Capitalism

Not only did the aftermath of the Second World War bring vast advances in technology, it also brought a shift in the balance of forces, known as the Cold War. The capitalists were no longer the only world power or the only pole. With the advancement of the Soviet Union and the rise of a block of socialist states, including China, the world was now multi-polar. In response to this global class war or Cold War, the United States established a permanent military industry with state management institutionalized. Political scientists such as Seymour Melman (1970) explained the rising poverty at the time as a direct consequence of resources diverted to maintain this military industrial complex.

US capitalists worried that a new economic depression would emerge as the stimulus of the full-employment war economy dissipated. The ruling-class was therefore committed to keeping the price of labor (i.e. wages) suppressed even as productivity increased. So dominant was their position with the only intact industrial infrastructure intact that it accounted for 60 percent of the world's productive output, but with only 6 percent of the global population. Within this context labor fought back with thousands and thousands of strikes.

Franz Schurmann (1972/1995), in an introduction to a collective of writings and speeches by Black Panther Party co-founder and theoretician, Huey P. Newton, constructs a narrative with a slightly different orientation. Schurmann argues that if the US economy had continued to expand as dynamically as it did in the nineteenth century, "Black people would have been absorbed into the ever-expanding industrial labor force" (xvi). Schurmann notes that the predominantly white labor unions, fearing the coming job losses due to automation, kept Brown and Black people out of the unions contributing to racial apartheid in the United States. It is within this context that Schurmann situates the emergence of the Black Panther Party in the 1960s.

Eugene Puryear (2012) notes that because the manufacturing jobs available to African Americans after the great migration North tended to be on the lowest rung, they were the first to lose their jobs as a result of developments in automation and other labor-saving technologies. The state responded to this shift in production with mass incarceration and the cutting of social services. Suffering from widespread unemployment "huge numbers of African Americans were trapped in either neglected inner-city 'hoods' or the cruelties of the prison system" (Puryer 2012: 46). Outlining this scenario in 1966 James Baldwin remains timely:

The jobs that Negroes have always held, the lowest jobs, the most menial jobs, are now being destroyed by automation. No remote provision has yet been made to absorb this labor surplus. Furthermore, the Negro's education, North and South, remains, almost totally, a segregated education, which is but another way of saying that he is taught the habits of inferiority every hour of every day that he lives.

The social unrest emerging from this situation is further agitated by the way in which the Black community has always been "policed like occupied territory" as Baldwin describes it. The ultimate function of the police, for Baldwin, is to "keep the Negro in his place and to protect white business interests, and they serve no other function." This is why, Baldwin elaborates, that "calls to 'respect the law,' always to be heard from prominent citizens each time the ghetto explodes, are so obscene." Heading this call then to "respect the law," situated "in the context in which the American Negro finds himself, is simply to surrender his self-respect."

Enter Police Unions

It was within the era of civil rights mobilizations and the escalation of police brutality that police unions were formed. Baldwin summarizes the demands civil rights activists were making of the repressive state:

> [T]he Police Department investigates itself, quite as though it were answerable only to itself. But it cannot be allowed to be answerable only to itself. It must be made to answer to the community which pays it, and which it is legally sworn to protect.

Responding to organizers bringing attention to "the role of police and police violence in defending racism and segregation" the armed wing of the state began forming unions "to give credibility to" its "efforts to protect police officers from police oversight and the criminal investigation of officer misconduct" (Correia &Wall 2018: 163). The consequence has been that:

> Through collective bargaining, police unions have transformed police violence into a contractually protected condition of their employment. This has had the effect of expanding the right of police to choose when and where to use violence at the same time that it has limited civilian police oversight or criminal investigation of that use of force by police.

(164)

As the repressive state was continuing its intensification and consolidation or pooling of power, African American communities were also winning concessions in education.

Critical Role of Education

During and following the Second World War and the recovery from the Great Depression, African Americans continued the struggle for civil rights, including in the area of education. This mass movement, combined with the national liberation struggles spreading through the colonized world following the Russian and then the Chinese revolutions, compelled the Supreme Court to overturn *Plessy v. Ferguson* in *Brown v. Board of Education*. To be sure many of the nine white male Supreme Court Justices who voted unanimously in favor of *Brown* had been in favor of upholding Jim Crow Apartheid. It was therefore not the Supreme Court that dismantled Jim Crow but one of the largest mass movements in US history led by the African American community in the epicenter of Southern apartheid.

The contradiction of African American soldiers fighting overseas against fascism for *their* country then coming home to legalized segregation enforced by the racist terror of the police/KKK was too stark. On their return to the United States African American soldiers had experiences in train terminal diners where they had to eat segregated in kitchens while their German prisoners of war were permitted to dine, smoke, and laugh with the white soldiers in white-only dining rooms. One African American solider, disgusted by the hypocrisy, reflected,

> I stood on the outside looking on, and I could not help but ask myself these questions: Are these men sworn enemies of this country? Are they not taught to hate and destroy all democratic governments? Are we not American soldiers, sworn to fight for and die if need be for this country? Then why are they treated better than we are? Why are we pushed around like cattle? If we are fighting for the same thing, if we are to die for our country, then why does the Government allow such things to go on? Some of the boys are saying that you will not print this letter. I'm saying that you will.
>
> (Yank Magazine 1944)

As Black veterans returned from the Second World War they led numerous civil rights campaigns, many involving armed self-defense as a necessity of the context. The fearless military of this struggle rattled the white supremacist economic and state power structure to its core.

This mass movement not only led to the *Brown* ruling, but it led the US Congress to pass the 1964 Civil Rights Act and the 1965 Voting Rights Act (Fisher 2008). If the Supreme Court is in fact not a neutral body objectively enforcing the law of the land, but perhaps the last line of defense for the capitalist class, then *Brown* and these subsequent pieces of progressive legislation can be understood as concessions/acts of self-preservation.

Brown is perhaps one of the most widely known Supreme Court rulings in the United States. The court famously concluded that "in the field of public education the doctrine of 'separate but equal' has no place. Separate educational facilities are inherently unequal." History of education texts tend to focus on how the ruling left undecided when and to what extent schools would be desegregated, finally determining fourteen months later, "with all deliberate speed."

Because Southern state courts were controlled by the white ruling-class power structure, integration or desegregation in public education depended, initially, on the willingness of whites, and eventually on the intervention of a hesitant federal government. The white Southern elite responded to desegregation with *school choice* campaigns. Conservative economist Milton Freedman laid the theoretical groundwork for school choice as a market-based alternative to the public system. Deceptively couched in progressive language *choice* was in fact a reactionary counter-revolution. While those intended to do the choosing were white conservatives, the initiative was marketed to poor communities as a market solution to the so-called monopolization of "failing" government schools.

The mechanism that would allow students and their families (i.e. "consumers") to choose the best product (i.e. school) was the voucher (i.e. the tax dollars allocated for each individual student). However, the voucher could only ever cover part of the tuition for private or religious schools. Consequently, the only students who could actually afford to remove their state-collected education dollars from public schools were those with preexisting economic advantages. The result has been a counter-force that subverts attempts to equalize the distribution of educational resources.

It was from within this counter-revolution that the charter school movement was hatched. The racist reaction to school integration erupted across the country. The racists were ultimately defeated by a mass movement of hundreds of thousands of African Americans and their supporters. The struggle to defeat

Jim Crow was no doubt heroic as it refused to back down or give up in the face of police dogs, beatings, jailing, torture, and even death.

Smashing Jim Crow segregation meant that legalized apartheid in the South was over. *Brown* was far reaching as it had immediate implications for pending rulings on racial discrimination in housing, public beaches, restaurants, and recreation facilities. It is within this era that many progressive education initiatives would become law. Among them was the Elementary and Secondary Education Act of 1965, the Bilingual Education Act of 1968, and the Education for All Handicapped Children Act of 1975 (renamed Individuals with Disabilities Education Act in 1990).

However, while these measures signaled a major political shift, as a whole, they have been critiqued for identifying the individual as deficient and in need of correction rather than the system or structure. In other words, poverty and racial inequality were viewed as the product of individual deficiencies such as a lack of educational opportunities rather than the internal logic of capitalism itself that can only function as such through the exploitation of labor hours. This was the premise behind the *Brown* ruling and the subsequent measures designed to correct so-called separate but equal. What was never implemented, for example, was the nationwide anti-racist curriculum Civil Rights leaders and countless educators demanded. The bourgeois state, being compelled to act against its own reason for being by the power of a mass movement, would only ever do the bare minimum in terms of meeting the peoples' demands.

As a result, racist police brutality and the super-exploitation of African American, Latino, Native American, and other working-class communities persisted. As automation began replacing manufacturing jobs and African Americans found themselves the first ones pushed onto the chopping block, the shift from mass education to mass incarceration reared its ugly head. The emergence of the Black Panther Party (as well as the American Indian Movement, the Brown Berets, and others) around the time of this shift would signal a new era in the Black liberation movement.

The Resistance

From the fringes of the Civil Rights movement the Black Panther Party for Self-Defense (BPP) was started in 1966 in Oakland, CA. After witnessing the Watts uprising in 1965 cofounder Huey P. Newton sensed a shift in the consciousness of the Black working-class. Since the non-violent peaceful protest movement had not stopped the police killing of unarmed African Americans, people began directing their pent-up outrage at the symbols of racist oppression (i.e. capitalist enterprises and police cars). The non-violent leaders of the Civil Rights movement were not even safe from the murderous impulse of the white supremacist repressive state.

Meeting the people where they were at in their political development the Panthers would be conceptualized employing a class analysis of capitalism and the increasingly repressive role of the police. Remember, the police had begun forming so-called unions to protect themselves from being held responsible for their often-deadly violence. Newton and the Panthers were well aware of the more centralized, pooled, and protected repressive state apparatus they faced. Political prisoner and former Panther, Mumia Abu-Jamal (2000), describes Newton as "a youth of rare brilliance, who molded mass militancy into a national black political movement that lit an age into radical incandescence" (137).

For example, responding to ongoing incidents of police killing African Americans in Oakland in particular, one of the Panthers' first campaigns was a *cop watch*. These included armed self-defense Panther patrols designed to monitor the activity of the occupying police presence. Aiming to counter racist police terror many cop watch actions brought Newton into locally famous face-offs with the armed wing of the state. These confrontations quickly made Newton a police target.

The Panthers would surge to national prominence after a traffic stop, not during a cop watch, where a compliant Newton was assaulted and shot by Officer Frey. However, the incident ended with the death of the cop and the arrest of Newton on murder charges. A campaign to "Free Huey" gripped the attention of a new generation of progressive activists from New York to Los Angeles. The BPP quickly became a national organization with branches springing up in cities across the country.

The Panther's ability to capture the hearts and minds of the African American community was not just in their recognition that the broadest masses, at the time, were ready for armed resistance, but in their recognition that "oppression would not be resolved through armed struggle alone" (Hilliard 2002). Rather, Hilliard (2002) describes the Panther's Ten Point Program as approaching:

> [S]elf-defense in terms of political empowerment, encompassing protection against joblessness and the circumstances that excluded blacks from equal employment opportunities; against predatory business practices intended to exploit the needs of the poor; against homelessness and inferior housing

conditions; against educational systems that denigrate and miscast the histories of oppressed peoples; against a prejudiced judiciary that convicts African Americans and other oppressed people of color by all-white juries; and, finally, against the lawlessness of law enforcement agencies that harass, abuse, and murder blacks with impunity.

(12)

The mass appeal of the Panthers, in other words, resided in their overall program that laid out a vision for and path to a world beyond racialized capitalism. In short, the BPP offered a socialist program tailored to African American experiences and consciousness at the end of the era of mass education and the dawn of the era of mass incarceration. Such a program inverts the capitalist value system moving the basic needs of the people (i.e. housing, education, health care, jobs with livable dignified wages, etc.) from the last priority to the first priority negating the priority of accumulating profit from the reasons for which a community produces. To serve the people in practice the Black Panther Party "fed hungry children, escorted senior citizens to banks to cash their checks, administered a model elementary school, and tested people for the rare blood disease, sickle cell anemia" (Abron 1998: 177).

The Panthers' fifth point in their Ten Point Program addresses education and offers a glimpse into how they saw the relationship between consciousness and social transformation:

We want education for our people that exposes the true nature of this decadent American society. We want education that teaches us our true history and our role in the present-day society. We believe in an educational system. If a man does not have knowledge of himself and his position in society and the world, then he has little chance of to relate to anything else.

(Newton 1973: 4)

The mechanism that allowed the Panthers to carry their revolutionary message deep into working-class African American communities throughout the United States was their Survival Programs (Abron 1998). To survive and build until revolutionary transformation. The programs were designed to meet the people's basic needs that the system, by design, fails to meet, including health care and adequate food and nutrition. There were also programs that addressed the people's educational needs with "liberation schools, community political education classes, and the Intercommunal Youth Institute" (Abron 1998: 185).

The liberation schools taught children Black history through the lens of class struggle, which only makes sense since capitalism, made possible by the super-profits of slave labor, has always been a racialized capitalism. The Panthers' liberation schools were a natural outgrowth of their Free Breakfast Program. The comrades running the program became frustrated with the lack of time they had to engage children in political discussions driving them to establish liberation schools.

The liberation school equivalent for adults were the community political education classes, which included not only content and analysis, but literacy skills trainings as well. The longest running of the Panthers' educational Survival Programs was the Intercommunal Youth Institute, which graduated its last class in 1982 after having been renamed the Oakland Community School in 1974 (Abron 1998). The school's people's curriculum was matched with a people's pedagogy. At its zenith the Institute had a waiting list of 400 students and even earned awards from the Governor of California for setting the standard for excellence in elementary education.

Ultimately, it was the FBI's domestic Counter Intelligence Program (COINTELPRO) that destroyed the Panthers and other revolutionary peoples' organizations. The FBI's tactics included things such as infiltrating the BPP sowing internal dissent, assassinating members of its leadership, and piling up false charges on members incarcerating many for decades, including Jalil Muntaqim (since 1971), Mutulu Shakur (since 1986), Russell "Maroon" Shoatz (since 1970), Sundiata Acoli (since 1973), Joseph Bowen (since 1971), and Mumia Abu-Jamal (since 1981). Police unions are perhaps the most responsible for these insanely long sentences as they consistently exert their influence to pressure public officials and the legal system to deny political prisoners parole.

Despite the state's war on revolutionaries, the revolution ebb and flow, but it lives on. The legacy of the Pathers continues to thrive in today's movement for Black lives and uprising against racism.

Part Four

History's Future and the Role of the Many

11

A Unipolar Imperialist Power

Introduction: Connection to the Previous Chapter

In Chapter 10 we saw the African American struggle for social justice force the state to take steps toward equality and make concessions in education. We also saw industrial automation, the displacement of African American workers, and the emergence of mass incarceration.

However, the US repressive state also worked to undermine the spread of progressive movements and governments around the world. By the mid-1960s the United States had engaged in around thirty military and CIA interventions abroad. As a result, the global working-class counter-weight had been weakened even though the Soviet Union would not fall for another three decades. When the Soviet Union did collapse around 1989, the United States had intervened nearly sixty times in every corner of the world.

The present chapter examines this tumultuous time and the aftermath. What emerged within the United States in the realm of social policy, including education, was a shift from a war on poverty to a war on the poor. As we will see the Reagan administration symbolizes the beginning of this new era called neoliberalism. It is within this context that the critical pedagogy movement emerged, which will be examined in the resistance.

Critical Role of Capitalism

The collapse of the Soviet Union was not the inevitable outcome of a defective socialist system. Rather, it was the combined consequence of internal bureaucratic errors and decades of external imperialist attacks led by the United States. However, contrary to the claims of imperialist propaganda, its demise was not celebrated by the Soviet people, 77 percent of whom supported it at the time of its fall (La Riva 2017; Marcy 1976).

When the Soviet Union disappeared from the world stage and the Cold War ended, the balance of global politics shifted. With the Cold War over some believed a new era of peace and stability would emerge. However, more than three decades later the United States continues to operate roughly 900 military bases throughout the world.

The official US foreign policy position after the Cold War was to prevent another rival on par with the Soviet Union from emerging. This was the time of unipolar imperialist power.

The Reagan administration was the instrument the capitalist class mobilized to reverse the New Deal tax codes. Consequently, access to the revenue needed to fund social programs was cut off. Conservative propaganda worked to manipulate working people convincing many the source of their problems was each other and their unions rather than a capitalist-class political establishment. The ruling-class goal was to transform working people from the grave diggers of an oppressive system to the grave diggers of their own livelihoods and futures.

Neoliberalism

Facing the mounting economic crisis of capitalism the Clinton administration signed the repeal of the Banking Act. Repealing the Banking Act, which limited the percent of overall deposits banks are required to hold as an insurance reserve, would free up more capital for investment. In other words, this example of deregulation increased the pool of capital banks would have to lend out and, in theory, stimulate the economy. Additional counter-acting measures designed to increase the profitability of capitalism were also mobilized, such as suppressing wage increases. Consequently, as productivity or the efficiency of production increased, wages flatlined. These measures would further the wealth gap between the capitalist-class and working-class.

Paradoxically, ballooning wealth at the top and immiseration at the bottom degrades profit returns thereby disincentivizing capitalists from investing and producing jobs perpetuating a system of not only inequality but it also destroys the very basis for capitalists to produce. This is one of the deepening or intensifying contradictions of capital: the process of wealth accumulation is also self-negating. With the undoing of New Deal policies, the inequality that led to the Great Depression reemerged. The 2008 housing market crash reflects this tendency. Growing poverty and the lowering of wages erodes workers ability to consume the products produced further intensifying the crisis in realization.

Economically, this era has been called neoliberalism. Situating neoliberalism within this context Malott and Ford (2015) argue, "that neoliberalism is part of a global class strategy and not merely a class strategy within capitalism" (8). Neoliberalism, in other words, is part of the larger counter-revolutionary strategy of the unipolar era. While popular conceptions of neoliberalism tend not to connect it to capital's global class strategy, Ford (2015) argues that it "is not so much about capital *accumulation* as it is about *class power*—a class strategy *within* capitalism" (99).

The thesis is that the US working-class, in the post-Second World War era, through union militancy, had been able to reduce the rate of exploitation (i.e. increase wages and benefits) to such an extent that the capitalist-class felt less than secure in their position. Neoliberalism, therefore, is about shifting the balance of power back to capital and away from labor.

In practice, neoliberalism has shifted the balance of power from labor to capital within imperialist countries, such as the United States, by bringing everything in the public sphere into the private sphere, "under the rule and logic of the market" (98). The role of the state has been fundamental here in facilitating the construction of new markets in publicly funded institutions such as education (Ford 2015, 2017). New markets in education have been created, for example, by deregulating how public education tax dollars can be spent paving the way for the charter school movement (Tell 2016). This can be described as counter-revolutionary because it is the mechanism through which resources for educating the *many* are being redirected to charter school corporations and accumulated as profit rather than spent on education. As we will see below, this process has been legitimated by inventing a crisis in education.

The US capitalist-class's neoliberal assault on the working-class within its own borders is part of the same offensive as its imperialist assault on socialist and independent states. Ford (2015) concludes that "the neoliberal war on US public education" is "one facet in a broader neoliberal war against the public everywhere. We can then see that a victory for neoliberal imperialism" abroad "is a defeat for the movement against neoliberalism in the US" (107).

Critical Role of Education

In the world of education, the final chapter of Cold War concessions was the Carter administration successfully creating a federal Department of Education for the first time since Reconstruction. The beginning of the neoliberal era in education, for Ford, is symbolized by Reagan's National Commission on Excellence in Education 1983 report *A Nation at Risk*. What follows is a brief review of the three most significant examples of neoliberalism in education in the unipolar era: Ronald Reagan's *A Nation at Risk*; George W. Bush's *No Child Left Behind* (NCLB); and Barack Obama's *Race to the Top* (RTTT).

A Nation at Risk

According to Ford (2015) *A Nation at Risk* 'in many ways inaugurated the winding path of neoliberal education reform that is currently treading us today' (96). Rather than waging a war on poverty, *A Nation at Risk* represents the conservative, neoliberal war on the poor. Mobilizing Cold War rhetoric, the White House and the Secretary of the Department of Education, Terrel Bell, in unprecedented fashion, blamed teachers and education for the economic recession of the 1970s (Ford 2017). The report claims the United States was falling behind its global competitors in education and technological innovation to such an extent that if it had been the result of an external imposition, it would have been considered an act of war. Rather, the report claimed the assumed mediocrity was self-imposed.

The report claimed that the average scores on standardized tests were lower than they were twenty-six years before when the Soviet Union launched Sputnik. However, nothing was said about the changing composition of college and university's student body in the intervening years. For example, it was not mentioned that the most privileged white male student scores on tests like the SAT had not declined. The report also did not mention that Civil Rights-era educational reforms had begun opening the doors of higher education to previously excluded oppressed communities. Scores of these groups were actually increasing. Educational initiatives were in fact making progress toward eliminating the achievement gap.

However, when the scores of the traditionally excluded and the traditionally privileged were lumped together, the result could be manipulated to make it appear that scores were declining. In other words, when test takers were broken down by subgroup, examining men, women, whites, Latinas/os, African Americans, Native Americans, and working-class students separately, it was revealed that scores were improving slightly over time. Seven years later a nearly identical study was conducted that found that student test scores, even when subgroups were lumped together, were in fact increasing. But such studies received little attention in the national spotlight (Berliner & Biddle 1995; Oaks & Lipton 1999).

Nevertheless, conservative counter-revolutionaries needed a scapegoat to justify their attack on progressive, Civil Rights-era reforms. The mountain of evidence regarding educational attainment was therefore "deliberately ignored, distorted, and suppressed" (Oaks & Lipton 1999: 24). Again, data demonstrated that schools were doing surprisingly well given the growing economic crisis and escalating poverty (Berliner & Biddle 1996). Summarizing the logic of the reactionary orientation of the Reagan administration Oaks and Lipton (1999) note,

> Their conclusion, however illogical, was that school reforms that focused on educational equity were largely to blame for both the achievement decline and for the faltering economy ... Schools were told that their poor students and students of color must do better, but programs designed to help them do that were cut back. Efforts to equalize money and resources between rich and poor schools were vigorously fought by wealthy communities.
>
> (24)

In addition, by the 1980s the number of Americans with high school diplomas had increased dramatically and US students led the world in academic achievement. These developments could have been celebrated as a huge success of the war on poverty-era reforms. However, the conservative counter-revolution, led by Reagan, was more interested in ending progressive education policies and redistributing educational resources to the elite. Remember, this was the era of mass incarceration and the war on the poor. Rather than continue to support what we could call the school to job pipeline, the school to prison pipeline emerged characterized by the criminalization of Black, Brown, and working-class youth and more punitive disciplinary measures that contributed to increasing push-out (i.e. drop out) rates.

The false message or lie the phrase *a nation at risk* was intended to convey was that underserving, criminal minorities and immigrants were taking the jobs and resources that belonged to hard-working whites. It was a message designed to decimate the working-class unity that had been built during the Civil Rights era. Creating a scapegoat that diverted attention from the capitalist-driven automation revolution as the real cause of growing joblessness and poverty while simultaneously sowing divisiveness within the working-class served the ruling-class well.

Even though *A Nation at Risk* was a report and not a policy, and therefore did not require "any particular actions to be taken," it has been "tremendously influential in delimiting the discursive field regarding education's purposes and goals" (Ford 2017: 38). For example, beyond influencing even some progressive educator's orientations, Ford notes that both Bush's *No Child Left Behind* and Obama's *Race to the Top* "follow from the framing provided by *A Nation at Risk*" (39).

No Child Left Behind

If *A Nation at Risk* signaled the beginning of the neoliberal era in education at the level of discourse, then the *No Child Left Behind Act* (NCLB) of 2001, which was a revised and reauthorized reversion of the *Elementary and Secondary Education Act* of 1965, represented the beginning of the neoliberal era in full-fledged practice. That is, it was the specific formula and approach of NCLB that successfully opened the door to begin privatizing public education. Privatization as contributed to both re-segregating education and making educational tax dollars available as a new source of wealth for the education industry. Previous administrations, such as the Clinton administration, attempted to implement neoliberal reforms through an undisguised voucher system, for example, but it never really caught on.

The idea behind vouchers is that students and their caregivers, as consumers, should be able to take their education tax dollars to the education market place where schools, as vendors, compete with each other for customers. The logic, which has since proven faulty, is that competition would force merchants (i.e. schools) to improve their products to attract customers and schools offering substandard products would go out of business. This idea never gained currency among working people in the United States who were not so quick to abandon the common schooling ideal. For example, David Hursh (2015), citing public opinion polls, reports that in the early twenty-first century, "77% of the public felt that placing education policy decision making in the hands of business and political leaders, effectively ignoring teachers … was exactly the wrong approach" (4).

NCLB advanced this wrong approach by employing a clever title, that, at face value, no caregiver or parent would reject. Educator and activist George Wood (2004a) elaborates on how the name of the policy extended the gap between the object (i.e. NCLB) and the idea of it:

> Who could object to a law that promises no child left behind when it comes to our schools? After all, isn't this the great promise of our public school system—

that all children, regardless of race, socioeconomic status, gender, creed, color, or disability will have equal access to an education that allows them to enjoy the freedoms and exercise the responsibilities of citizenship in our democracy?

(vii)

Indeed, leaving no children behind in educational improvement sounds great. But beyond the title NCLB was pure neoliberalism. Picking up where *A Nation at Risk* left off NCLB takes up the false assumption that there is a crisis in public education caused by a lack of teacher accountability due to the unjust protection offered by powerful teacher unions. NCLB's solution to this manufactured crisis was to increase the stakes for standardized tests. That is, every school in the country would be expected to achieve 100 percent proficiency by 2014. Every school would be tested in basic skills. If every student in every subgroup did not test at grade level, the school would be designated needs improvement and annual test score goals would be set called Adequate Yearly Progress (AYP). If AYP goals continued to not be met, schools would be designated failing (Darling-Hammond 2004).

Sanctions for missing AYP targets included notifying students' caregivers of the school's label. Failing schools would also be expected to cover the costs of transferring students to other schools. Another penalty was the loss of school funding and handing the control of schools over to private management corporations. Critics have charged NCLB as being nothing more than a "backdoor maneuver" (Kohn 2004: 84) allowing private for-profits to take over public education—paving the way for *market reform*. Supporting this claim Darling-Hammond (2004) notes that "it is impossible to attain 100 percent proficiency levels for students on norm-referenced tests (when 50 percent of students by definition must score below the norm)" (9). Since it is clear that NCLB was not really about improving education, but setting schools up to fail to create a justification for privatization, it is not surprising that the results have tended to be devastating.

When private management companies take over public schools and the public education tax dollars the schools receive, they tend to immediately implement cost-cutting reforms. For example, a common practice is to lay off the teaching and administrative staff and only hire back the teachers and administrators with the fewest years of service because they are at the bottom of the pay scale. By reducing the cost of labor with the goal of having some of the education tax dollars left at the end of the year to be accumulated as profit rather than spent on education, the private management company excludes valuable knowledge held by the most experienced staff. Summarizing what NCLB has done to the practice of education at the level of teaching, George Wood (2004b) notes:

> Teachers across the map complain that the joy is being drained from teaching as their work is reduced to passing out worksheets and drilling children as if they were in dog obedience school. Elementary 'test prep' classroom methods involve teachers snapping their fingers at children to get responses, following scripted lessons where they simply recite prompts for students or have children read nonsense books, devoid of plot or meaning ... good literature and meaningful stories are being banished from classrooms around the country. Who would have thought we would long for the days of Dick and Jane? At the high school level teachers race to cover mountains of content, hoping their charges will memorize the right terms for true/false or multiple-choice exams ... What this has meant for curriculum and the school day is that test preparation crowds out much else.
> (39–42)

Driving the point home even further that NCLB was a destructive force Alfie Kohn (2004) reminds his readers that it is false to assume that higher test scores should automatically be equated with educational improvement when, in fact, they "may even indicate the opposite" (p. 85). Indeed, Kohn notes that rather than leaving no children behind, NCLB did much more to ensure all of the children of the many would be left behind by intensifying segregation based on ethnicity, ability, and age while simultaneously criminalizing so-called misbehavior. That is, teachers, faced with losing their jobs if their students test scores decline, have turned more and more to the practice of removing so-called bad kids rather than addressing their needs.

NCLB therefore only enhanced an already white supremacist system that suspends students of color at twice the rate as white students for the same infractions. With NCLB-related budget cuts reducing school-based mental-health services, the presence of police in schools has increased accordingly. Black girls in particular are targeted at even higher rates comprising just "16 percent of the female student population in public schools ... but more than one-third of all female school-based arrests" (Stoltzfus 2018: 251). It is clear that NCLB, as a neoliberal policy, is part of the capitalist-class offensive against the working-class. Given this stark reality, the name *No Child Left Behind* represents the cruelest of deceptions. As we will see below Obama's education agenda represents not only a continuation of neoliberalism, but an intensification "by requiring more standardized testing, increasing the role of the tests in teacher accountability, and promoting more charter schools" (Hursh 2015: 3). The Obama deception, which we will now turn to, was particularly cynical (Ahlquist 2015; Berlak & Madeloni

2015; Carlson 2015; Carr & Porfilio 2015; Christianakis & Mora 2015; Garrison 2015; Hoover 2015; Hursh 2015; Lea 2015; Montaña 2015; Sleeter 2015).

Race to the Top

Barack Obama, marketed as the *change* and *hope* candidate offering a *real* alternative to *the status quo in Washington* and the hated George W. Bush, became the United States' first Black president in 2008. Coming out of Bush's imperialist wars, such as the war in Iraq, and NCLB, progressives were excited about Obama's promises of transformation. Progressive educator's hopes were not unfounded. While campaigning Obama sought out education professor and staunch critic of NCLB Linda Darling-Hammond as his education advisor. This was a good sign. Appealing to the mood of the many on the campaign trail, Obama even promised to phase out NCLB-related high stakes testing acknowledging the harm of an education system focused on filling in bubbles. At the same time, Obama conceded that the goal of NCLB was correct. Speaking directly to teachers and teacher educators Obama "proposed improving the teaching profession by upgrading teacher education, developing mentoring programs, rewarding teachers through career ladders rather than individual bonuses, and engaging with teacher educators" (Hursh 2015: 5). Saying all the right things on the campaign trail educators had good reason to be hopeful that Darling-Hammond would be chosen as secretary of education if Obama was elected.

However, Obama not only faithfully held the imperialist line in terms of foreign policy, but also held the neoliberal line in the realm of education reform. The sobering truth would begin to emerge when Obama turned to Arne Duncan as his first Secretary of Education. Duncan became notorious for supporting Bush's *No Child Left Behind Act* while CEO of Education in the incorporated city of Chicago. Before joining Obama in Washington Duncan was known for laying off teachers, increasing class size, enforcing external curriculum standards, and contributing to the increasing alienation of students and teachers. Perhaps most significantly Duncan advanced the neoliberal agenda of privatization in Chicago by shuttering many public schools and replacing them with charter schools (Tell 2016). That is, responding to Duncan Chicago teachers protested: "he spent a lot of time using NCLB and test scores to close down quite a few public schools and turn them over to charters" (Malone & Sadovi 2008).

Duncan's record therefore made him the perfect henchman to spearhead Obama's RTTT program. At the heart of the program was replacing the traditional federal funding model under the Elementary and Secondary Education Act that allocated resources based on poverty rates with a naked system of competition. While it is true that RTTT provided a way for states to avoid the 2014 proficiency goal of NCLB, the alternative "would be far more odious" (Hursh 2015: 6). That is, for states to compete for an increasingly limited supply of education dollars, they would have to pass laws allowing for charter schools. For states that already permitted charter schools, they would have to remove any caps limiting the number of charters allowed. Whereas NCLB created a backdoor for deregulating how education tax dollars could be used, RTTT made privatization a requirement. In this way, RTTT is an intensified neoliberal approach to education policy. Rather than invent an accountability excuse to privatize public education, RTTT practically just deposited money that was supposed to be used for education straight into the bank accounts of private charter school companies.

In addition, state-granted NCLB waivers would be required to implement the Common Core State Standards funded by the Gates Foundation, which would increase standardized testing to determine where to inflict punishment. Making matters worse student test scores would become a large part of how teachers and administrators were evaluated. Given the fact that the number one predictor of student achievement is rate of poverty, coupled with the fact that the national poverty rate has been escalating throughout the neoliberal era, many teachers and teacher unions understood that educators working in the most oppressed and exploitation communities would be increasingly punished for a situation they have absolutely no control over. Again, if neoliberalism is a capitalist-class war on the working-class, RTTT fits the bill. Understanding this larger context, in 2012, the Chicago Teachers Union (CTU) went on strike. That is, the CTU not only struck over wages and working conditions, but took a stand for social justice issues. However, the CTU faced challenges stemming from the nature of the policy itself. Summarizing this situation retired educator and union activist Howard Ryan (2016) explains:

> [T]he problem is that even the most progressive teachers union locals that are trying to eliminate the use of test scores in teacher evaluations are usually hamstrung by state and federal policies. For example, the 2012 strike of the ... CTU was partially over this issue: the union opposed the use of any test scores in evaluating teachers. The problem was that state law required a minimum of 25 percent of teacher ratings to be based on test scores. This meant that CTU, forced to negotiate from a position of weakness, could only minimize the use of test scores, not eliminate it altogether.
>
> (144)

As we will see in Chapter 12, more and more teachers are creating alternative centers of progressive power within their unions called caucuses "in response to the failure of state and national teachers unions to aggressively organize against the corporate agenda" (141). In addition to the traditional salary demands progressive teacher caucuses are pushing their unions to fight for smaller "class size, wraparound student services, restorative justice, parent engagement, reducing counselor loads, and opposing high stakes testing" (141). This burgeoning teacher movement began as a response to *A Nation at Risk*.

The Resistance

Ira Shor (1986) locates the beginning of the counter-revolution embodied in *A Nation at Risk* in Richard Nixon's narrowly successful 1969 bid for the presidency. The revolutionary upheaval of the 1960s was so fundamentally all-encompassing that it included radical movements in education calling not just for progressive reforms, but for "the inevitable and imminent demise of public education in the face of a new" radical "consciousness spreading through society" (Shor 1986: 2).

The ruling-class moved quickly protecting their monopoly on state power. We already saw the escalation in the use of violence and other forms of state repression against the era's mass movements. In the field of education the Nixon team introduced *career education* with a curriculum emphasizing basic skills and work discipline. Coupled with this were elite reformers desperately pleading to go *back-to-the-basics* to combat an assumed crisis in literacy. By basics the reformers meant a Euro-centric curriculum, which functioned as a thinly veiled racist attack on multicultural education. By 1983 "a new crisis of 'mediocrity' was officially declared" in *A Nation at Risk,* and "a new war for excellence was launched" (Shor 1986: 4).

A Nation at Risk was a significant driving factor that led many educators to a new movement in education called *critical pedagogy*. Many teachers were outraged at what they understood to be the state using them as a scapegoat in their counter-revolution. Data, in fact, showed that schools were actually doing remarkably well given the difficult circumstances stemming from the crisis in capitalism's rising poverty rates (Berliner & Biddle 1995).

While Bowles and Gintis's (1976) *Schooling in Capitalist America* offered a Marxist analysis of the reproductive role of education in capitalist society, especially in times of crisis and upheaval, critics argued such work did not offer a viable educational alternative or a critical pedagogy. The claim was that social reproduction theories were guided by a pessimistic economic determinism leaving educators no room to conceptualize and enact a transformative education (Cho 2017). What was missing, the critics argued, was a pedagogy of possibility and hope capable of not only critiquing, but challenging, in practice, the reaction embodied within *A Nation at Risk*.

US educators found a concrete example to learn from in the Brazilian educator Paulo Freire. The English translation of Freire's (1970) *Pedagogy of the Oppressed* is largely regarded as critical pedagogy's most influential and formative text. Freire's influence on the North American critical pedagogy movement was so central that Ana Maria Araûjo Freire and Donaldo Macedo's (1998) Introduction to the *Paulo Freire Reader* takes the Reagan administration's attack on teachers as their place of departure. For example, Araûjo Freire and Macedo (1998) begin with the observation that "the Reagan era educational legacy can be best characterized by an unrelenting assault on schools and public school teachers" (1). Freire, it is implied, played a central role in teachers' pedagogical response.

Henry Giroux and Ira Shor were among the first US educators who would reach out to and build relationships with Freire. The name "critical pedagogy" was coined by Giroux (1983) in one of his early texts. Because Freire's approach included a focus on the development of critical consciousness, critical pedagogy has had a tendency to focus on individualized projects. With the emphasis on agency in the classroom the mainstream of critical pedagogy has operated at the individual level of micro-politics.

Critical pedagogy's most common active subject of change is the individual critically conscious teacher acting *for* the many rather than *with* the many. Despite the general absence of a collective, organized conception of critical pedagogical action within the mainstream, the vastness of the critical pedagogical movement has resulted in a progressive gravitational shift within the field of education. At the same time, the locus of change here is not systemic or revolutionary. Freire's *Pedagogy of the Oppressed*, however, conceptualizes educational change, not as a micro-level process but part of a larger, collective society-wide transformation.

Early critical pedagogies such as Ira Shor (1986) picked up on aspects of Freire's work that educators too often interpreted within an individual framework. For example, Shor (1986) highlights the following passage taken from a talk Freire gave in the United States in 1981, "there is always space for education to act. The question is to find out what are the limits of this space" (quoted in Shor 1986). The subject could be easily taken here to be an individual. Even so, Freire offered North American educators a pedagogy of hope and possibility for transformation in even the most restricted environments.

Freire's praxis of possibility would also find value and help give expression to collective movements. The Rethinking School collective is a case in point. Functioning as a collective organization of progressive classroom teachers Rethinking Schools publishes theoretically informed examples of teaching for social justice in the most restricted contexts. Rethinking Schools takes the same inspiration as Freire in their insistence on a theoretically rigorous and indeterminant creativity engaging the totality of systemic injustices in the pursuit of liberation.

As the concrete context of society is in a permanent state of development, Freire and the critical tradition have been engaged, extended, interpreted, and reinterpreted. Antonia Darder, Marta Baltodano, and Rodolfo Torres (2017) note that once *Pedagogy of the Oppressed* was translated into English in 1970 it "became a watershed for radical educators in schools, communities, and labor organizations, struggling to bring about social change to public health, welfare, and educational institutions across the country" (5).

Making a similar point the late Joe L. Kincheloe (2008) notes that "with Freire, the notion of critical pedagogy as we understand it today emerges" (69). Situating the significance of Freire within the international context of education Peter McLaren (2000) argues that he "was one of the first internationally recognized educational thinkers who fully appreciated the relationship among education, politics, imperialism, and liberation" (141).

Offering concrete examples of his revolutionary pedagogy Freire (1978/1998) has offered invaluable insights on transformation that go far beyond individualist approaches. For example, Freire (1978/1998) wrote *Pedagogy in Process: The Letters to Guinea-Bissau* about his participation in the transformation of the colonial education system in Portugal's African colony, Guinea-Bissau, after a successful national liberation struggle in 1975.

After the revolution Freire was invited as part of a team from the Institute for Cultural Action of the Department of Education within the World Council of Churches to Guinea-Bissau to assist the revolutionary government with their education program. Their task was to uproot the colonial residue that remained as a result of generations of colonial education designed to de-Africanize the people.

Freire's approach to education was firmly grounded in the insight that the gap between *what is* and what *can be*, and what the *can be* will look like, are unknown entities. In other words, Freire rejected predetermination and dogmatism. To prepare for their visit to Guinea-Bissau Freire and his team therefore did not construct lesson plans or programs to be imposed upon the people. Rather, they studied the work of Guinea-Bissau's revolutionary leaders, such as Amilcar Cabral, and learned as much as possible about the context.

Upon arrival they continued to listen and discuss learning from the people. Only by learning about the revolutionary government's education work could they assess it and make recommendations. What an education that can contribute to the process of decolonization/liberation will look like cannot be known outside of the concrete reality of the people and their struggle. It also cannot be constructed without the active participation of the learners as a collective.

This is the central component of Freire's dialectical approach and the reason why he was so adamantly opposed to what he called a banking model of education. A banking model of education with predetermined outcomes is the primary model of colonialist and capitalist schooling that seeks to dominate learners by turning them into passive objects.

Such insights were fundamental in critiquing the US model of education embodied within *A Nation at Risk*. Critical pedagogues in the United States therefore did not take the methods Freire co-developed either in his home country of Brazil or Guinea-Bissau and dogmatically apply them to the United States. Rather, the task was to understand the context in which *A Nation at Risk* articulated its assumptions and forge a critical pedagogy designed to challenge them.

The result was a critical pedagogy that refused to accept the assumptions that the Civil Rights-era progressive reforms put the United States as a whole *at risk*, or that there was a single US interest. In other words, in a racialized class society like the US progressive, anti-racist reforms shift the balance of forces to the many. In the context of progressive, Civil Rights-era reforms the only thing *at risk* is the ability of the white supremacist capitalist class from maintaining their dominance over the many.

Conclusion

Far from peace, the end of the Cold War signaled an intensified attack on all of the concessions reluctantly given up during the Civil Rights era. While neoliberalism continues to hold sway, a new counter-weight is emerging with its center of gravity located in China. The savageness of neoliberal capitalism has led to a renewed worldwide interest in socialism, including the United States. The trajectory of this context is explored in the next and final chapter.

12

An Emerging Counter-Force

Introduction: Connection to the Previous Chapter

In Chapter 11 we saw the effects of the move from the war on poverty to the war on the poor. In this final chapter we discuss the emergence of a new counterforce with its center of gravity in China.

After reviewing the assent of China and the imperialist response, we will turn to a discussion of the mega crisis of 2020 resulting from the converging of multiple crises: racist police terror and the public lynching of George Floyd at the hands of Derek Chauvin of the Minneapolis Police Department, the US governments' failure to adequately respond to Covid-19, unprecedented corporate bailouts in the face of mass unemployment and economic disintegration, and mass evictions as the government failed to cancel the rents and bailout the people.

Leading up to the mega crisis of 2020 was a wave of teacher strikes that began in 2018. Having already been mobilized we see teachers continue to fight for the safety of themselves and their students during the 2020 pandemic.

This final chapter is concluded with a survey of the uprising against racism that swept the United States and the world during the summer of 2020. A final assessment is then offered regarding the future direction of the global balance of forces.

Critical Role of Capitalism

After the death of Mao in 1976 Chinese policy shifted toward more capitalist-oriented approaches in a bid to access Western production technologies in an effort to speed up economic development and lift the vast peasantry out of poverty. Toward these ends China legalized and encouraged private property and the state monopoly on foreign investment was gradually relaxed. Consequently, the door was opened for Western capitalists and bankers to invest and produce in China (Becker 2012; Mills 2012).

These reforms allowed Western investors to overcome their own falling rates of profit by accumulating super profits in China. The recovery of the global economy after the 2007–8 housing market crash "had largely been based by 2013 on the rapid expansions in so-called 'emerging' markets" (Harvey 2014: 170). Despite this Western exploitation of Chinese labor, 800 million people in China have been lifted out of poverty. China even managed to maintain an unprecedented average annual growth rate of 10 percent for forty straight years. As a result, China now has the second largest economy in the world and is on the fast track to replace the United States as the dominant global economy.

China's success has transformed it into an increasingly powerful global counter-weight. Over-extended militarily in Iraq and the Middle East, the United States has been slow in its attempts at turning its energies east, which, in 2015, Obama called a pivot toward Asia. This pivot is designed to contain or slow down China's growth (Enfu & Xiaoqin 2017; Singh 2018).

Toward these ends the Trump administration announced 60 billion dollars of tariffs on Chinese imports in 2019. Trump claimed such measures were designed to equalize an unfair trade imbalance that favored China. However, beyond the public rhetoric it is clear that the real intention was to attempt to sabotage the growth and status of China's economy (Klare 2019). US Pacific Commander Admiral Harry Harris went so far as telling Congress in February of 2018 that the United States must prepare for war with China (Singh 2018). In August 2020 the Trump administration escalated their rhetoric even further calling for outright regime change in China.

So determined to undermine what is clearly an ascending China the United States responded to the Coronavirus (i.e. Covid-19) pandemic with anti-Chinese attacks. After the first reported Covid-19 death on February 29, 2020, the US government did nothing in preparation to contain the virus. Even after making the Covid-19 genome available to the global scientific community on January 10th, Secretary of State Mike Pompeo continued to falsely claim that China had hidden vital information.

Trump and his administration also used anti-Chinese racism to characterize the virus calling it the "Chinese virus" resulting in an escalation in anti-Asian racism and hate crimes in the United States. Before in-person schooling was shut down stories proliferated of high school students attacking classmates accusing them of being infected and college students posting anti-Asian tweets about dropping classes with Asian students.

Mega Crisis of 2020

Not only have many economists and social scientists described the economic crisis of 2020 as deeper than the Great Depression of the 1930s, but some such as Richard Wolff (2020) have characterized it as so severe that it likely represents a moment in the process of the irreversible disintegration of US capitalism. If the fascistic repeal of civil liberties is reflective of a desperate capitalist class attempting to hold on to state power, then the police repression of the protests against racism that erupted during the summer of 2020 represents such a turn.

The conditions for the mega crisis that erupted during the summer of 2020 were laid during the neoliberal decades during and following the Reagan administration. The inequality between the capitalist-class and the working-class, for example, has been deepening for decades.

The privatization and subsequent hollowing out of institutions have rendered them unable to deal with the stresses put on the system. The privatization of the health care system is a prime example. The Coronavirus pandemic is therefore one of the stresses put on the system that institutions cannot handle.

Even before the US economy began to shut down in mid-March Congress prepared to bail out mega banks and large corporations with trillions of no strings attached, no questions asked dollars. When the stock market began to plummet mid-summer trillions more were injected.

While the money to bail out the banks has been bottomless, calls to bail out the people have been met with cries of financial distress. Rather than allocate resources and formulate a plan to mitigate the spread of Covid-19, Trump downplayed its seriousness until March 11th. While publicly downplaying the severity of Covid-19, privately, Trump acknowledged its danger. In a number of interviews in early February and March of 2020 with *Washington Post* journalist Bob Woodward, Trump admitted how deadly and contagious the virus was (Smolarek 2020).

Still, the president refused to put people before profits rejecting calls to fully mobilize the Defense Production Act to compel relevant corporations to mass produce testing kits, ventilators, and personal protection equipment (PPE) at cost. Consequently, widespread testing was not implemented and without this vital information needed for contact tracing, the virus spread wildly.

Washington also failed to provide 100 percent unemployment insurance or the cancellation of rents and mortgages. As a result, the virus continued to be transmitted as millions of already impoverished sick workers kept going to their jobs as an economic necessity.

Given the racialized stratification of the labor force it is no wonder that Black and Brown workers, who disproportionately do essential labor from driving busses to collecting garbage, account for a disproportionate number of Covid-19 deaths.

As a result of the criminal neglect of the Trump administration, the United States became the global epicenter with 4 percent of the world's population but 25 percent of Covid-19 deaths. With tens of millions of people having lost their jobs and therefore facing evictions and uncertainty, and with corporate profits nevertheless surging from government bailouts, the public execution of George Floyd on May 25th by the Minneapolis Police Department proved to be the trigger that would spark an unprecedented nationwide uprising against racism.

The fact that racist police terror would continue even in the midst of a pandemic and society-wide lockdown was a reality too obvious to ignore. George Floyd was one of many victims of racist police terrorism during Covid-19. Not only did the police continue murdering, but they also unleashed their tear gas, pepper spray, rubber bullet, baton-wielding violence on protesters (i.e. the millions of people of all backgrounds taking to the streets demanding justice for all of the victims of racist police terror).

By July the call to defund the police had developed into a mainstream demand. It had become far too obvious that it made little sense that roughly 40 percent of many city budgets funded racist police departments that contributed nothing to decreasing so-called crime and creating safe and sustainable communities. Rather than funding terror people all over the country began to demand that those resources be used for housing, education, and health care.

Just as the police killings continued, so did the protests. On August 23rd the Kenosha, Wisconsin, police shot a young African American man, Jacob Blake, seven times in the back for walking away from them. As a result, Blake's spinal cord was severed leaving him paralyzed from the waist down. On the second day of the angry protests in Kenosha a right-wing militia group seen collaborating with the police gathered to supposedly protect private property from the protesters' indignation.

In the course of events one of the racist counter-protesters, seventeen-year-old Kyle Rittenhouse, shot and killed two Black Lives Matter protesters and injured a third. With the barrel of his assault rifle undoubtedly still hot the police let a surrendering Rittenhouse walk right past them. What is more, the crowd, addressing the police as they let Rittenhouse stroll past them, loudly and persistently identified him as the shooter. Without even questioning him the police told Rittenhouse to go home.

By the end of the summer of 2020 banks had prepared for the looming fallout by enacting a nearly complete moratorium on loans. The objective was to stockpile cash for the massive wave of foreclosures, bankruptcies, and defaults on student loans, credit cards, and car payments they knew were coming. Even during the pandemic when the poor became poorer, the wealth concentrated at the top increased by more than 500 billion dollars.

Critical Role of Education

With the Trump administration came the nomination and then confirmation of Betsy Devos, arguably by far the most incompetent Secretary of the Department of Education since its establishment under the Carter administration in 1972. So close was Devos' confirmation that the vice president, unprecedented in US history, had to intervene with the deciding vote.

Trump's selection of incompetence was certainly no accident. Devos represents the billionaire class's desire to abolish the Department of Education and privatize public education. From this point of view, Devos is well qualified given her record of privatizing public education in her home state of Michigan, one of the few states that allow for openly for-profit charter schools.

In response to public schools moving to an online format during the pandemic Devos argued that "American investment in education is a promise to students and their families. If schools aren't going to reopen and not fulfill that promise, they shouldn't get the funds, and give it to the families to decide to go to a school that is going to meet that promise" (Richardson 2020). Devos's use of the Coronavirus pandemic to opportunistically advance the agenda to privatize public education should come as no surprise.

The Resistance

In the two years preceding the Coronavirus pandemic of 2020 US school teachers had engaged in a nation-wide wave of strikes. This wave of strikes offered teachers vital experience to draw from rendering them well positioned to organize against unsafe school reopening plans. Before discussing the resistance to unsafe plans to reopen schools, the teacher strikes beginning in 2018 and their larger context are briefly discussed.

The Supreme Court Delivers a Blow to Unions

On June 27, 2018, in *Janus v. AFSCME* the Supreme Court of the United States, in a 5-4 decision, dealt a blow to organized labor overturning *Abood v. Detroit Board of Education* (1977) effectively rendering the public sector throughout the whole country right to work.

In *Abood* the Supreme Court ruled that public-sector unions may collect agency or fair share fees from non-members to pay their fair share of the costs associated with *collective bargaining, contract administration, and grievance adjustments*. *Abood* was a partial correction of the 1947 Taft-Hartley Act that required unionized shops to represent all workers even if they were not union members thereby providing a legal mechanism for bankrupting unions by encouraging freeloaders.

In *Janus v. AFSCME* the court ruled in favor of AFSCME union member Mark Janus's claim that compulsory agency fees violate his first amendment rights. Agency fees typically account for roughly 80 percent of union dues. Only political action funds can be spent on political speech to support pro-labor politicians, which are separate from membership dues and are contributed on a purely volunteer basis. Nevertheless, the position Janus represented was that unions in and of themselves are political in nature rendering the purely mechanical agency fees also political.

Part of the irony in the first amendment argument is that there is no free speech or democracy in the workplace. Historically, unions have been the mechanism through which workers have fought for a collective voice challenging the anti-democratic nature of capitalism. Despite the clear distinction between compulsory dues for services all employees benefit from and non-compulsory donations for political speech, SCOTUS ruled that:

> "The State's extraction of agency fees from nonconsenting public-sector employees violates the First Amendment. *Abood* erred in concluding otherwise, and *stare decisis* cannot support it. *Abood* is therefore overruled."
>
> Mark Janus does not represent a grassroots movement of workers fighting back against the so-called tyranny of unions. Mark Janus was nothing more than a patsy for the anti-union lobby groups, such as the Center for Individual Rights and the National Right to Work Legal Defense Foundation, that have put millions of dollars toward undermining unions.

Teachers Go on Strike

Immediately following the Janus decision, in cities across the United States, teachers, students, and workers took to the streets rallying and demonstrating against the *Janus* decision demanding it be overturned and committing themselves to fighting back.

On February 23, 2018, four months before the *Janus* ruling was released, teachers in West Virginia set off what would develop into a nation-wide wave of teacher union strikes. Following West Virginia, teachers in Arizona, Oklahoma, Colorado, North Carolina, Kentucky, California, and Massachusetts either went on strike or staged massive rallies for more education funding and better working and learning conditions. The fact that these strikes and actions occurred in states already right to work, many of whom also have laws making it illegal for public sector employees to strike, provided valuable lessons for the struggle ahead (Wilcox 2018). In this sense, West Virginia teachers stepped up as the country's teachers demonstrating that a more militant approach to union activism would be necessary in the *Janus* era.

One of the things that made the West Virginia strike unique was that it was a wildcat strike. That is, it was a teacher-led strike that went against their own union leadership who had reached a tentative agreement with West Virginia Governor Justice. In the original agreement the union signed off on a 2 percent pay raise and increases in health insurance costs. Being forced to work multiple extra jobs just to make ends meet, West Virginia teachers could not accept what their union signed off on and began organizing amongst themselves through social media county by county until a majority of teachers throughout the whole state decided to reject their union leadership's contract and went on strike anyway. It was not only courageous, but from the teachers' point of view, it was necessary. A 2 percent raise would not change the concrete conditions of their lives. To live they had to take more militant actions and go on strike. What is more, for years the standard length of time for teachers' strikes had been two to three days. That is, short symbolic strikes where teachers were allowed to blow off some steam before going back to work without much in the way of gains had been the norm. West Virginia teachers broke that mold staying on strike for nearly three weeks (Martin 2018; West 2018).

Less than a month after West Virginia teachers' wildcat strike, Oklahoma teachers, working in another right-to-work (for less) state, were able to strike on April 2nd against an uncompromising management without calling a wildcat. Choosing to follow the new, successful precedent set by West Virginia teachers,

Oklahoma teachers rallied under the slogan, "as long as it takes." Consequently, Oklahoma teachers stayed out on the pick-line strike for nearly two weeks from April 2nd to April 12th. Like striking teachers across the United States, Oklahoma teachers struck over low pay, over-crowded classrooms, and education budget cuts leading to dramatically reduced per-pupil appropriations.

Following the Oklahoma work action teachers in Arizona walked out on strike from April 26th to May 3rd when Governor Doug Ducy finally agreed to extend his wage increase offer to staff. That is, demonstrating classic union solidarity teachers refused to accept a deal that did not also include a substantial pay raise for support staff. Roughly 20,000 teachers in Arizona protested against stagnating wages and seemingly endless cuts to school funding. The Arizona strike coincided with a similar action in Colorado that began April 27th and lasted two and a half weeks ending May 12th. Again, teachers struck over low pay, cuts to education spending, and the mismanagement of pension funds.

The next major teacher action came early in 2019 in Los Angeles after months of tense, nationally covered build-up. From January 14th to 22nd, 33,000 teachers, nurses, counselors, librarians, and other staff in Los Angeles, the second largest school district in the country, went on strike. Organized under the United Teachers of Los Angeles (UTLA) the union was fighting against the Los Angeles Unified School District's Superintendent and former investment banker Austin Beutner's plans to break up and privatize the system. It was reported that Beutner intended to apply the "portfolio" model, which entails breaking up large districts into dozens of smaller ones, which was used by Corey Booker when he was the mayor of Newark, New Jersey, enabling him to privatize more than a third of the city's public schools (Feldman 2019).

So outraged by these privatization schemes in September of 2018 LA teachers voted to authorize their union to call a strike. By December teachers had firmly rejected what could have been a tempting 6 percent pay increase and no reductions in health care benefits and demanded, instead, for improved learning conditions such as smaller classes and more librarians, nurses, and counselors. In addition, the UTLA demanded a moratorium on the creation of more charter schools as well as an increase in per-pupil education funding.

Following Los Angeles teachers in Oakland, California went on strike between February 21st and March 4th. Confronted with the same deteriorating conditions teachers across the United States are faced with, Oakland teachers struck for higher wages, more education funding for students, and an end to the trend toward greater and greater privatization utilizing the charter school mechanism. Demanding a 12 percent salary increase Oakland teachers won an astonishing 11 percent increase. Teachers also won slight reductions in class size and caseloads for counselors, resource specialists, psychiatrists, and speech therapists (Hrizi 2019). Like the improvements in teaching conditions and learning conditions won by striking teachers across the United States, the concessions won by Oakland teachers reaffirm the effectiveness of the strike. Teachers are also demonstrating, in the post-Fair Share era, that their unions are by far the most effective vehicle they have to fight for their students' learning needs.

On March 9, 2019, the Indiana State Teachers Association brought thousands of teachers and education workers to the state capital in Indianapolis, following the national trend, to rally for a higher wages and a larger state appropriation for student resources (Ford 2019). Building off the militant energy of the nationwide wave of strikes Ford reported that the rally's chants focused on the theme of fighting back and doing whatever it takes.

Similarly, on March 20th more than 600 teachers, staff workers, students, and community members rallied at the Bruce C. Bolling Municipal Building, headquarters of Boston Public Schools. In addition to rallying for a fair contract since the Boston Teachers Union (BTU) has been without a contract for nearly a year, the crowd demanded that the city remediate the high levels of lead in many of the school's drinking water. The BTU's president, Jessica Tang, stressed the connections between teaching and learning conditions demanding higher wages, larger appropriations for education funding, and more staff essential for meeting student needs such as counselors and social workers. Student activists also pointed out that Boston is the only district in Massachusetts where every school does not have a full-time nurse. Finally, teachers directly addressed the Janus decision noting that it has made it necessary for teacher unions to adopt an organizing model of unionism pointing to the wave of strikes since West Virginia as evidence for its effectiveness (Rothmel 2019).

Another significant development in the *Janus* era is that the recently organized charter school teachers have begun to go on strike. This is significant because one of the attractions of privatizing public education is that it has been a method of undermining teacher unions. That is, when the management of a public school gets handed over to a private management company, it tends to leave the district leaving the newly chartered school without a union. Eventually, charter school teachers began organizing.

The first charter school strike occurred in Chicago and lasted for four teaching days beginning on Tuesday December 4, 2018. Teachers were back in the classroom Monday December 10th. Teachers demanded a shorter school year, a larger salary and yearly wage increase to better reflect rising housing costs, more funding for teaching materials, and an official sanctuary school status for students and their care givers to foster a safer learning environment. Unlike public schools proper, charter schools, which operate under more deregulated mandates for using public education funds, can deny ICE agents access to school grounds without a warrant or subpoena.

Teachers Take a Stand during Covid-19

Riding the wave of these strikes teachers sprang into action after the CDC lowered their safety guidelines for reopening schools on July 24, 2020. Teachers were quick to point out that urging in-person returns to school downplayed the dangers Covid-19 continued to pose to students, teachers, and the community. The progressive teacher group *Reds in Ed* (2020) pointed out that reopening plans stressed the benefits to the economy but offered virtually no scientific proof that such plans were safe.

Advocating for their students *Reds in Ed* noted that 76 percent of parents of color believed that schools should open later rather than sooner as protection against Covid-19. This comes as no surprise since African American Covid-19 deaths are three times higher than whites. It was painfully obvious that the state was far too willing to sacrifice African American and Latina/o lives, disproportionally represented among essential workers, for profit.

Undeterred, teachers and their unions fought back in defense of their own and their students' safety. In Florida, for example, teachers organized many demonstrations protesting against reopening schools before it was safe. The Florida Education Association even sued the state for neglecting to put safety first in regards to their reopening plans. Teacher unions in Arizona, California, and New York, for example, issued statements against reopening in-person schooling without proper safety guidelines in place. On July 28, 2020, the National Education Association even published a statement saying that they would support their members who struck over workplace safety issues (*Reds in Ed* 2020).

Facing looming unsafe reopening plans teachers in NYC mobilized on August 3, 2020, marching from the UFT headquarters to the Department of Education ending at the Federal Building at Foley Square where they rallied. Situating working-class consciousness at the center of analysis, many speakers connected the struggle over reopening schools and properly funding public education, especially in African American and Latina/o communities, to defunding the police (Salem 2020).

Speakers argued that reopening schools before it is safe because it benefits the economy only tells part of the story. That is, many noted that it benefits the billionaire class while sacrificing the health and safety of African American and Latina/o working people especially. Rather than enacting 100 percent unemployment insurance so all workers can shelter in place, thereby eliminating the pressure to send children back to in-person school before it is safe, the state, once again, pursued a path that traded the lives of the working-class for the sake of profit (Salem 2020). NYC teacher Karla Reyes argued that "teachers are playing a key role in exposing the real enemy and the shortcomings of this government. Teachers are making an active choice to fight for what we all deserve, which is the right to live" (Salem 2020).

After some states resumed in-person instruction in the spring of 2020, teachers in at least five of those states contracted and died from Covid-19 (Kenific 2020). Of course, "the loss of a teacher in any community constitutes a traumatizing experience; the death of a beloved teacher forced to work in unsafe conditions compounds the tragedy" (Kenific 2020). Teachers have therefore continued to struggle against a white supremacist capitalist system that puts profits before the lives of teachers, students, and their communities.

It is clear that unions are the most important mechanism that pools teacher power enabling them to fight back against the bourgeois state. That is, four of the five states where there was a returning teacher who died from Covid-19 had right-to-work legislation in place before the *Janus* ruling resulting in smaller, weaker unions. Proportionally larger, stronger unions are more able to defend the fights of their members and students they serve. The Syracuse Teachers Association in upstate New York, for example, successfully lobbied to delay unsafe reopening plans (Kenific 2020).

Abolitionist Teaching

As the movement for Black lives continues to gain momentum more and more works that can be considered to be a part of the critical pedagogical tradition are moving away from the individual subject and toward the collective. Betina Love's (2019) text on abolitionist teaching frames the possibility within the pedagogical as the struggle to matter. Love gives special attention to the collective struggle that has historically taken to the streets shutting down society fighting for the movement to matter by demanding housing rights, economic justice, universal health care, etc.

Rather than conceptualizing educational justice as the pursuit of individual teachers Love (2019) notes that it is going to take "people power" and "radical collective freedom-building" (9). Mobilizing movement language and invoking the spirit of the rally Love (2019) proclaims that "we must struggle together not only to reimagine schools but to build new schools that we are taught to believe are impossible" (11). Directly answering the question of what abolitionist teaching might look like in practice Love (2019) describes it as "teachers working with community groups in solidarity to address issues impacting their students and their students' communities" (11).

More specifically Love (2019) imagines teachers and "local and national activists" "reimagining and rewriting curriculums" "to provide students with not only examples of resistance but also strategies of resistance" (11). In addition to joining the movement for immigrant rights Love (2019) describes abolitionist teaching as "refusing to take part in zero-tolerance policies and the school-to-prison pipeline" (11). In addition to many other characteristics Love (2019) argues abolitionist educators:

> [M]ust embrace theories such as critical race theory, settler colonialism, Black feminism, dis/ability, critical race studies, and other critical theories that have the ability to interrogate anti-Blackness and frame experiences with injustice, focusing the moral compass toward a North star that is ready for a long and dissenting fight for educational justice. These theories additionally help in understanding that educational justice can happen through a simultaneous fight for economic justice, racial justice, housing justice, environmental justice, religious justice, queer justice, trans justice citizenship justice, and disability justice.
>
> (12)

The spirit of revolutionary love guiding the Black radical tradition is on full display in Love's conceptualizations of abolitionist teaching. With Love perhaps we are seeing a return to the revolutionary vision of radical educators in the 1960s highlighted by Shor (1986). Perhaps the upheaval that began during the summer of 2020 has already made unprecedented progress toward the negation of the negation in North America.

Conclusion

From setting their economic and military sights on the new counter-weight led, globally, by Chinese state power to attacking collective bargaining rights through

Janus, US imperialism, out of desperation, has intensified its war on its opposing interests globally and domestically. The re-emerging socialist movement and the mega crisis of 2020 has rendered US imperialist capitalism less likely to regain its former dominance.

Nevertheless, if the US state department and multinational corporations gain an upper hand against China, however unlikely, their acquired power would strengthen their hand domestically. At the same time, if the *Janus* outcome successfully reduces the power of labor unions, thereby increasing the power of the capitalist-class, in general, their relative strength and ability to challenge China will be intensified. Again, the mega crisis of 2020 and the nationwide uprising against racism have weakened the hand of capital. It is therefore not surprising that another counter-revolution led, in part, by far-right, white supremacist terror groups, usually with the full support of the repressive state, has emerged to beat back the movements of the many.

Within this context teachers and workers are pushing back refusing to be intimidated by the forces of reaction. As the socialist movement for Black lives grows, pulling in people who had never participated in a mass movement before, the horizon of a new system beyond racialized capitalism comes ever closer.

Conclusion: The Dialectics of History

Throughout this book we have seen a complex dialectical struggle between a balance of forces. On one hand we have seen various centers of European and settler ruling-class power in competition with each other. Intertwined with the other hand we have seen a vast and diverse working and oppressed class emerge in North America pushing and pulling in struggle with this developing capitalist and enslaving class. In other words we have seen the quantitative development of essential contradictions within capitalism moving toward an unknown negation of the negation.

More specifically, we saw the struggle between European powers for control over the American colonies as slavery was their primary model of economic development until the mid-nineteenth century. As part of this contest we saw the struggle not only between competing enslavers, but between the enslaved and those enslavers. We saw the use of an education policy designed to force the enslaved into a position of illiteracy and disempowerment. At the same time we saw the enslaved resist disempowerment and oppression.

We saw 1776 as a counter-revolution against rebelling enslaved Africans designed to ensure slavery was not abolished in the thirteen colonies. We saw the yeomen rise up against the tyranny of the newly formed US merchant class. We saw the Constitutional Convention of 1787 as a move to more centrally pool the collective power of the US ruling-class. We saw an education policy designed to create consent to the newly formed Constitution designed to ensure state power forever remain in the hands of monied interests.

With the invention of the machine factory and the cotton gin we saw the expansion of slavery and its atrocities. Out of this growth in slave wealth we saw the growth of US capitalism in the North. From the deteriorating conditions we saw the rise in working-class militancy and the creation of new police forces and common schooling to suppress and prevent further disruption.

After the rise of slavery we saw its fall. Subverting their bid to reformulate the United States into one large slave oligarchy, we saw the enslaved end slavery by taking advantage of a dramatic tactical miscalculation of the expansionist enslaver class. After the Civil War we saw US capitalism develop into US imperialism and then the defeat of Reconstruction. We therefore saw the rise of Jim Crow as another counter-revolution against the gains African Americans won in education and democracy.

We then saw the re-emergence of African American mobilization after the Second World War despite the continued rise of US global capitalism. We saw the African American-led Civil Rights movement force the US Supreme Court to abolish Jim Crow segregation in *Brown v. Board of Education* in 1954. After a period of progressive education policy, we saw another counter-revolution symbolized in the Reagan Administration's *A Nation At Risk*.

After decades of neoliberal capitalism and reaction in education, we are now seeing the decline of US imperialism and the rise of a new counter-weight in China and in the mass mobilizations in the United States. The crisis of the hollowed-out neoliberal state (Jessop 2001) unable to meet the demands of multiple stressors simultaneously converging in the mega crisis of 2020 is on full display.

Widely understood to have significantly contributed to the deadliness of the Corona-virus and the devastation to the US economy and general immiseration, more than 70 million voted out Donald Trump in the 2020 US Presidential election. The exit poles made it clear that this was not a vote for the uninspiring Biden who only became the nominee after the Democratic Party ruling-class establishment united to stop Bernie Sanders from getting the nomination. The unprecedented voter turnout, in other words, did not reflect support for Biden's campaign promises including the refusal to ban fracking, the refusal to defund the police, the refusal to support universal health care, and the refusal to pull back militarist aggression against China. The movement against the current system of policing and mass incarceration that Biden played a key role in constructing through the 1994 Crime Bill has therefore not stopped since he won the presidency.

If Biden is to be taken at his word while on the campaign trail promising his Wall Street supporters that if he becomes president nothing will fundamentally change regarding the US capitalist system, then we should also expect the status quo in the field of education. If the Biden administration pursues any substantive progressive policies, such as transforming the national rent moratorium into a rent cancellation, it will be the result of popular, collective pressure from below.

***

We are once again facing an unknown gap. This time between the mega crisis of 2020 and the future. Are capitalism and capitalist education on the verge of sublation? *A History of Education for the Many* suggests it is increasingly possible. However, no *history of education* can offer a magic window into the details of what a sublated future will look like or exactly how the process of sublation will occur. In other words, even though history can offer insights into possible future trajectories, the outcome of sublation can never be reduced to altering pre-existing options, alternatives, or outcomes (Ford 2018).

Ford's (2018) notion of exodus is therefore indispensable for constructing historical narratives flexible enough to accommodate the insight that the future will likely include possibilities unimaged within the narrow limits of what is. At the same time we do know that the process of systemic sublation involves collective organization and effort.

What will ultimately determine the future and the potential for exodus is the outcome of competing forces. The working-class's ability or inability to counter capitalist divisiveness and unite as a class for itself could very well be the deciding factor.

Notes

Chapter 1

1. The "totality" is a philosophical term that refers to the total of existence in any given moment.
2. "The discovery of gold and silver in America, the extirpation, enslavement and entombment in mines of the aboriginal population, the beginning of the conquest and looting of the East Indies, the turning of Africa into a warren for the commercial hunting of black-skins, signalized the rosy dawn of the era of capitalist production. These idyllic proceedings are the chief moments of primitive accumulation" (Marx 1867/1967: 751).
3. A page whose writing has faded away and a new text superimposed upon the old so the past text can still be viewed under the new text. Used to conceptualize history, past eras lay visibly below the transparent present. Rather than linear calendar time, we conceptualize time here as layers upon layers.

References

Abron, J. (1998). "Serving the People": The Survival Programs of the Black Panther Party. In Charles E. Jones (Ed.). *The Black Panther Party Reconsidered*. Pp. 177–92. Baltimore: Black Classic Press.

Abu-Jamal, M. (2000). *All Things Censored*. New York: Seven Stories Press.

Abu-Jamal, M. (2003). *Faith of Our Fathers: An Examination of the Spiritual Life of African and African-American People*. Trenton, NJ: Africa World Press.

Adams, D.W. (1995). *Education for Extinction: American Indians and the Boarding School Experience 1875–1928*. Lawrence, KS: University of Kansas Press.

Ahlquist, R. (2015). Dismantling the "Commons": Undoing the Promise of Affordable, Quality Education for a Majority of California Youth. In Paul R. Carr and Brad J. Porfilio (Eds.). *The Phenomenon of Obama and the Agenda for Education: Can Hope (Still) Audaciously Trump Neoliberalism? Second Edition*. Pp. 143–68. Charlotte, NC: IAP.

Ahmed, S. (2006). *Queer Phenomenology: Orientations, Objects, Others*. Durham, NC: Duke University Press.

Allen, T. (2012). *The Invention of the White Race*. New York: Verso.

Althusser, L. (1971/2014). *On the Reproduction of Capitalism: Ideology and Ideological State Apparatuses*. New York: Verso.

Anderson, J. (1988). *The Education of Blacks in the South, 1860–1935*. London: The University of North Carolina Press.

Au, W. (2007). Vygotsky and Lenin on Learning: The Parallel Structures of Individual and Social Development. *Science & Society*. 71(3). Pp. 273–98.

Au, W., Brown, A., & Calderon, D. (2016). *Reclaiming the Multicultural Roots of US Curriculum: Communities of Color and Official Knowledge*. New York: Teachers College Press.

Axtell, J. (1975). The White Indians of Colonial America. *The William and Mary Quarterly*, vol. 32, No. 1 (January 1975), pp. 55–88

Beal, T. (2005). *North Korea: The Struggle against American Power*. Ann Arbor, MI: Pluto Press.

Becker, B. (2012). What Do Socialists Defend in China Today? In Keith Pavlik (Ed.). *China: Revolution and Counterrevolution*. Pp. 3–22. San Francisco, CA: PSL Publication.

Becker, B. (2015). *Imperialism in the 21st Century: Updating Lenin's Theory a Century Later*. San Francisco, CA: Liberation Media.

Berkey, C. (1992). United States-Indian Relation: The Constitutional Basis. In Chief Oren Lyons and John Mohawk (Eds.). *Exiled in the Land of the Free: Democracy, Indian Nations and the US Constitution*. Pp. 189–225. Santa Fe, NM: Clear Light.

Berlak, A. & Madeloni, B. (2015). From PACT to Pearson: Teacher Performance Assessment and the Corporatization of Teacher Education. In Paul R. Carr and Brad J. Porfilio (Eds.). *The Phenomenon of Obama and the Agenda for Education: Can Hope (Still) Audaciously Trump Neoliberalism? Second Edition.* Pp. 193–214. Charlotte, NC: IAP.

Berliner, D. & Biddle, B. (1995). *The Manufactured Crisis: Myths, Fraud, and the Attack on America's Public Schools.* Cambridge, MA: Perseus Books.

Blue Jacket (1807/1995). Relations with the United States and Britain. In Wayne Moquin with Charles Van Doren (Ed.). *Great Documents in American Indian History.* Pp. 131–2. New York: Da Capo Press.

Bowles, S. & Gintis, H. (1976). *Schooling in Capitalist America: Educational Reform and the Contradictions of Economic Life.* New York: Basic Books.

Boyanton, D. (2010). Behaviorism and Its Effect on Upon Learning in School. In Greg Goodman (Ed.). *Educational Psychology Reader: The Art and Science of How People Learn.* Pp. 49–65. New York: Peter Lang.

Buhle, P. (1987/2013). *Marxism in the United States: A History of the American Left.* New York: Verso.

Button, H. & Provenzo, E. (1989). *History of Education & Culture in America.* Second Edition. New York: Prentice Hall.

Carr, E.H. (1979). *The Russian Revolution: From Lenin to Stalin.* New York: The Free Press.

Carr, P. & Porfilio, B. (2015). Introduction: Audaciously Espousing Hope (Well into a Second Mandate) within a Torrent of Hegemonic Neoliberalism: The Obama Educational Agenda and the Potential for Change. In Paul R. Carr and Brad J. Porfilio (Eds.). *The Phenomenon of Obama and the Agenda for Education: Can Hope (Still) Audaciously Trump Neoliberalism? Second Edition.* Pp. xxxix–li. Charlotte, NC: IAP.

Carlson, D. (2015). Afterword: Reclaiming the Promise of Democratic Public Education in New Times. In Paul R. Carr and Brad J. Porfilio (Eds.). *The Phenomenon of Obama and the Agenda for Education: Can Hope (Still) Audaciously Trump Neoliberalism? Second Edition.* Pp. 337–50. Charlotte, NC: IAP.

Chanca, C. (1496/1969). The Letter Written by Dr. Chanca to the City of Seville. In J.M. Cohen (Ed. and trans.). *The Four Voyages of Christopher Columbus.* Pp. 129–57. New York: Penguin Classics.

Cho, S. (2017). Historical Origins of Critical Pedagogy. In Michael Peters (Ed.). *Encyclopedia of Educational Philosophy and Theory*, vol. 1. A–F. Pp. 291–6. Singapore: Springer.

Christianakis, M. & Mora, R. (2015). Charter Schools and the Privatization of Public Schools. In Paul R. Carr and Brad J. Porfilio (Eds.). *The Phenomenon of Obama and the Agenda for Education: Can Hope (Still) Audaciously Trump Neoliberalism? Second Edition.* Pp. 95–116. Charlotte, NC: IAP.

Churchill, W. (2004). *Kill the Indian, Save the Man: The Genocidal Impact of American Indian Residential Schools.* San Francisco, CA: Clear Light.

Churchill, W. & Vander Wall, J. (1990). *The COINTELPRO Papers: Documents from the The FBI's Secret Wars against Dissent in the United States.* Boston: South End Press.

Columbus, C. (1493/1969). Letter of Columbus to Various Persons Describing the Results of His First Voyage and Written on the Return Journey. In J.M. Cohen (Ed. and trans.). *The Four Voyages of Christopher Columbus.* Pp. 115–23. New York: Penguin Classics.

Correia, D. & Wall, T. (2018). *Police: A Field Guide.* New York: Verso.

Counts, G. (1931). *The Soviet Challenge to America.* New York: The John Day Company.

Counts, G. (1932). *Dare the Schools Build a New Social Order?* New York: The John Day Company.

Cremin, L. (1957). *The Republic and the School: Horace Mann on the Education of the Free Man.* New York: Teachers' College Press.

Cremin, L. (1970). *American Education: The Colonial Experience 1607–1783.* New York: Harper & Row Publishers.

Cremin, L. (1980). *American Education: The National Experience 1783–1876.* New York: Harper & Row Publishers.

Daggett, D. (1787/1981). Oration Delivered in New Haven. In John Kaminski and Gaspare Saladino (Eds.). *The Documentary History of the Ratification of the Constitution. Volume XIII: Commentaries on the Constitution Private and Public: Volume 1: 21 February to 7 November 1787.* Pp. 160–3. Madison: State Historical Society of Wisconsin.

Darder, A., Baltodano, M., & Torres, R. (2017). Critical Pedagogy: An Introduction. In Antonia Darder, Marta Baltodano, and Rodolfo Torres (Eds.). *The Critical Pedagogy Reader.* Third Edition. Pp. 1–23. New York: Routledge.

Darling-Hammond, L. (2004). From "Separate but Equal" to "No Child Left Behind": The Collision of New Standards and Old Inequalities. In Deborah Meier and George Wood (Eds.). *Many Children Left Behind: How the No Child Left behind Act Is Damaging Our Children and Our Schools.* Pp. 3–32. Boston: Beacon.

De Las Casas, B. (1552/1992). *A Short Account of the Destruction of the Indies.* New York: Penguin Classics.

Deloria, V. & Lytle, C. (1984). *The Nations Within: The Past and Future of American Indian Sovereignty.* New York: Pantheon.

Douglass, F. (1845). *Narrative of the Life of Frederick Douglass, an American Slave: Written by Himself.* Boston: The Anti-Slavery Office.

DuBois, W.E.B. (1896/2007). *The Suppression of the African Slave Trade in the United States of America.* London: Oxford University Press.

DuBois, W.E.B. (1935/1992). *Black Reconstruction in America 1860–1880.* New York: Free Press.

Enfu, C. & Xiaoqin, D. (2017). A Theory of China's "Miracle." *Monthly Review.* https://monthlyreview.org/2017/01/01/a-theory-of-chinas-miracle/.

Engels, F. (1870/2006). *The Peasant War in Germany.* New York: International Publishers.

Engels, F. (1892/2007). *Socialism: Utopian and Scientific.* New York: Pathfinder.

Engels, F. (1894/1987). Anti-Duhring. In Karl Marx and Frederick Engels. *Karl Marx and Frederick Engels: Collected Works* (vol. 25). Pp. 5–309. New York: International Publishers.

Ewing, E.T. (2006). The "Virtue of Planning": American Educators Look at Soviet School. In E. Thomas Ewing and David Hicks (Eds.). *Education and the Great Depression: Lessons from a Global History.* Pp. 41–61. New York: Peter Lang.

Feldman, D. (2019). Solidarity with LA Teachers! *Liberation News.* https://www.liberationnews.org/solidarity-with-the-la-teachers-strike/

Fisher, S. (2008). The Supreme Court: Last Line of Defense of the Ruling Class. In Andy McInerney (Ed.). *Democracy and Class Society.* Pp. 49–57. San Francisco, CA: PSL Publications.

Foner, E. (2009a). *Give Me Liberty! An American History. Volume One, Second Edition.* New York: W. W. Norton.

Foner, E. (2009b). *Give Me Liberty! An American History. Volume Two, Second Edition.* New York: W. W. Norton.

Ford, D. R. (2015). From Standardized Testing to the War on Libya: The Privatization of U.S. Education in International Context. In Mark Abendroth and Brad J. Porfilio (Eds.). *Understanding Neoliberal Rule in K-12 Schools: Educational Fronts for Local and Global Justice Volume I.* Pp. 95–109. Charlotte, NC: IAP.

Ford, D. R. (2017). *Education and the Production of Space: Political Pedagogy, Geography, and Urban Revolution.* New York: Routledge.

Ford, D. R. (2018). Pedagogy of the "Not": Negation, Exodus, and Postdigital Temporal Regimes. *Postdigital Science and Education.* 1(1), 104–18. https://doi.org/10.1007/s42438-018-0009-4

Ford, D.R. (2019). Red4Ed in Indianapolis: The Next State to Strike? *Liberation News.* https://www.liberationnews.org/red4ed-in-indianapolis-the-next-state-to-strike/.

Freire, A.M. & Macedo, D. (1998). Introduction. In Paulo Freire (Au). *Paulo Freire Reader.* Pp. 1–44. New York: Continuum.

Freire, P. (1978). *Pedagogy in Process: Letters to Guinea-Bissau.* New York: Continuum.

Garrison, M. (2015). Value-Added Measures and the Rise of Antipublic Schooling: The Political, Economic, and Ideological Origins of Test-Based Teacher Evaluation. In Paul R. Carr and Brad J. Porfilio (Eds.). *The Phenomenon of Obama and the Agenda for Education: Can Hope (Still) Audaciously Trump Neoliberalism? Second Edition.* Pp. 215–34. Charlotte, NC: IAP.

Gates, H.L. & McKay, N. (1997). *The Norton Anthology of African American Literature.* New York: W. W. Norton.

Genovese, E. (1969). *The World the Slaveholders Made: Two Essays in Interpretation.* New York: Pantheon Books.

Genovese, E. (1979). *From Rebellion to Revolution: Afro-American Slave Revolts in the Making of the Modern World.* Baton Rouge, LA: Louisiana State University Press.

Giroux, H. (1983). *Theory & Resistance in Education: A Pedagogy for the Opposition.* New York: Bergin & Garvey.

Goldscheider, T. (2015). Shay's Rebellion: Reclaiming the Revolution. *Historical Journal of Massachusetts.* 43(1). Pp. 63–93.

Gutek, G. (1970). *An Historical Introduction to American Education.* New York: Cowell.

Hadden, Sally (2001). *Slave Patrols: Law and Violence in Virginia and the Carolinas.* Cambridge, MA: Harvard University Press.

Harvey, D. (2014). *Seventeen Contradictions and the End of Capitalism.* New York: Oxford University Press.

Hilliard, D. (2002). Introduction. In David Hilliard and Donald Weise (Eds.). *The Huey P. Newton Reader.* Pp. 9–19. New York: Seven Stories Press.

Hobsbawn, E. (1978). From Feudalism to Capitalism. In Rodney Hilton (Ed.). *The Transition from Feudalism to Capitalism.* Pp. 159–64. New York: Verso.

Holt, T. (1995). *Thinking Historically: Narrative, Imagination, and Understanding.* New York: The College Board.

Hoortunian, H. (2015). *Marx after Marx: History and Time in the Expansion of Capitalism.* New York: Columbia University Press.

Hoover, R. (2015). The Neoliberal Metrics of the False Proxy and Pseudo Accountability. In Paul R. Carr and Brad J. Porfilio (Eds.). *The Phenomenon of Obama and the Agenda for Education: Can Hope (Still) Audaciously Trump Neoliberalism? Second Edition.* Pp. 235–50. Charlotte, NC: IAP.

Horne, G. (2014). *The Counter-Revolution of 1776: Slave Resistance and the Origins of the United States of America.* New York: New York University Press.

Horne, G. (2018). *The Apocalypse of Settler Colonialism: The Roots of Slavery, White Supremacy, and Capitalism in Seventeenth Century North America and the Caribbean.* New York: Monthly Review Press.

Horne, G. (2020). *The Dawning of the Apocalypse: The Roots of Slavery, White Supremacy, Settler Colonialism and Capitalism in the Long Sixteenth Century.* New York: Monthly Review Press.

Hrizi, N. (2019). Oakland Teachers Settle Seven-day Strike. *Liberation News.* https://www.liberationnews.org/oakland-teachers-settle-seven-day-strike/.

Hursh, D. (2015). Even More of the Same: How Free Market Capitalism Dominates Education. In Paul R. Carr and Brad J. Porfilio (Eds.). *The Phenomenon of Obama and the Agenda for Education: Can Hope (Still) Audaciously Trump Neoliberalism. Second Edition.* Pp. 3–19. Charlotte, NC: IAP.

Jensen, M. (1976). Introduction. In Merrill Jensen (Ed.). *The Documentary History of the Ratification of the Constitution: Volume I: Constitutional Documents and Records, 1776–1787.* Pp. 176–79. Madison: State Historical Society of Wisconsin.

Jessop, B. (2001). 'Bringing the State Back in (Yet Again): Reviews, Revisions, Rejections, and Redirections', published by the Department of Sociology, Lancaster University, Lancaster LA1 4YN, at http://www.comp.lancs.ac.uk/sociology/papers/Jessop-Bringing-the-State-Back-In.pdf

Jessop, B. (2004). On the Limits of *Limits to Capital. Antipode.* 36(3), 480–96.

Kelley, R. (2015). *Hammer and Hoe: Alabama Communists during the Great Depression.* Chapel Hill, NC: The University of North Carolina Press.

Kenific, S. (2020). Six Teacher Deaths at Start of Fall Semester Heighten Public Health Concerns. *Liberation News.* https://www.liberationnews.org/six-teacher-deaths-atstart-of-fall-semester-heighten-public-health-concerns/.

Kincheloe, J. (2008). *Critical Pedagogy Primer.* Second Edition. New York: Peter Lang.

Kliebard, H. (2004). *The Struggle for the American Curriculum: 1893–1958.* Third Edition. New York: Routledge.

Kohn, A. (2004). NCLB and the Effort to Privatize Public Education. In Deborah Meier and George Wood (Eds.). *Many Children Left Behind: How the No Child Left behind Act Is Damaging Our Children and Our Schools.* Pp. 79–97. Boston: Beacon.

La Riva, G. (2017). Why We Continue to Defend the Soviet Union. In Jane Cutter (Ed.). *Storming the Gates: How the Russian Revolution Changed the World.* Pp. 45–52. San Francisco, CA: Liberation Media.

Lea, V. (2015). "The Hunger Games": A Fictional Future or a Hegemonic Reality Already Governing Our Lives? In Paul R. Carr and Brad J. Porfilio (Eds.). *The Phenomenon of Obama and the Agenda for Education: Can Hope (Still) Audaciously Trump Neoliberalism? Second Edition.* Pp. 21–44. Charlotte, NC: IAP.

Lenin, V.I. (1916/1986). *Imperialism, the Highest Stage of Capitalism.* Moscow: Progress Publishers.

Lenin, V.I. (1919/2019). First All-Russia Congress on Adult Education: Speech of Greeting. In Derek Ford and Curry Malott (Eds.). *Learning with Lenin: Selected Works on Education and Revolution.* Pp. 23–5. Charlotte, NC: IAP.

Lenin, V.I. (1920/2016). *"Left-Wing" Communism, an Infantile Disorder: A Popular Essay in Marxist Strategy and Tactics.* New York: International Publishers.

Linebaugh, P. & Rediker, M. (2000). *The Many Headed Hydra: Sailors, Slaves, Commoners, and the Hidden History of the Revolutionary Atlantic.* New York: Beacon.

Loomba, A. (2005). *Colonialism/Postcolonialism.* Second Edition. New York: Routledge.

Love, B. (2019). *We Want to Do More Than Survive: Abolitionist Teaching and the Pursuit of Educational Freedom.* New York: Beacon Press.

Lyons, J. (2006). Regional Variations in Union Activism of American Public Schoolteachers. In E. Thomas Ewing and David Hicks (Eds.). *Education and the Great Depression: Lessons from a Global History.* Pp. 19–39. New York: Peter Lang.

Malone, T. and Sadovi, C. (2008). Head of the Class: City School Reform Goes National. *Chicago Tribune*, December 17.

Malott, C. (2011). *Critical Pedagogy and Cognition: An Introduction to a Postformal Educational Psychology.* New York: Springer.

Malott, C. & Ford, D. (2015). *Marx, Capital, and Education: Toward a Critical Pedagogy of Becoming.* New York: Peter Lang.

Mann, H. (1852). Immigration and Education. In Horace Mann (Ed.). *The Common School Journal, Volume 14*. Pp. 43–45. Boston: Morris Cotton.
Marcy, S. (1976). *The Class Character of the USSR*. New York: World View.
Martin, A. (2018). Striking Teachers Give Lesson in Labor Struggle. *Liberation News*. https://www.liberationnews.org/striking-teachers-lessons-labor-struggle/.
Marx, K. (1853/2007). Revolution in China and in Europe. In James Ledbetter (Ed.). *Dispatches for the New York Tribune: Selected Journalism of Karl Marx*. Pp. 3–11. New York: Penguin Classics.
Marx, K. (1861/2007). The North American Civil War. In James Ledbetter (Ed.). *Dispatches for the New York Tribune: Selected Journalism of Karl Marx*. Pp. 280–91. New York: Penguin Classics.
Marx, K. (1867/1967). *Capital: A Critique of Political Economy* (vol. 1). New York: International Publishers.
Mattick, P. (1978). *Economics, Politics and the Age of Inflation*. New York: Taylor & Francis.
McLaren, P. (2000). *Che Guevara, Paulo Freire, and the Pedagogy of Revolution*. New York: Rowman & Littlefield.
McNamee, G.D. (1990). Learning to Read and Write in an Inner-city Setting: A Longitudinal Study of Community Change. In Luis C. Moll (Ed.). *Vygotsky and Education: Instructional Implications and Applications of Sociohistorical Psychology*. Pp. 287–303. Cambridge, UK: Cambridge University Press.
Melman, S. (1970). *Pentagon Capitalism: The Political Economy of War*. New York: McGraw-Hill.
Mills, C. (2012). Independent Development versus Imperialist Domination. In Keith Pavlik (Ed.). *China: Revolution and Counterrevolution*. Pp. 43–8. San Francisco, CA: PSL Publication.
Mitchell, J. (1903). *Organized Labor: Its Problems, Purposes and Ideals and the Present and Future of American Wage Earners*. Philadelphia, PA: American Book and Bible House.
Montaña, T. (2015). Obama, Escucha! Estamos en la Lucha! Challenging Neoliberalism in Los Angeles Schools. In Paul R. Carr and Brad J. Porfilio (Eds.). *The Phenomenon of Obama and the Agenda for Education: Can Hope (Still) Audaciously Trump Neoliberalism? Second Edition*. Pp. 169–92. Charlotte, NC: IAP.
Moree, D. & Mitchell, M. (2006). *Black Codes in Georgia*. Atlanta, GA: The APEX Museum.
Movement for Black Lives. The Movement for Black Lives Stands with the People of Palestine. https://www.facebook.com/mvmt4bl/posts/1805376756424461 (accessed April 1, 2019).
Naison, M. (2005). *Communism in Harlem during the Pression*. Chicago: University of Illinois Press.
Newton, Huey P. (1973). *To Die for the People: The Writings of Huey P. Newton. Edited by toni morrison*. New York: Writers and Readers Publishing.

Noble, D. (1984). *Forces of Production: A Social History of Industrial Automation.* New York: Alfred A. Knopf.

Oaks, J. & Lipton, M. (1999). *Teaching to Change the World.* New York: McGraw-Hill.

Paine, T. (1775). African Slavery in America. https://www.constitution.org/tp/afri.htm.

Powhatan. (1609/1995). Remarks to Captain John Smith. In Wayne Moquin with Charles Van Doren (Eds.). *Great Documents in American Indian History.* Pp. 111. New York: De Capo Press.

Pratt, R. (1892). Kill the Indian, Save the Man. http://historymatters.gmu.edu/d/4929

Prins, N. (2014). *All the Presidents Bankers: The Hidden Alliances That Drive American Power.* New York: Nation Books.

Puryear, E. (2012). From Liberation to Thermidor: Phases of China's Socialist Revolution. In Keith Pavlik (Ed.). *China: Revolution and Counterrevolution.* Pp. 139–52. San Francisco, CA: PSL Publication.

Reds in Ed (2020). CDC Shifts under Pressure, Weakens Safety Standards for School Reopening, Parents and Educators Resist. https://redsined.org/cdc-shifts-under-pressure-weakens-safety-standards-for-school-reopening-parents-and-educators-resist/

Richardson, H. (2020). Assault on Public Schools: Why Betsy Devos Is Using the Pandemic to Privatize Education across the Nation. *Milwaukee Independent.* http://www.milwaukeeindependent.com/special/covid-19/assault-public-schools-betsy-devos-using-pandemic-privatize-education-across-nation/

Robertson, L. (2005). *Conquest by Law: How the Discovery of America Dispossessed Indigenous Peoples of Their Lands.* London: Oxford University Press.

Rothmel, H. (2019). Boston Teachers Union "All in" to Fight for a Fair Contract. *Liberation News.* https://www.liberationnews.org/boston-teachers-union-all-in-to-fight-for-a-fair-contract/.

Rury, J. (2013). *Education and Social Change: Contours in the history of American schooling.* Fourth edition. New York: Routledge.

Rury, J. (2014). *Education and Social Change: Contours in the History of American Schooling.* Fourth Edition. New York: Routledge.

Rush, B. (1773). "An Address to the Inhabitants of the British Settlements, upon Slave Keeping." https://quod.lib.umich.edu/cgi/t/text/text-idx?c=evans;cc=evans;rgn=div1;view=text;idno=N10229.0001.001;node=N10229.0001.001%3A2

Rush, B. (1787/1981). "Address to the People of the United States." In John Kaminski and Gaspare Saladino (Eds.). *The Documentary History of the Ratification of the Constitution. Volume XIII: Commentaries on the Constitution Private and Public: Volume 1: 21 February to 7 November 1787.* Pp. 45–49. Madison: State Historical Society of Wisconsin.

Ryan, H. (2016). *Educational Justice: Teaching and Organizing against the Corporate Juggernaut.* New York: Monthly Review Press.

Salem, A. (2020). NYC Educators Fight Life-threatening Reopening Plan. *Liberation News*. https://www.liberationnews.org/nyc-educators-fight-life-threatening-reopening-plan/#.XzIIMPhKjow.

Schurmann, F. (1972/1995). "Introduction." In Huey P. Newton (Au). *To Die for the People: The Writings of Huey P. Newton. Edited by Toni Morrison*. Pp. xiii–xxii. New York: Writers and Readers Publishing.

Shor, I. (1986). *Culture Wars: School and Society in the Conservative Restoration 1969–1984*. Boston: Routledge & Kegan Paul.

Singh, A. (2018). China's Rise Threatens U.S. Imperialism, Not American People. Hampton Institute. http://www.hamptoninstitution.org/china-rise-threatens-us-imperialism-not-people.html#.XJaZAi2ZPq0.

Sleeter, C. (2015). Foreword: Challenging the Empire's Agenda for Education (2011, for the first edition). In Paul R. Carr and Brad J. Porfilio (Eds.). *The Phenomenon of Obama and the Agenda for Education: Can Hope (Still) Audaciously Trump Neoliberalism?* Second Edition. Pp. xxv–xxviii. Charlotte, NC: IAP.

Smith, A. (1763/1978). *Lectures on Jurisprudence: Lectures on Justice, Police, Revenue, and Arms*. New York: Oxford University Press.

Smolarek, W. (2020). Trump's Stunning Admission: As Pandemic Spread, President Lied to the World. *Liberation News*. https://www.liberationnews.org/trumps-stunning-admission-as-pandemic-spread-president-lied-to-the-world/

Spring, J. (2014). *The American School: A Global Context: From Puritans to the Obama Administration*. Ninth Edition. New York: McGraw Hill.

Stannard, D. (1992). *American Holocaust: The Conquest of the New World*. New York: Oxford University Press.

Stoltzfus, K. (2018). How K-12 Schools Push Out Black Girls: An Interview with Monique W. Morris. In Dyan Watson, Jesse Hagopian, and Wayne Au (Eds.). *Teaching for Black Lives*. Pp. 251–5. Wilwaukee, WI: Rethinking Schools.

Szatmary, D. (1980). *Shay's Rebellion: The Making of an Agrarian Insurrection*. Amherst, MA: The University of Massachusetts Press.

Takaki, R. (2008). *A Different Mirror: A History of Multicultural America*. New York: Back Bay Books.

Taylor, C. (2011). *Reds at the Blackboard: Communism, Civil Rights, and the New York City Teachers Union*. New York: Columbia University Press.

Tell, S. (2016). *Charter School Report Card*. Charlotte, NC: IAP.

Therborn, G. (1978). *What Does the Ruling-class Do When It Rules? State Apparatuses and Atate Power under Feudalism, Eapitalism and Socialism*. New York: Verso.

Thorndike, E. (1910). *Educational Psychology*. Albany, NY: Teachers College Press.

Tumulty K. & Layton, L. (2014). Changes in AP History Trigger a Culture Clash in Colorado. *Washington Post*. October 5.

Tyack, D. (1974). *The One Best System: A History of American Urban Education*. Cambridge, MA: Harvard University Press.

Urban, W. (1978). Preface. In George Counts (Au.). *Dare the School Build a New Social Order?* Pp. v–xiv. Carbondale, IL: Southern Illinois University Press.

Urban, W. & Wagoner, J. (2009). *American Education: A History.* New York: Routledge.

Urban, W. & Wagoner, J. (2014). *American Education: A History.* Fifth edition. New York: Routledge.

US Congress, Sixty-Fifth. (1917). Espionage Act. Session I. Chapters 29, 30. Washington, DC: Library of Congress.

Venables, R. (2004a). *American Indian History: Five Centuries of Conflict & Coexistence. Volume I: Conquest of a Continent 1492–1783.* Santa Fe, NM: Clear Light.

Venables, R. (2004b). *American Indian History: Five Centuries of Conflict & Coexistence. Volume II: Confrontation: Adaptation, and Assimilation 1783–Present.* Santa Fe, NM: Clear Light.

Vitale, A. (2018). *The End of Policing.* New York: Verso.

Vygotsky, L. (1978). *Mind in Society: The Development of Higher Psychological Processes.* Cambridge, MA: Harvard University Press.

Vygotsky, L. (1986). *Thought and Language.* Edited by Alex Kozulin. London: MIT Press.

Washington, B.T. (1901/2004). *Up from Slavery: An Autobiography.* West Berlin, NJ: The Townsend Library.

Watkins, W. (2001). *The White Architects of Black Education: Ideology and Power in America, 1865–1954.* New York: Teachers' College Press.

Weir, F. (2016, January 29). Maybe the Soviets Weren't So Bad? Russian Nostalgia for USSR on the Rise. The Christian Science Monitor. http://www.csmonitor.com/World/Europe/2016/0129/Maybe-the-Soviets-weren-t-so-bad-Russian-nostalgia-for-USSR-onthe-rise?cmpid=gigya-fb

Wertsch, J. (1985). *Vygotsky and the Social Formation of Mind.* Cambridge, MA: Harvard University Press.

West, T. (2018). West Virginia's Lesson Plan: Solidarity and Working-class Power. *Liberation News.* https://www.liberationnews.org/west-virginias-lesson-plan-solidarity-and-working-class-power/.

Wilcox, P. (2018). The Historic Teachers' Strikes: What Do They Mean? *Liberation News.* https://www.liberationnews.org/the-historic-teachers-strikes-what-do-they-mean/.

Wison, J. (1787/1976). 'Plain Truth.' In Merrill Jensen (Ed.). *The Documentary History of the Ratification of the Constitution. Volume II: Ratification of the Constitution by the States: Pennsylvania.* Pp. 289–92. Madison, WI: State Historical Society of Wisconsin.

Wolff, R. (2020). *The Sickness Is the System: When Capitalism Fails to Save Us from Pandemics or Itself.* New York: Democracy at Work.

Wood, G. (2004a). Introduction. In Deborah Meier and George Wood (Eds.). *Many Children Left Behind: How the No Child Left behind Act Is Damaging Our Children and Our Schools.* Pp. vii–xv. Boston: Beacon.

Wood, G. (2004b). A View from the Field: NCLB's Effects on Classroom and Schools. In Deborah Meier and George Wood (Eds.). *Many Children Left Behind: How the No Child Left behind Act Is Damaging Our Children and Our Schools*. Pp. 33–50. New York: Beacon.

Yank Magazine (1944). Quoted in "Sixty Years after Brown v. Board of Ed" by Admin. Liberation School, August 12, 2014. https://liberationschool.org/sixty-years-after-brown-v-board-of-ed/

Zinn, H. (1980/2015). *A People's History of the United States*. New York: Harper Perennial.

Index

abolitionist teaching 201–2
Abood v. Detroit Board of Education 196
Abu-Jamal, M. 44, 171, 173
Act of Supremacy (1534) 15
actual devaluation 64, 149, 150
Adams, J. 100
Adequate Yearly Progress (AYP) 183
African American 66, 105, 107, 110, 111, 113–19, 121, 122, 124, 127, 128, 134, 136, 153–5, 165, 166, 168–72, 177, 201, 206
African Muslims 45, 46
AFT. *see* American Federation of Teachers (AFT)
age of printing 26, 27
Agricultural Adjustment Administration 150
Ahmed, S. 31
Allen, T. 38
All Russian Congress 133
Althusser, L. 2
American Communist Opposition (ACO) 155
American Education (Cremin) 70
American Federation of Teachers (AFT) 155, 158, 159, 162
American Revolution 55, 60, 67, 70–2, 81
Anderson, J. 116
Annual Yearly Progress (AYP) 183
Arawak 18, 19

Bacon's Rebellion 37–9
Baldwin, J. 166–7
Baltodano, M. 189
Banking Act of 1933 148
Bartolomé De Las Casas 20
behaviorism 137, 147
Bilingual Education Act 170
Birmingham 153–4
Black church 118
Black Codes 113

Black Communist in the Freedom Struggle, A (Haywood) 134
Black Lives Matter 194
Black Panther Party (BPP) 90, 166, 170–3
Blue Jacket 83
boarding schools 97, 100, 147
Bolshevik Revolution 131, 133, 134, 139, 140, 160
Boston Teachers Union (BTU) 199
bourgeois 26, 29, 51, 122, 123, 132, 133, 170, 201
Bowles, S. 4, 89–93, 187
Brant, J. 81–2
Brewery Workers Union 129
Brinsley, J. 28
Brown v. Board of Education 168–70, 206
Buhle, P. 92, 127, 128, 133, 153, 158
Button, H. W. 70

capital 8
capitalist imperialism 122, 123, 129
Cato, G. 48–9
Chicago teachers 98, 152–5, 160, 164
Chicago Teachers Union (CTU) 152, 186
child labor 86, 98, 99
China 95, 166, 190–2, 203, 206
Chinese Communist Party 135, 136, 153, 155, 158
Choctaw 102, 103
Christianity 20, 29, 30, 34, 42–4
circulation 41, 95, 148–51
Civil Rights Act 114, 169
Civil Rights movement 165, 170, 171, 206
Civil War 107–10, 114, 115, 119, 121, 122, 124–8, 206
Classroom Teacher Group (CTG) 157
cognitive development 99, 139–41
Cold War 166, 178–80, 190
colonial education 26, 28, 30, 42, 55, 189
colonial expansion 16–24
colonialism 7, 13, 19–21, 23, 26, 27, 31, 37, 202

Index

colonial repressive state apparatus 24–6
Columbus, C. 4, 13, 15, 17–20, 113
Common Core 186
common schooling 87, 89–94, 96, 98, 114, 116, 117, 126, 182, 205
Common School Journal (Mann) 93
communism 133–6, 153, 155, 159, 162
Communist Control Act 135
Communist Party 155
Congress of Industrial Organizations (CIO) 159
Conquest by Law (Robertson) 79
Constitutional Convention of 1786 68
Constitutional Convention of 1787 55, 56, 67, 71, 72, 74, 78, 80, 85, 96, 205
containment 91
Corona Virus (Covid-19) 191–4, 200–1, 206
corporate education 125–7
corporeal schema 7
cotton gin 86, 94, 95, 105, 107, 108, 205
counter-revolution 34, 62, 63, 71, 85, 117, 155, 169, 179, 181, 187, 203, 205, 206
Counts, G. 152, 159–64
Cremin, L. 21, 26, 27, 70, 74–6, 159
crisis
　1893 149
　of capitalism 151, 178
　economic 15, 61–7, 121, 126, 136, 147, 148, 150, 178, 181, 193
　mega crisis of 2020 191, 193–5, 203, 206, 207
critical pedagogy 38, 177, 187–90
cultural genocide 20, 23, 25, 92

Daggett, D. 72
Darder, A. 189
Dare the School Build a New social Order? (Counts) 159–62
Darling-Hammond, L. 183, 185
day-to-day resistance 49–51
debtor states 124
De Las Casas, B. 20
Deloria, V. 89
democratic centralism 68, 69, 90, 126, 137
deteriorated conditions 15–16
determinism 29, 141, 188
Devos, B. 195

Dewey, J. 131, 137, 138, 159
dialectics 1, 2, 5, 7–8, 41, 74, 138, 139, 205–7
dichotomy 61, 74
Douglas, F. 42–4, 50, 86, 103, 105
dual power 132
DuBois, W. E. B. 36–8, 40, 94, 95, 107–10, 113–19
Duma 132
Dunmore, Lord 79

education
　common schooling 89–94
　corporate 125–7
　for extinction 88, 96–7
　higher 26, 46, 180
　mandatory ignorance 94–6
　Soviet Union 138–44
　United States 136–8
Education of a Christian Prince, The (Erasmus) 28
Elementary and Secondary Education Act (ESEA) 170, 182, 185
Engels, F. 16, 22, 26, 148, 150
England 15, 16, 21–7, 29, 34, 36, 37, 40, 46, 51, 59
enlightenment 27, 56, 70, 71
enslaved 103–5
Equiano, O. 39–40
Erasmus, D. 28, 29
Espionage Act 134–5
Europe 14–16, 23, 29, 31, 36, 41, 51, 78, 107, 131, 149

FBI 158–9, 173
feudalistic education 27
feudal state 15–16, 22
finance capital 108, 123–5, 127, 151
financial oligarchy 123
Foner, E. 124
Ford, D. 8–9, 179, 180, 182, 207
Foxe, J. 28, 29
Free Breakfast Program 173
free colonization 109
freedom 31, 39, 44, 47, 49–51, 57, 68, 70, 71, 77, 98, 103, 111–13, 119, 156, 183
free-soil movement 109
Freire, A. M. 188
Freire, P. 188–90

gap between 6, 41, 141, 142, 144, 161, 178, 182, 189
Gates Foundation 186
Gates, H. L. 118–19
General Intelligence Division (GID) 136
general strike 110
Genovese, E. 36–7, 41, 42, 44, 46, 47, 50, 51
Georgia 57–8, 96, 115–17
German immigrants 128–9
Gintis, H. 4, 89–93, 187
Giroux, H. 188
Glorious Revolution of 1688 39, 57
Goldscheider, T. 60
Great Depression 147–51, 164, 168, 178, 193
  Birmingham 153–4
  Chicago 152–3
  Counts and 152, 159–64
  NCY 154–9
Grievance Committee 157
Gutek, G. 91

Hadden, Sally 88, 113
Harlem 153, 155
Harmar, J. 81
Harootunian, H. 5, 6, 9
Harrison, W. H. 100–2
Harvey, D. 147–50
Haywood, H.. 134
head start 127
higher education 26, 46, 180
Hilliard, D. 171
Historical Introduction to American Education, An (Gutek) 91
Hoortunian, H. 7
Horne, G. 13–14, 16, 17, 19, 21, 22, 24, 36–9, 56, 57, 59–66, 109
Hursh, D. 182

ideology 2, 26, 29, 42, 46, 51, 101, 140
Indiana State Teachers Association 199
Indian territory 96
indigenous 100–3
industrial capitalism 88, 96
Inquisition 16
Intercommunal Youth Institute 173
interpenetration of opposites 8

Janus v. AFSCME 196, 197
Jefferson, T. 76–8, 100–1

Jensen, M. 71–2
Jessop, B. 2, 4
Jubilee 44

Kansas-Nebraska Bill of 1854 108
Kelley, R. 154
Kincheloe, J. 189
Kliebard, H. 125
Kohn, A. 184
Ku Klux Klan (KKK) 122

labor 8
labor aristocracy 26, 107, 131, 132
labor saving technology 150–1
Lenin, V. I. 5, 86, 123–4, 128, 132–3, 138–41, 143
Lincoln, A. 109–11
Linebaugh, P. 30, 33
Lipton, M. 181
Little Turtle 81–3, 101
London 15, 19–24, 29, 40, 57–60, 63, 76, 79, 81
London Company 23, 34
Love, B. 201–2
Lyons, J. 154–5
Lytle, C. 89

Macedo, D. 188
McKay, N. 118–19
McLaren, P. 189
Madrid 13, 14, 17, 19–21, 30, 31, 35, 36, 49, 56–9, 63
Malott, C. 179
mandatory ignorance 35, 45, 46, 51, 94–6, 103, 114, 116
Mann, H. 90–1, 93–4, 98
Maroons 39, 44
Marxism 93
Marxism in the United States: A History of the American Left (Buhle) 127
Marx, K. 22, 85, 92, 109, 139, 143
mass incarceration 165–7
  Black Panther Party 170–3
  Brown v. Board of Education 168–70
  police unions 167–8
Mattick, P. 149–50
mega crisis of 2020 191, 193–5, 203, 206, 207
militant labor 124–5
Missouri Compromise 108

Mitchell, J. 97–100
Mohawk 30, 81
monopolization 47, 88, 89, 94, 169
More, T. 29, 30
Morgan, J. P. 123

Naison, M. 153, 154
National Economic League 152
National Industrial Recovery Act (NRA) 151
National Labor Relations Act 151
National Recovery Act 158
A Nation at Risk 180–3, 187, 188, 190, 206
Nat Turner's rebellion 88
NCY 154–9
negation of the negation 8, 9, 79, 202, 205
Negro 96, 110, 117–18, 122, 167
neoliberalism 177–80, 183, 184, 186, 190
Nixon, R. 187
No Child Left Behind (NCLB) 182–6
normative discourse 143
North America 21, 23, 26, 27, 29, 30, 34, 44–7, 60, 79, 80, 101, 121, 202, 205
Northwest Ordinance, The 80–1

Oaks, J. 181
Obama, B. 135, 184, 185, 192
organized labor 97, 98, 127, 196
Orient 19
orientation 2, 4–7, 18, 19, 23, 25, 26, 29, 33, 41, 42, 44, 45, 56, 60–2, 64, 65, 70, 74, 75, 90, 97, 98, 105, 114, 127–9, 131, 152, 155, 157–9, 166, 181, 182
Ottoman Empire 14, 35, 49

Paine, T. 74–5
pan-Indian alliance 56, 80, 83, 85, 100–2
patrolling 113–14
peasants 132–3
Pedagogy in Process: Letters to Guinea-Bissau (Freire) 189–90
Pedagogy of the Oppressed (Freire) 188, 189
Pennsylvania State Police 124–5
pivot toward Asia 192
Plessy v. Ferguson 121–2, 168
police, the 1–7, 9, 29, 34, 69, 84, 86, 87, 90, 91, 113, 122, 124–5, 154, 167, 168, 171, 193–5, 200, 206
police unions 167–8, 173
Powhatan 22–3, 30–4
Pratt, R. 97

primitive accumulation 6, 93
producers 22, 23, 132, 150, 163
production
    advances in 47
    of cotton 95, 132
    modes of 61
    phases of 149
    revolution in 96
    technological revolutions in 86
Progressive Education Association 160
Progressive Group 133, 155, 157
proletariat 92, 132, 133
Provenzo, E. 70
Provisional Government 132
Puryear, E. 166
Pushmataha 102

race
    dialectics of 41, 74
    and unipolar imperialist power 185–7
Race to the Top (RTTT) 185–7
racialization 7, 26, 46, 138
racism 19, 97, 121, 162, 165, 167, 173, 191, 192–4, 203
Rank and File 153, 155–7
Reagan, R. 177, 178, 180, 181, 188, 193, 206
realization 64, 149–53, 164, 165, 178
Reconstruction 111, 113, 114, 117, 119, 121, 122, 128, 154, 165, 179, 206
Reconstruction Act of 1867, The 114
Rediker, M. 30, 33
Reds In Ed (2020) 200
remote ancestry 138
Republican Party 109
Requerimiento 17
reservation system 88–9
resistance 30–4
Rethinking Schools 189
Robertson, L. 79–80
Rockefeller, J. D. 123
Roman Catholic Church 14, 15, 27, 29
Roosevelt, T. 148, 150, 151, 157, 158
Royal African Company (RAC) 37, 57, 59
Rury, J. 70
Rush, B. 55–6, 72–7, 84
Russian Revolution of 1917 131–3
    communism 133–4
    educational theory 136–44
    state repression 134–6
Ryan, H. 186

schooling, common 89–94
Schooling in Capitalist America (Bowles and Gintis) 89, 187–8
Schurmann, F. 166
Scott, D. 108
Second World War 164–6, 168, 179, 206
Sedition Act 135
settler colonialism 21, 202
1776 55–6. *see also* Shay's Rebellion
   economic crisis 62–7
   factors 57–60
   resistance 79–83
   state representatives 67–70
Shawnee 80–1, 83, 100–2
Shay's Rebellion 55, 56, 60–2, 65, 72, 73, 77, 85
Shor, I. 187, 188, 202
slave masters religion 42–3, 78
slave patrols 87–8
slaves, wage 97–100
slave trade 36–7
   African 37–8
   Bacon's Rebellion 38–9
   enslavement and patrolling 39–42
   resistance 46–51
   whiteness 38
Smith, A. 69–70
Smith Act 135
Smith, J. 32–3
socialism 51, 91–3, 127–9, 134, 140, 143, 144, 147, 151, 162, 190
Social-Revolutionary Party 132
South Carolina 20, 25, 29, 30, 40, 47, 57, 58, 68, 72, 115, 116
Soviet Commissariat of Education 161
Soviet Union 133, 134, 136, 147, 159–61, 166, 177, 178, 180
   educational theory 138–44
Spring, J. 70
stagism 6, 9
Stannard, D. 20
state power 14–15, 24, 68, 77, 78, 92, 169, 187, 193, 202, 205
state repression 4, 6, 68, 84, 85, 129, 132–6, 147, 154, 156, 164, 187
state, the 2, 3, 9, 14, 15, 28, 46, 55, 60, 65, 67, 69, 72, 73, 87, 88, 99, 112, 116, 117, 119, 121, 125, 129, 132, 136, 150, 151, 166, 167, 171, 173, 177, 179, 187, 191, 196, 199–201

stock market 193
Stono's Revolt 57
story of arrival 25, 85, 90
strike 33, 47, 65, 87, 97, 110, 132, 152, 156, 157, 166, 186, 191, 195–200
sublation/sublate 8–9, 13, 18, 27, 36, 55, 56, 61, 65, 86, 107, 140, 141, 165, 207
Summerset case 59, 79
Supreme Court, US 68–9, 108, 121–3, 135, 168, 169, 196, 206
Survival Programs 172, 173
Szatmary, D. 61–3, 65, 66

Taft-Hartley Act 196
Takaki, R. 24, 39
Taylor, C. 155–7, 159
teachers
   abolitionist teaching 201–2
   in Chicago 98, 152–5, 160, 164
   covid-19 and 200–1
   strikes 191, 196–200
Teachers Union (TU) 155, 156, 158
Tecumseh 83, 100–3, 109, 147
tender laws 64, 65, 67
Ten Point Program 171–2
Therborn, G. 3, 14, 16–17
Thorndike, E. 137, 138
Thought and Language (Vygotsky) 143
tobacco 23, 24, 37, 39, 56
Torres, R. 189
Treaty of Greenville, The 83, 100
Trump, D. 135, 192–5, 206
Tsenacommacah 22, 23
Turkestan 132
Tuskegee Institute 119
Tyack, D. 126–7

Union of Soviet Socialist Republics (USSR) 133
unions, teacher 105, 152, 155, 158, 183, 186, 197, 199, 200
unipolar era 179, 180
unipolar imperialist power 177
   Nation at Risk, A 180–3, 187, 188, 190
   neoliberalism 178–9
   No Child Left Behind Act 182–5
   race and 185–7
United Nations 82

United States 2, 13, 21, 45, 47, 51, 55–7, 62, 63, 76–83, 86, 92, 93, 95, 97–9, 105, 107–9, 124, 125, 128, 129, 131–3, 147, 150, 161, 166, 177–80, 190–2
  communism 133–4
  educational theory 136–8
  state repression 134–6
United Teachers of Los Angeles (UTLA) 198
Up from Slavery (Washington) 119
Urban, W. 70, 76–7, 159–60
US imperialism 123–4
  corporate education 125–7
  German immigrants 128–9
  state police and militant labor 124–5
usurer states 124
Utopia (More) 29, 30

Vitale, A. 87
Volunteer Emergency Committee (VEC) 155
Vygotsky, L. 138–44

wage slaves 97–100
Wagoner, J. 70, 76–7
War of 1812 103
war of conquest 109–11
war on poverty 177, 180, 181, 191
Washington, B. T. 118–19
Watkins, W. 114
Webster, N. 55–6, 64
White Architects of Black Education, The (Watkins) 114
whiteness 7, 20–5, 28, 31, 34, 35, 38, 41, 42, 46, 49, 58, 74, 76, 113, 127
Wolff, R. 193
Wood, G. 182–4
Wyandot 83, 100

Yamasee War 29–30
yeomen 60–70, 73, 75–8, 81, 82, 84, 128, 205

Zinn, H. 60
zone of proximal development (ZPD) 142

www.ingramcontent.com/pod-product-compliance
Lightning Source LLC
Chambersburg PA
CBHW062219300426
44115CB00012BA/2141